Who Was Jesus?

D1211308

Contributors

Herb Basser is Professor of Religious Studies at Queens University (Ontario). He has written *Studies in Exegesis: Christian Critiques and Rabbinic Responses, 70-300 C.E.* (Brill), *Pseudo-Rabad*, and *In the Margins of Midrash* (both with University Press of America).

Bruce Chilton is Bernard Iddings Bell Professor of Religion at Bard College (New York). He has written extensively on Jesus and the relationship of Judaism and early Christianity. His books include *Rabbi Jesus: An Intimate Biography* (Doubleday), *Pure Kingdom: Jesus' Vision of God* (Eerdmans), and *Judaic Approaches to the Gospels* (University Press of America).

Carsten Claussen teaches New Testament at the Evangelisch-Theologische Fakultät at the University of Munich. He has written (in German) *Assembly, Community, Synagogue* [Versammlung, Gemeinde, Synagoge]: *Studies on the Hellenistic-Jewish Environment of Early Christian Communities* (Vandenhoeck & Ruprecht, forthcoming).

Paul Copan is Visiting Associate Professor at Trinity International University (Illinois) and is on staff with Ravi Zacharias International Ministries (Georgia). He has edited *Will the Real Jesus Please Stand Up?* (Baker) and coedited *Jesus' Resurrection: Fact or Figment?* (InterVarsity Press).

William Lane Craig is Research Professor at Talbot School of Theology (California). He has authored *Assessing the New Testament Evidence for the Historicity of the Resurrection of Jesus* (Edwin Mellen) and has contributed to *Will the Real Jesus Please Stand Up?* (with John Dominic Crossan) and *Jesus' Resurrection: Fact or Figment?* (with Gerd Lüdemann).

Craig A. Evans is Professor of Biblical Studies at Trinity Western University (British Columbia), where he founded the Dead Sea Scrolls Institute and directed the Graduate Program in Biblical Studies. He is an active member of the Historical Jesus Section of the Society of Biblical Literature and has written several books on Jesus and the Gospels.

Donald A. Hagner is the George Eldon Ladd Professor of New Testament at Fuller Theological Seminary and is author of numerous articles and books including *The Jewish Reclamation of Jesus* (Zondervan). He is coeditor of *Conflicts and Challenges in Early Christianity* (Trinity Press International).

Scot McKnight is the Karl A. Olsson Professor in Religious Studies at North Park University (Illinois). He has authored *A New Vision for Israel: The Teachings of Jesus in National Context* (Eerdmans) and *A Light Among the Gentiles: Jewish Missionary Activity in the Second Temple Period* (Fortress). He is on the advisory board of the Historical Jesus Section for the Society of Biblical Literature.

Jacob Neusner is Research Professor of Religion and Theology at Bard College (New York) and is known for his contribution to Judaic studies. His books include *A Rabbi Talks with Jesus* (McGill Queens University Press), *Introduction to Rabbinic Literature* (Doubleday) and, as coeditor, *The Encyclopedia of Judaism* (Continuum).

Peter Zaas is Professor of Religious Studies at Siena College (New York) and is Director of the Hayyim H. Kieval Institute for Jewish-Christian Studies there. He has been involved in Jewish-Christian dialogue, has published articles on Jewish-Christian dialogue as well as Pauline moral language, and is currently working on *The New Testament: A Jewish Scholar's Translation*.

Who Was Jesus?

A Jewish-Christian Dialogue

Edited by

Paul Copan
and
Craig A. Evans

Westminster John Knox Press
LOUISVILLE
LONDON • LEIDEN

© 2001 Westminster John Knox Press

All rights reserved. No part of this book may be reproduced or transmitted in any form or by any means, electronic or mechanical, including photocopying, recording, or by any information storage or retrieval system, without permission in writing from the publisher. For information, address Westminster John Knox Press, 100 Witherspoon Street, Louisville, Kentucky 40202-1396.

Scripture quotations, unless otherwise indicated, are from the New Revised Standard Version of the Bible, copyright © 1989 by the Division of Christian Education of the National Council of the Churches of Christ in the U.S.A., and used by permission. Scripture quotations from the Revised Standard Version of the Bible are copyright © 1946, 1952, 1971, 1973 by the Division of Christian Education of the National Council of the Churches of Christ in the U.S.A. and are used by permission. Scripture quotations marked NIV are from The Holy Bible, New International Version. Copyright © 1973, 1978, 1984 International Bible Society. Used by permission of Zondervan Bible Publishers. Scripture quotations marked NASB are taken from the New American Standard Bible, copyright © 1960, 1962, 1963, 1968, 1971, 1972, 1973, 1975, 1977 by The Lockman Foundation. Used by permission.

Material from the *Weekday Prayerbook*, edited by Moses Hadas, is reprinted with permission. Copyright © 1961 by the Rabbinical Assembly.

Book design by Sharon Adams
Cover design by Cynthia Dunne
Cover illustration: Jesus Carrying the Cross by Sebastiano del Piombo (c. 1485–1547); Prado, Madrid, Spain/Bridgeman Art Library

First edition
Published by Westminster John Knox Press
Louisville, Kentucky

This book is printed on acid-free paper that meets the American National Standards Institute Z39.48 standard.

PRINTED IN THE UNITED STATES OF AMERICA

01 02 03 04 05 06 07 08 09 10 — 10 9 8 7 6 5 4 3 2 1

Library of Congress Cataloging-in-Publication Data

Who was Jesus? : a Jewish-Christian dialogue / edited by Paul Copan and Craig A. Evans.
  p. cm.
  Includes bibliographical references and indexes.
  ISBN 0-664-22462-8 (pbk. : alk. paper)
  1. Jesus Christ—Person and offices. 2. Jesus Christ—Jewish interpretations. 3. Christianity and other religions—Judaism. 4. Judaism—Relations—Christianity. I. Copan, Paul.
II. Evans, Craig A.

BT203 .W48 2001
232—dc21   2001035040

Contents

Preface

Who was Jesus? This question more than any other has divided "Judaism" and "Christianity." Was Jesus of Nazareth a prophet, holy man, social/political reformer, Messiah, Son of God? Was he one who "practiced magic" or "sorcery" so that he enticed and led Israel astray,"[1] as early rabbinic texts indicate?

And *who is a Jew?* The answer to the first question will have significant bearing on the second. As odd as it may seem today, many in the earliest Christian community (which was undoubtedly ethnically Jewish) believed one must embrace Judaism in order to be a disciple of Jesus—a "Christian"—in the fullest sense. Even today, not all informed non-Christian Jews believe a "Jewish Christian" is a contradiction in terms. After all, if one can be an atheistic Jew, why then does a Jew's embracing Jesus as Messiah automatically de-Judaize that person?

Summarizing the second Durham-Tübingen Research Symposium on Earliest Christianity and Judaism (September 1989), James Dunn notes that rabbinic Judaism, which began to emerge in the wake of the first-century destruction of Jerusalem by Rome, indeed came to define Judaism and Jewishness. But between 70 and 135,[2] "it was still by no means clear that rabbinism was going to triumph and so also that Christianity was going to be excluded from 'the Jewish community.'"[3] As is mentioned in one essay in this volume, the origins of Judaism and Christianity are like interwoven threads that should not, in our view (as co-editors), be unraveled.[4] Identifying and tracing these threads constitute the principal concern of the essays that make up this book.

This book involves the contribution of scholars who identify themselves as "Christians" and "Jews." The event that actually inspired this book was a friendly dialogue on the question of Jesus between Jewish New Testament scholar Peter Zaas and Christian scholar/philosopher William Lane Craig. Their dialogue raises a number of issues at the very heart of

Jewish-Christian discussion: Who was Jesus? What was his setting? What were his aims? Why did he die? Do the Gospels reliably depict the historical Jesus? Does his resurrection make a difference? Can a Jew be a Christian? Is Christianity inherently anti-Semitic?

We would like to thank each of the contributors for their thoughtful—and sometimes controversial—viewpoints. Indeed, controversy is not limited to the Zaas-Craig dialogue; controversial issues are raised in the essays also. We hope that this book will encourage further friendly dialogue between Jews and Christians—and even (dare we say!) Christians who happen to be Jewish.

We thank Ginny Evans for her assistance in the preparation of the indexes. We are especially grateful to Carey C. Newman of Westminster John Knox Press, who immediately deemed our proposal worthy of publication and has moved forward the publishing process with "unperturbed pace, deliberate speed, and majestic instancy."

Paul Copan
Craig A. Evans

Introduction

Paul Copan

Background to the Dialogue

Back in 1993 in upstate New York, I was organizing a series of lectures and debates for a friend, former professor, and now fellow-collaborator, William Lane Craig. He frequently speaks on university campuses—on any number of topics—in order to present an intellectual defense of biblical Christianity. Since Bill is not only a fine philosopher but also at home with biblical and theological studies, I thought he would be interested in debating a Jewish New Testament scholar I had heard of: Dr. Peter Zaas, Professor of Religious Studies at Siena College in Loudonville, New York, and Director of its Institute for Jewish-Christian Studies.

I promptly contacted Peter Zaas about a debate on the subject, "Who Is Jesus?" slated for October 3, 1993. Zaas wrote me a letter in June of that year, stating that he was uncomfortable with framing this session as a *debate*: "This term seems to me to imply that the participants will perforce be taking different sides in a question that has specifically defined 'sides.'" There simply is no "orthodox" Jewish view of Jesus to defend nor for Bill Craig to attack, he wrote. In closing, he humorously remarked: "If you insist on the competitive format, I guess I'm game, but I think you'd have to pay me more!" Needless to say, Zaas didn't have to be paid more.

Zaas's perspective intrigued me. Here was a conservative Jewish New Testament scholar—a *non*-messianic Jew—asserting that there was no "orthodox" view of Jesus for a Jew to hold. In another dialogue, Zaas noted: "As far as Jews are concerned, the distinction between Jew and Christian is not theological; there is no theological test which defines Judaism. There is no historical base for this doctrine; the Church's belief is founded upon its own need for separateness."[1]

Here was a perspective one is not often accustomed to hearing, and this viewpoint was partly the source of inspiration for this book. The

1

Zaas-Craig interaction was not only a kind of politically incorrect discussion about Jesus; it was also an illuminating dialogue about Jewish identity (i.e., whether a Jew is defined by history/ethnicity or by adherence to a core of theological doctrines). Zaas claims that while Jews and Christians share a common understanding of the revelatory force of history, they interpret this revelation differently.[2] In large measure, this difference hinges upon the identity of Jesus of Nazareth.

Summarizing the Dialogue

In terms of the dialogue itself, Zaas opens the discussion by stating that the identity of Jesus "is not a question that has been of great concern to Jews throughout their history" (p. 15). He notes that the books of the New Testament are "primarily Jewish books, books by Jewish authors" (p. 15). As a New Testament scholar, Zaas asserts his right to appreciate their Jewishness, regardless of what others in the Jewish community think of those books. Zaas contends that Judaism is non-creedal—namely, that Jewish *beliefs* have never defined *Jews* in the same way that Christian beliefs have generally defined Christians (contrary to what certain Jews or Christians have assumed). Jewishness, rather, is to be understood in terms of *peoplehood—without* any "concomitant religious dimension at all, without theism, without messianism, without eschatology, for some even without the dimension of ethics. It is certainly possible to be an atheistic Jew, or an immoral one" (p. 16).

In Zaas's estimation, Jesus of Nazareth was the third most popular messianic figure among Jews—after the seventeenth-century Shabbatai Zvi and (much more recently) Menachem Schneersohn, the Lubavitcher Rebbe. One difference between Jesus and other Messiah-like figures in Jewish history, though, is that "Jesus' messianic proclamation was carried on by his followers after his death" (p. 17). But in terms of most first-century Jews, if they heard the Christian proclamation at all, they found it to be "largely irrelevant" to their own concerns (p. 17).

The anti-Jewish zeal of some early Christian theologians has, of course, carried over through the Crusades to Czarist pogroms and the Holocaust. For their part, Jews throughout history have "persisted in imagining Christianity to be a righteous and proper mode for Gentiles to worship God" (p. 18). As for Zaas, he is fascinated by the apostle Paul and by Jesus—by their Jewishness and the situations and issues they addressed. He studies them "even if the claims that [Jesus'] followers made about his person are irrelevant to my religious life" (p. 19).

He concludes with this moral: "Read the Bible. Read it the way it was written, in Hebrew, in Aramaic, and in Greek. That's the way to approach the story of the works of God" (p. 20).

William Craig opens his part of the dialogue with the declaration of a kind of consensus in New Testament scholarship about the self-identity of Jesus, who, in an unprecedented way, assumed himself an authority to stand and speak in God's place. In his person, the kingdom of God had come. But why think these claims are true? For Jesus' earliest followers—and for us today, Craig claims—the key to answering the question of Jesus' identity can be found in coming to terms with the historicity of Jesus' resurrection.

Craig points to three strands of evidence accepted by the majority of New Testament scholars[3] which reinforce the resurrection thesis: (a) the resurrection appearances, (b) the empty tomb, and (c) the origin of the Christian faith. Regarding *the resurrection appearances*, the resurrection tradition and witness list in 1 Corinthians 15 is very early, going back to the Jerusalem church. If the bodily resurrection of Jesus were legendary, how could it have emerged and taken hold in such a short time—with the purported eyewitnesses still alive? Citing classical historian A. N. Sherwin-White, Craig argues that far more time would have been needed.

Regarding *the discovery of the empty tomb*, Craig offers five supporting points here. First is that the historical reliability of the burial story supports the empty tomb, which was known to friend and foe alike. Second, the empty-tomb story is pre-Markan and thus quite old. Third, the empty-tomb story is simple and does not reflect legendary embellishment. Fourth, the tomb was discovered empty by several of Jesus' women followers; the fact that their testimony would have been deemed worthless within their societal context is telling: these appearances to the women are not fabrications. Fifth, the empty tomb was presupposed in early Jewish polemic. Craig concludes that, given the strength of the evidence for the empty tomb, it is not *historical* considerations, but *philosophical* and *theological* ones that move persons to reject Jesus' resurrection.

Regarding *the origin of the Christian Way*, the earliest followers of Jesus *believed* that Jesus had been raised from the dead. But what could adequately account for that belief? Not *Jewish* theology, which held to a corporate and eschatological resurrection rather than an individual one prior to the eschaton. Nor was it *Christian* belief since Christianity did not then exist. The bodily resurrection of Jesus best explains this otherwise-enigmatic emergence of the Christian church.

In Craig's assessment, all three of these facts point, by way of inference to the best explanation, to the resurrection of Jesus. It is this event that helps us most adequately to answer the question, "Who was Jesus?"

Then in their interactive discussion, Zaas asks Craig, "With whom are you arguing?" (p. 29). Craig points out that he is not directing an argument *against* anyone but is presenting positive justification for his belief in the resurrection, which helps us treat the question regarding Jesus' identity. Obviously many people *do* reject the historicity of Jesus' bodily resurrection, but it is precisely *because* God raised Jesus from the dead that this is "good news" worth proclaiming.

Zaas then mentions the charge of blasphemy (a vague term in Jewish law) leveled at Jesus—in addition to that of his anti-Temple activity. Zaas doubts that Jesus was truly charged with blasphemy; rather, mention of it was more likely Mark's attempt to make Jesus look good in "a Roman kind of way" (p. 31). For Zaas, a more likely explanation for the basis of Jesus' execution is the more unambiguous—at least, to the Roman authorities— threat of revolutionary activity. Craig points out that it was precisely those anti-Temple actions or the authoritative claim to forgive sins that precipitated the charges of blasphemy. After all, Jesus sought to "replace the Temple as the focus of Judaism with himself and the kingdom of God as the focus of belief" (p. 31). This kind of authority is reflected in Jesus' Sermon on the Mount ("but I say to you"). Yet Zaas questions whether or not speaking with such authority can be considered blasphemy (which was typically understood by Jews as cursing God).

Zaas and Craig then proceed to discuss the stance that Jesus took on the Torah and its food laws (Jesus had declared all foods "clean"). For Zaas, Jesus is entering into a hermeneutical dispute of his day. But Craig sees this as one part in a cumulative case for Jesus' radical self-awareness, as one standing in the very place of God.

When the discussion advances to the topic of how Jewish identity should be understood, Zaas reaffirms what he said earlier: "Judaism *isn't* a religion. . . . Judaism is a sense of peoplehood, and Jews believe all kinds of things and still remain Jews. . . . Jews cannot be read out of Judaism for their beliefs, nor are they admitted into the community by their beliefs" (p. 34). So despite the typical thing to say—that "Jews believe in at most one God"—this is not what defines Jewishness (p. 34). And the converse is true: "If Jews are not going to be identified by their lack of belief in Jesus, then they ought not to be *un*identified by their belief in Jesus as the Messiah" (pp. 34–35).

Following this interactive discussion are questions from the floor. They cover such topics as the nature of atonement and blood sacrifice within

Judaism and their relationship to Jesus' death; the basis for Jesus' execution; how to "categorize" messianic Jews within the broader Jewish community; the impact (or non-impact) of Jesus' resurrection; the difference between resurrection and revivification (such as with Lazarus or Jairus' daughter); and the radical and authoritative claims of Jesus.

During the Q&A time, Zaas states his position about the resurrection: "I don't dispute the fact of the resurrection. It's not something I'm involved in, but it doesn't seem to be an event that's made much positive difference to Jewish history" (p. 38). For him, this resurrection claim is just a Christian claim.

In his closing remarks, Zaas expresses his appreciation for the nature of this kind of dialogue—one in which the sides don't agree in advance about what *not* to talk about or in which they agree to talk about only what they have in common—such as what to do with the Muslims! Zaas again stresses the importance of history and God's workings in the past as well as in the present—a notion which Jews and Christians share.

Craig, too, stresses how refreshing this politically incorrect dialogue is. He then reiterates the main points for believing that God raised Jesus from the dead. Citing theologian Horst Georg Pöhlmann, Craig closes with this statement: "With regard to Jesus, there are only two possible modes of behavior: either to believe that in him God encounters us or nail him to the cross as a blasphemer. There is no third way" (p. 42).

Responses to the Dialogue and Reflections on Jesus and Jewishness

To varying degrees, the respondents interact with the Zaas-Craig dialogue. Some of them respond directly to the dialogue while others address the question of Jesus in the context of the Jewish-Christian interface without really touching on the dialogue at all. I offer here some of my own thoughts; Craig Evans will add his in the Conclusion.

Donald A. Hagner brings the first response ("Jesus: Bringer of Salvation to Jew and Gentile Alike"). Contrary to Zaas, he defines Jewishness religiously rather than ethnically. But believing in Jesus as Lord and Messiah does not prevent a Jew from remaining Jewish. In fact, in the early church an emotionally charged topic was whether or not one could be a Christian without being Jewish! Hagner indicates that while blasphemy in first-century Palestine is difficult to nail down, "if Jesus insulted God by arrogating to himself prerogatives that belong to God alone, this could well have been regarded as blasphemous" (p. 47).

Further, Hagner is surprised that Zaas does not engage the question of the Gospels' reliability—something many Jewish scholars are inclined to do. Yet their general historical trustworthiness can be ably defended. Regarding the *aims* of Jesus, Hagner states that Jesus' self-awareness makes him something more than a Jewish reformer (*contra* Zaas); given the lofty and authoritative claims he makes, Jesus is taking upon himself *divine prerogatives*. Jesus' ethical teaching cannot adequately fit within the Judaism of his day since it is inextricably linked with his *personal claims*.

Hagner agrees with Craig that the resurrection of Jesus is foundational for understanding the birth of the church, and any other attempt to explain the phenomena surrounding its origination is simply inadequate. Hagner concludes by noting that the question of Jesus is no armchair topic. As in his day (if he was who he is reported to be in the Gospels), so today Jesus makes demands upon us all—Jew and Gentile alike: "The fact is that no Christian can answer the question 'Who is Jesus' without becoming an evangelist!" (p. 57).

Craig A. Evans' essay, "The Jesus of History and the Christ of Faith: Toward Jewish-Christian Dialogue," also interacts much with the Zaas-Craig exchange. Evans observes that the *relevance* of Jesus and his resurrection depends on "one's philosophical and religious interpretation" (p. 59). Rabbi Pinchas Lapide, for instance, believes that historical evidence for Jesus' bodily resurrection is solid. But this does not mean he is Messiah—only that he is the means of bringing God's salvation to the Gentiles. Rabbi Peter Levinson, on the other hand, interprets the implications of Jesus' resurrection differently: "If I believed in Jesus' resurrection I would be baptised tomorrow" (p. 60). We must thus distinguish between *what happened* and *what the event means*.

Evans claims that Jesus accepted all the major tenets of the Judaism of his day. For example, he accepted (rather than attacked) the Torah's authority, but he opposed certain interpretations and applications of it. Evans sees Jesus as "the anointed, eschatological prophet who proclaims the kingdom (or . . . reign) of God" (p. 62). Jesus' claim to be a prophet is historically authentic, and he participated in priestly activity (such as pronouncing persons "clean" and also forgiving individuals—in addition to "cleansing" the Temple). He was crucified as "King of the Jews" and as one who claimed to be "God's Son" (Mark 14:61–62), which likely stems from the deliberate messianic mission he had embarked on. And Jesus viewed his own miracles (e.g., exorcisms) as evidence of the kingdom's appearing.

He offered salvation to the Jewish people and the leaders of his day, but when they rejected him as their king at the triumphal entry (after which he cleansed the Temple and his authority was challenged), his message changed. Once national repentance (along with restoration) was no longer on the horizon, Jesus spoke of coming judgment upon Jerusalem and its Temple. Thus Jesus died because of his messianic claims and because of his threat against the Temple establishment.

The early church then emerged because of the firm belief that Jesus had been raised from the dead. The Gospels themselves are a trustworthy record of Jesus' deeds—rather than being a mirror reflection of the needs of early Christian communities. (After all, if this were the case, why don't the Gospels treat issues such as food sacrificed to idols, spiritual gifts, circumcision, Jew-Gentile relations, and the like?)

Evans closes by expressing agreement with Zaas that Jews are not "prevented by reason of their Jewishness from accepting this Christian notion [of Jesus as *the* Messiah]" (p. 71). To be Jewish today does not entail being religious. And none of us should forget that the "story of Christian origins is a Jewish story" (p. 72).

Scot McKnight ("Jesus' New Vision within Judaism") bypasses Peter Zaas's somewhat cavalier attitude toward Jesus as well as Craig's arguments regarding the personal claims made by Jesus (not to mention his bodily resurrection), choosing instead to focus on how Jesus fits into the first-century context of diversified Judaism.

He offers some clarifying comments on Zaas's and Craig's understanding of "Judaism" and "Christianity." He suggests, for instance, that the "Judaisms" of Jesus' day should not be construed *religiously* per se ("personal relationship to God") but as a "vision for Israel"—namely, "who a Jew is, who God is, how Jews are supposed to live before this God, how the nation is to conduct itself with outsiders, in short, a Jewish way of life in terms of God's covenant with Abraham, Moses, and David" (p. 75).

McKnight seeks to show that Jesus is believably Jewish and that his vision for Israel was a viable form of Judaism. Jesus saw himself at the "epicenter" of God's new work among his people (thus ruling out any charge of anti-Semitic beliefs allegedly held by the earliest Christians). Both Jesus' *baptism* and *death* tell us much about his vision for Israel. John's baptism (through which one passed through the Jordan River, beginning from the eastern side and into the "promised land"—reenacting what took place under Joshua's leadership) was both purificatory and unique in its theological import. And in his baptism, Jesus identified with this new movement among God's people.

Like Moses and Joshua in their redemptive activities, Jesus *acted out* his vision for Israel ("sign-acts"), indicating that he was self-consciously a new

Moses and a new Joshua. Jesus' teaching and his ethic exhibit a fully Jewish context. And when it comes to the death of Jesus, he sees his mission to be that of national restoration, offering himself on behalf of "the many" to the fatal power of his enemies. Thus, McKnight writes, "the *death of Jesus is his personal national sacrifice to bring about the completion of the story of Israel, to restore the fortunes of Israel, to end the exile, to bring forgiveness, peace, and righteousness*" (p. 92, his emphasis).

At the outset of his essay ("Early Christianity in the Synagogue: A Parting of the Ways"), Carsten Claussen places Jesus squarely in a Jewish setting. In fact, "Jesus did not found a new institution" (p. 98). His apocalyptic message—again, a *Jewish* phenomenon—concerned a new world order. Claussen agrees with Craig that Christianity stands or falls on the historicity of Jesus' bodily resurrection. He disagrees with Zaas's understanding of Jewishness as solely ethnic (once the religious element is left out, the necessary cohesiveness is lost). Claussen later points out that *monotheism, election, covenant* (focused on Torah), and *land* (focused on the Temple) served as a fourfold foundation on which various Judaisms were built. Claussen notes that the earliest Christians were *Jewish* (cp. Acts 2:42–47). What unified them was not simply creedal belief in Jesus' resurrection, but their experience of God's *Spirit*.

Just as there were Jewish "sects" (a non-pejorative term back then) such as the Essenes, Zealots, Pharisees, and Sadducees, so Christians came to be identified as "the Nazarene sect" (Acts 24:5). Claussen briefly tracks some of the historical developments of the relationship between Christians and the synagogue. Of the four parts of the "foundation" for Judaism, *monotheism* and *Torah* would become the key matters of dispute between Jews and Christians, and the apostle Paul was often seen to be in conflict with Jews of his day (particularly on Torah-related matters).

But the larger question is: "Who was Jesus?" Jesus saw himself as God's Son, and his earliest followers prayed to him, included him in their creeds, etc. What is remarkable is that there is no tension in Paul's lofty Christology and his monotheism. Monotheism and the confession of Jesus as Lord were smoothly integrated by the early Christians.

In "The Gospels Would Have Been Greek to Jesus," Herbert Basser hits hard: "A central goal of the Gospel writers was to instill contempt, an odium, against Judaism: Jews were children of hell, their leaders a brood of vipers" (p. 111). Yet if we strip away this "nasty rhetoric" embedded in the Gospels, Basser sees "little controversy" (p. 111); the "early formulations" of Jesus' encounters "could not at all have been confrontational" (p. 111). Basser expresses strong disagreement with Craig on several points—

the reliability of the Gospels as they now stand, the historical basis for the resurrection, and soundness of the earliest Christian traditions. According to Basser, we "simply do not know" why Jesus died (p. 113). But the Jesus of the Gospels "shows us no reason" why Jewish or Roman authorities would have him executed through due process (p. 114).

Basser refers to Lapide's sympathy with Jesus' resurrection as historical as an exception among reputable Jewish/rabbinic scholars. He agrees with Zaas that Jews really don't think about Jesus—any more than most Christians think about Buddha. He disagrees with Zaas, though, regarding the essence of Jewishness: "Unlike Zaas, I affirm that Jewish belief exists as an essential part of all Judaic systems and is important for Jewish self-definition" (p. 114). Thus while Zaas is "certainly correct . . . that belief does not define who is a Jew," it does "determine the culture of the community" (p. 115).

Basser tackles certain passages in the Gospels to show what Jesus does and says is not very radical. He does not contradict biblical or scribal law, and Basser devotes space to certain Sabbath pericopae to make his point. The statement "the Son of Man is lord of the Sabbath" is a Matthean comment, and one should not draw overblown christological conclusions from it. As with David's taking the *showbread* from the priest (mentioned in Matt. 12:1–8 and par.), Basser acknowledges that biblical law may be overridden in such circumstances. Basser claims that Mark 7:19 (in which Jesus is said to declare all foods clean) deals with the eating of carrion by Jewish-Christian missionaries; but we cannot ascribe to Jesus the statement "things that enter the body do not defile" since in Jesus' lifetime there were no such missionaries.

Basser concludes that we can know *nothing* about Jesus from history. Also, a Jew *cannot* remain a Jew in good standing if he or she has become a follower of Jesus; such an idea is "preposterous" (p. 122). We can't know what the relationship of Jesus was to the Judaism of his day since nothing reliable is historically accessible to us. Jesus' own aim could have been multifaceted (healer, teacher of righteousness, etc.), but at minimum, he was a Jew who cared for his people and the continuation of his religion and desired to know how best to serve God. In the end, all we can know is "what people *thought* he proclaimed" (p. 124).

Jacob Neusner titles his essay "At What Points Do Judaisms and Christianities Meet?" We don't have to wait long for an answer. He begins the sweep of his reflections with: "Judaisms and Christianities never meet anywhere" (p. 125). This is why Judaism (as defined by the Torah) and Christianity (as defined by the Bible) never intersect. Neusner pulls no punches in his Torah-centric treatment of Christianity. "Once God has made himself known in the Torah, the Torah must stand in judgment on all other claims to know God" (p. 125).

Neusner does not deal with the question of the historical Jesus per se—whether regarding the reliability of the New Testament, the identity claims of Jesus, the evidence for Jesus' resurrection, or the emergence of the early church. Rather, he discusses the essential conflicts between Judaisms and Christianities. One knows from the outset that he strongly disagrees with Zaas's view on what constitutes Jewish identity: "when Jews adopt Christianity or Islam, they can no longer claim a portion in the God of Jacob" (p. 125). Jews begin with Torah, the starting point for the knowledge of God, whereas Christians see Jesus as the means of knowing God, but this is in violation of the criterion of Torah. The teaching of Torah itself is carried forth by rabbis and sages in the Oral Torah—as well as in the liturgy of the synagogue and home life, defining the Jewish worldview. While various Jewish worldviews have come and gone, Torah remains. This is borne out by the writers of Jewish synagogue liturgies and by Jewish sages whose wisdom is laid out in the Oral Torah, and Neusner cites plenty of them to reinforce his point. They define the essence of Judaism, and in both cases, they draw upon the Written Torah for their inspiration: "when we define the theology of the Oral Torah, we state Judaism pure and simple, no more, no less" (p. 153). As a result, Judaisms and Christianities cannot meet or intersect "because they cannot afford a common prayer and do not share a common revelation" (p. 153).

In the final essay, "Jesus, a Galilean Rabbi," Bruce Chilton (Neusner's colleague at Bard College) summarizes the new body of evidence that has emerged, highlighting Galilee's resistance to Hellenistic culture and attesting to "the cultural integrity of Galilean Judaism" (p. 154). This runs contrary to the common assumption that it was "essentially non-Jewish" (p. 154). Evidences of stashed coins (including defunct ones) and purification jars from Galilee have "shattered the myth of a purely or mostly Hellenistic Jesus" (p. 155). Thus the "archaeological Galilee" is a "Jewish Galilee" insofar as Jesus and his movement are concerned (p. 155).

Prior to the second-century establishment of a more monolithic Judaism via the Mishnah (and then later via the Talmud), various Judaisms existed around the time of Jesus—a fact brought to light by the Dead Sea Scrolls discovery. (Hence Chilton urges caution in defining Judaism by Mishnaic standards since Christianity had become a competitor by this time.) These Judaisms shared the common hope that God would personally intervene in history for the sake of humanity. And Jesus articulated this message in proclaiming the kingdom of God. Before we get to the canonical Gospels (or even the Gospel of Thomas, which contains some authentic sayings of Jesus), the initial stage is critical—namely, "what we must infer of Jesus within his Jewish environment to explain how the texts emerged in their variety and in their agreement" (p. 159). This question must be taken in conjunction with another: how a Galilean boy, accused of illegitimate birth, could become a respected rabbi who challenged the established religious and Temple system and then be shamefully crucified, followed by the conviction among his followers that God had raised him from the dead.

So in which direction shall we move? In light of the two alternatives that Horst Georg Pöhlmann mentioned in Craig's concluding remarks, should we follow Zaas in believing that Jesus—given his authoritative claims and the historical evidence for the resurrection—can be safely ignored (the very "third way" Pöhlmann rejects)? Or must one take the position of, say, Jewish scholars such as Herb Basser or Jacob Neusner, who would forcefully disagree with Zaas on the relevance of Jesus' self-identity claims and evidence for the resurrection (and whether Jewishness is ethnic or religious)? Or, finally, is one to follow Craig and other contributors to this volume—that we are "to believe that in [Jesus] God encounters us," that "God was in Christ reconciling the world to himself"? In the essays that follow, these momentous alternatives receive the scrutiny they deserve.

Part One

The Dialogue

Chapter 1

Who Was Jesus? A Jewish Response

Peter Zaas

I t is with some trepidation that I approach tonight's topic.[1] It is a topic about which our guest, William Craig, has a great deal more to say than I do. He has written passionately and even brilliantly about the topic. His writing reflects his learning as well as the unique set of questions he brings to bear on the historical record. But I have been asked to join him in conversation about "Who is Jesus?" and to begin with a brief statement in answer to this question. I am pleased for the opportunity to converse with such an eminent scholar, but I have to tell you at the outset that this is not a question that has been of great concern to Jews throughout their history. Much of what I will have to say, in fact, will deal with the idea that there is no "Jewish" position on who Jesus was, and that the question of Jesus' precise historical identity bears very little weight among the range of Jewish religious concerns.

I am a Jew whose primary field of academic scholarship concerns the New Testament and the early history of the Christian communities. I think I am called upon tonight to speak to you more as a Jew than as a New Testament scholar, although I do not mean to suggest that these parts of me are in conflict. The books of the New Testament are, after all, primarily Jewish books, books by Jewish authors, and if most Jews have ignored them or worse, villified them, I am still entitled to appreciate their Jewishness. But I am not called upon tonight to give a Jewish appreciation of the books of the New Testament, but rather to try to give some kind of Jewish answer to the question "Who is Jesus?"

I must remind you at the outset that although I might be able to muddle through with a Jewish answer to this question, neither I nor any other Jew can possibly give *the* Jewish answer to this question since there is none. Judaism is not only non-creedal, not based on a set of beliefs that all Jews share; it does not have any central authority structure to determine what Jews should or should not believe about this or any other question.

Judaism has never had such a structure, although in antiquity there were bodies of authority who could enforce one or another *action* on Jews. Even today there are still some communities organized around an authoritative leader who might dictate how his followers might behave in a given situation. But still, Judaism is non-creedal, and Jewish *beliefs* have never defined *Jews* as, I think, Christian beliefs have sometimes defined Christians.

Jewish beliefs have never defined Jews, but the belief persists among some Christians that Judaism *is* defined by a belief, specifically by the belief that Jesus is not the Messiah. Jews are the ones, I'm very often told, who don't believe the Messiah has come yet. This is the definition of who Jews are that I hear most often from my students. Thus for some Christians, a Jew appears to be a kind of damaged Christian, a Christian in all respects except for the essential belief in the Messiahship of Jesus.

From a Jewish point of view, of course, this kind of definition, trying to define Jews by what they *don't* believe, is absurd. For most Jews (I say without any authority at all) Jewishness expresses itself most significantly as a consciousness of peoplehood, of belonging (with whatever degree of strain) to the Jewish nation. Many Jews experience this sense of peoplehood without any concomitant religious dimension at all, without theism, without messianism, without eschatology, for some even without the dimension of ethics. It is certainly possible to be an atheistic Jew, or an immoral one. The range of religious expressions among Jews today, not to mention throughout the thousands of years of Jewish existence, is extremely broad.

Although Judaism does not define itself as the people who believe that this or that person is or isn't the Messiah, Jews throughout history have followed after—or rejected—any number of Messiahs. In his writings my colleague Rabbi Pinchas Lapide has elaborated just how many. By my nonauthoritative count, Jesus probably ranks as the third most popular Messiah in Jewish history so far, coming in behind Shabbatai Zvi, an immensely popular Messiah of the seventeenth century, as well as behind Menachem Schneersohn, the Lubavitcher Rebbe, a contemporary Messiah, at least in the eyes of many of his followers, who are preparing for his bodily translation to the Holy Land even as he lies dying in Brooklyn.[2]

It will be interesting—and I imagine painful—to observe what difficulties those who claim the Lubavitcher Rebbe to be the Messiah will encounter should events come to teach them that he is not. Certainly, when Shabbatai Zvi converted to Islam in 1667, most of his followers, recognizing this as distinctly un-messianic behavior, experienced a period of tremendous religious letdown. (Curiously, though, a number of Zvi's followers proclaimed that his Messiahship was *demonstrated* by his refusal to fulfill the traditional expectations of what the Messiah would or wouldn't do. He *must* be the Messiah—else why would he have converted to Islam?)

Arguably, one difference between Jesus and Shabbatai Zvi and any number of other Messiahs in Jewish history is that Jesus' messianic proclamation was carried on by his followers after his death. If Jesus thought himself to be the Messiah—in the sense that his followers understood this slippery term—his self-proclamation was only understood by his disciples following his death. Individual women and men, families of people, even crowds follow Jesus in the Gospels, but not necessarily because they believe him to be the Messiah, even though his miraculous healings, his authoritative teaching, his confrontation with authority are all interpreted by the text as signs of his Messiahship. Jesus' followers, during his earthly ministry, followed him for a variety of reasons, to be healed or to observe him heal, to encounter his teaching about how the Jewish purity laws ought to be interpreted in the moral sphere, perhaps because, unlike Jesus' predecessor John the Baptizer, Jesus offered a new way of looking at Judaism that did not require the difficult pilgrimage to the Judean desert to be baptized by John. "Repent, for the kingdom of Heaven is very near," both John and Jesus say in the first gospel, but Jesus says this to the marginalized of society, in their own environment. Jesus was a pilgrimage who came to you.

All of Jesus' first followers, and nearly all of the people to whom he proclaimed his message, were Jews, but Jews made up only a tiny part of the church gathered in the name of the risen Lord. We should not assume, of course, that large numbers of Jews were even exposed to the kerygma of Jesus' earliest followers, or that they would have been able to distinguish this proclamation from the pronouncements of any of the myriad claims for the miraculous acts of God with which they were confronted in antiquity. The first century of the common era was not a time epoch in Jewish history that offered much by way of mass media, but it did offer a great number of religious claims and counterclaims from any number of groups and individuals. That those Jews who did hear this kerygma found it to be largely irrelevant to their concerns as Jews—concerns which after all involved a century-long, decimating war with Rome, with the need to rethink the structure of Judaism itself following the Roman destruction of the Temple in 70, the need simply to build communities in the harsh climate of late antiquity—is hardly portentous, from a Jewish point of view. What is fraught with portent is the zeal shown by the early theologians of the church to denounce the Jews for what they perceived as a deliberate rejection of a manifest act of God. The Jews had somehow "rejected" Christ, and God was therefore rejecting them, replacing them with the True Israel of the (almost-entirely-Gentile) church.

We know what effect this doctrine of the rejection of the Jews had on historical events leading up to our time. My generation is the generation of the children of Holocaust survivors, and, however much Christians may disavow this horror, these survivors remember that their tormentors all claimed to be Christians, all understood that the Messiah was the Jesus of Nazareth. There are still Jews alive who remember the pogroms of Czarist Russia, conducted in the name of Christ, and Jews may look in their history books to remember the horrors perpetrated by the Crusaders' attempt to rid the Holy Land of the infidel.

No matter how much Jewish history has been affected by Christianity's fury over this perceived rejection of Jesus, though, the central proclamation of Christianity, the question "Who is Jesus?" remains as it has always been, entirely irrelevant to the Jewish enterprise, as most Jews, at least, have defined that enterprise. But while Christianity flourished among Gentiles and gathered energy by vilifying Jews, Jews persisted in imagining Christianity to be a righteous and proper mode for Gentiles to worship God. Jewish thinkers in late antiquity wondered whether Christians could truly be described as monotheistic, dividing God up into three persons as they were wont to do, but these thinkers determined that Christians were indeed monotheists, not splitters of God. Jewish thinkers determined that Christianity, like Islam, could constitute righteousness for Gentiles, that these two monotheistic, Gentile faiths were respectable paths to the worship of the God of all.

Although some early sources in the tannaitic period tried their best to malign Jesus by circulating ugly rumors about his parentage or about his participation in arcane practices, these texts were themselves irrelevant to how Jews thought about Jesus, even before they were voluntarily expunged from talmudic manuscripts to avoid the potentially murderous wrath of medieval Christian authorities.

In more modern times, Jewish scholars have turned with renewed interest to the books of the New Testament, vital evidence as they are for a complex and consequential period in Jewish history. Largely their enterprise was not to debunk the claims of Christianity, but to try to understand them in their own context, using the linguistic, historical, and legal tools at their disposal. My own study of the writings of the apostle Paul were motivated by how struck I was at that man's concern over issues that are still at the forefront of religious thinking these days: What must a person do to be righteous? I was also struck by how revealing a self-portrait Paul's letters present of a Jew wrestling with issues of conscience and faith.

I continue to be struck, as a Jew, by many aspects of Jesus' life and teachings, even if the claims that his followers made about his person are irrelevant to my religious life. I am struck by the Jewishness of Jesus, and by the pointedness of the critique of Jewish hypocrisy which pervades his teachings in the Gospels. Jesus stood against the sin of religiosity, the notion that what God desires is religiousness rather than justice, the notion that persons whose religiousness is a mask for their viciousness are the worst sinners. This idea, born among the Hebrew prophets but expressed with Jesus' characteristic simplicity and vigor in the Gospels, links this teacher with what is best in Jewish ethical thinking. If Christian readers of the Gospels persisted, most of the time, in thinking of Jesus as standing in opposition to *Jewish* hypocrisy and not to religious hypocrisy in general, that does not detract from the force of what Jesus himself stood for, and stood against. The Jesus of the Gospels is a Jewish teacher of righteousness, no matter how unrecognizable to Jews the church has made him.

The flyer for this event asks a series of questions under the "Who is Jesus?" heading: Is Jesus a rabbi, a radical, a teacher, a Messiah, or a myth? As I approach the end of these remarks, I will venture out onto a shaky limb and suggest that in the eyes of this nonauthoritative Jewish teacher, Jesus was not a rabbi (because he said he wasn't), he was a radical (but not a political radical), he was certainly a teacher (and a very good one, whose lessons are still being learned by new hearers as well as old ones), and, although he may have been one Messiah among many in Jewish history who have been called by that title, Jews have no reason at all to consider him *the* Messiah, nor are Jews prevented by reason of their Jewishness from accepting this Christian notion.

I want to end these comments with the story of the best teaching I ever did, and nudge you to the moral of it. The best teaching I ever did—curiously not at Siena—was with a self-described evangelical Christian student named Linda, who found herself something of a misfit at the mainstream Protestant college where I taught. She was interested in Scripture but found herself in real conflict with being told by her professors about how the historical-critical method proves thus-and-so about this-and-that, where her religious perspective impelled her to accept the literal truth of God's word. I suggested that she pursue her biblical interest through simply starting at the beginning of the Bible and reading the text, which sounded good to her, even when I brought out my Hebrew Bible and turned to the first verses of Genesis. We began studying Hebrew, and then we studied Greek, and God's word spoke to Linda in a new, and even more convincing way. Before she could indulge in working out what the text meant to her and her life, she had to learn simply what the text said. I wasn't of much use to her ultimate questions about God and the world, but I greatly appreciated sitting with her while the mysteries of Scripture were revealed, watching her achieve real growth until she grew into a real scholar. She went on to become a successful biblical scholar on the graduate level, even though last I heard she works for Jack Kemp.

The moral? Read the Bible. Read it the way it was written, in Hebrew, in Aramaic, and in Greek. That's the way to approach the story of the works of God.

Chapter 2

Who Was Jesus? A Christian Perspective

William Lane Craig

I also have approached this evening with no small degree of trepidation. So I'm glad to hear that we're both in the same boat. As we near the end of the twentieth century after his death, Jesus of Nazareth now as ever continues to exert his power of fascination over the minds of men and women. But who was Jesus really? Was he, as Christians believe, God incarnate, or was he just a Jewish prophet or rabbi? Was he the highest embodiment of some human quality such as faith or love? Who *was* Jesus?

In recent years, New Testament scholarship has reached something of a consensus that the historical Jesus of Nazareth came on the scene with an unprecedented sense of divine authority—the authority to stand and speak in God's place. That's why the Jewish leadership instigated Jesus' crucifixion on the charge of blasphemy. He claimed that in himself the kingdom of God had come, and as visible demonstration of that fact, he carried out a ministry of miracle-working and exorcisms. He opened the doors of God's kingdom to sinners and believed that people's eternal destiny hinged on their response to his own person.

So radical was the person who Jesus thought himself to be that British New Testament scholar James D. G. Dunn at the end of his study of the self-understanding of Jesus feels compelled to say, "One last question cannot be ignored: 'Was Jesus mad?'"[1] Dunn rejects the hypothesis that Jesus was insane because it cannot account for the soundness and the balance of Jesus' whole life and teaching.

But the earliest followers of Jesus offered an even better reason for thinking his radical claims to be true—his resurrection from the dead. As the German theologian Wolfhart Pannenberg explains,

> The resurrection of Jesus acquires such decisive meaning, not because someone or anyone has been raised from the dead, but because it is Jesus of Nazareth, whose execution was instigated by the Jews because he had blasphemed against God. The resurrection can

only be understood as the divine vindication of the man who was rejected as a blasphemer.[2]

I believe, therefore, that the key to answering the question of who Jesus was lies in our assessment of the historicity of the resurrection of Jesus.

Now by the very nature of the case, a historical event such as this cannot be proved with any sort of certainty. Nonetheless, we can assess the credibility of the testimony to that event either positively or negatively within a certain range of probability. In the brief time allotted to me tonight, let me therefore share some of the reasons why I think that the resurrection of Jesus is most plausibly to be taken as a historical event.

We can approach this subject most conveniently by considering three inductive grounds for affirming the historicity of the resurrection of Jesus: first, the resurrection appearances; second, the empty tomb; and third, the origin of the Christian faith. Let's look briefly at each of these.

The Resurrection Appearances

The German New Testament critic Joachim Jeremias has demonstrated that in 1 Corinthians 15, Paul is quoting an old Christian saying which he received and in turn passed on to his converts.[3] In this saying, he lists the witnesses to six resurrection appearances of Jesus. According to his letter to the Galatian churches (in 1:18), Paul was in Jerusalem three years after his conversion on the Damascus road on a fact-finding mission, during which he conferred with both Peter and James over a two-week period. And he probably received the saying at this time if not before. Since Jesus died in A.D. 30 and Paul was converted around A.D. 33, this means that the list of witnesses goes back to the first five years after Jesus' death. Thus it is idle to dismiss the appearances as legendary. We can try to explain them away as hallucinations if we want to. But we cannot deny that they occurred.

Paul's information makes it certain that on separate occasions, different individuals and groups saw appearances of Jesus alive from the dead. According to Norman Perrin, the late New Testament critic of the University of Chicago, "The more we study the traditions with regard to the appearances, the firmer the rock begins to appear on which they are based."[4] This conclusion is virtually indisputable today.

Moreover, I would argue that the traditions underlying the Gospel appearance stories may well be as reliable as Paul's information. For in order for these stories to be (in the main) legendary, a very considerable length of time must be available for the evolution and development of the historical traditions until the historical elements have been supplanted by unhistorical elements. This factor has, unfortunately, been typically neglected in New Testament scholarship, as Professor A. N. Sherwin-White points out in his book, *Roman Society and Roman Law in the New Testament*. Professor Sherwin-White is not a theologian; he is a professional historian of Greek and Roman times—the era roughly contemporaneous with the New Testament. According to Professor Sherwin-White, the sources for Roman history that he has to work with are usually biased and usually removed at least one or two generations or even centuries from the events that they record. And yet he says historians reconstruct with confidence what really happened. He chastises New Testament critics for not realizing what valuable sources they have in the Gospels. The writings of the ancient Greek historian Herodotus furnish a test case for the rate of legendary accumulation, and the tests show that even two generations is too short a time span to allow legendary tendencies to wipe out the hard core of historical facts. When Professor Sherwin-White turns to Gospels, he states that for these to be legends, the rate of legendary accumulation would have to be "unbelievable."[5] More generations are needed.

All New Testament scholars agree that the Gospels were written down and circulated within the first generation—during the lifetime of the eyewitnesses. It's instructive to note in this connection that no apocryphal gospel appeared during the first century. These did not arise until the second century after the generation of the eyewitnesses had died off. These are, I think, better candidates for the office of legendary fiction than the biblical Gospels. There was simply insufficient time for sufficient accrual of legend by the time of the Gospels' composition. And thus I think we have quite good historical grounds for affirming the credibility of Jesus' appearances after his death as recorded in the Gospels.

The Discovery of Jesus' Empty Tomb

Once widely regarded as an offense to modern intelligence and an embarrassment to Christian theology, the empty tomb has come to take its place among the generally accepted facts concerning the historical Jesus. Allow me to review just briefly some of the evidence undergirding this conclusion.

(1) *The historical reliability of the burial story supports the empty tomb.* If the burial account of Jesus is accurate, then the site of Jesus' grave was known to both Jew and Christian alike. But in that case, it is a very short inference to the historicity of the empty tomb. For if Jesus had not risen and the burial site were known, then the disciples could never have believed in the resurrection of Jesus. For a first-century Jew, the idea that a man might be raised from the dead while his body still remained in the tomb was simply a contradiction in terms. Moreover, the Jewish authorities would have exposed the whole affair. The quickest and surest answer to the proclamation of the resurrection of Jesus would have been simply to point to his grave on the hillside. For these reasons, the accuracy of the burial story supports the historicity of the empty tomb.

Unfortunately for those who wish to deny the empty tomb, however, the burial story is widely recognized to be one of the most historically certain traditions that we have concerning Jesus. But if that is the case, then, as I have explained, the inference that the tomb was empty is not very far at hand.

(2) *The empty-tomb story was part of the pre-Markan passion story and is therefore very old.* The empty-tomb story was probably the end of Mark's source for the final week of Jesus' suffering and death in Jerusalem, the so-called "passion" of Jesus. Now since Mark is the earliest of our Gospels, this passion source is therefore itself quite old. In fact, the commentator Rudolf Pesch contends that it is an incredibly early source. He argues that at the very latest, the pre-Markan source must come from within seven years after Jesus' death.[6] This source thus goes back to the very first few years of the Jerusalem fellowship and is therefore an ancient and reliable source of historical information.

(3) *The empty-tomb story itself is simple and lacks legendary development.* The empty-tomb story is uncolored by the theological and apologetical motifs that would be characteristic of a later legendary account. Probably the most forceful way to appreciate this fact is to compare the Gospel accounts of the empty tomb with the accounts in apocryphal gospels of the second century. For example, in the so-called *Gospel of Peter*, a voice rings out from heaven during the night, the stone rolls back of itself from the door of the tomb, and then two men descend from out of heaven and enter the tomb. Then three men come out of the tomb, the two of them supporting the third. The heads of the two men reach up to the clouds, but the head of the third man overpasses the clouds. Then a cross comes out of the tomb, and a voice from heaven asks, "Hast thou preached to them that sleep?" And the cross answers, "Yea." Now

these are how real legends look. They are colored by theological and other motifs.

(4) *The tomb was probably discovered empty by women.* To understand this point, one has to recall two facts about the role of women in first-century Palestine.

(a) Women occupied a low rung on the Jewish social ladder. This is evident in such rabbinic expressions as, "Sooner let the words of the law be burnt than delivered to women," and again, "Happy is he whose children are male, but woe to him whose children are female."[7]

(b) The testimony of women was regarded as so worthless that they were not even permitted to serve as legal witnesses in a court of law. If a man was caught in the very act of committing a crime by a group of women, he could not be convicted on the basis of their testimony because it was regarded as so worthless that it would not even be admitted into court.

Now in light of these two facts, how remarkable must it seem that it is *women* who are the discoverers of Jesus' empty tomb. Any later legend would certainly have made the male disciples to discover the empty tomb. The fact that women, whose testimony was worthless, rather than men, are the chief witnesses to the empty tomb is most plausibly accounted for by the fact that, like it or not, they *were* the discoverers of the empty tomb, and the Gospels accurately record this somewhat embarrassing fact.

(5) *The earliest Jewish polemic presupposes the empty tomb.* In Matthew 28, we find the Christian attempt to refute the earliest Jewish polemic against the resurrection. That polemic asserted that the disciples stole away Jesus' body. The Christians responded to this by reciting the story of the guard at the tomb, and the polemic in turn charged that the guard fell asleep. Now the noteworthy feature of this whole dispute is not the historicity of the guards but rather the presupposition of both parties that the body was missing. The earliest Jewish response to the proclamation of the resurrection was an attempt to explain away the empty tomb. Thus, the evidence of the adversaries of the first disciples provides evidence in support of the empty tomb.

I could go on, but perhaps enough has been said to indicate why the consensus of scholarship affirms the historicity of the empty tomb of Jesus. According to Jacob Kremer, "By far most exegetes hold firmly to the reliability of the biblical statements concerning the empty tomb."[8] Thus it is today widely recognized that the empty tomb of Jesus is a simple historical fact. As New Testament critic D. H. van Daalen points out, "It is extremely difficult to object to the empty tomb on historical grounds; those who deny it do so on the basis of theological or philosophical assumptions."[9] But assumptions may simply have to be changed in light of the facts.

The Origin of the Christian Way

Even the most skeptical scholars admit that the earliest disciples at least believed that Jesus had been raised from the dead. Indeed, they pinned nearly everything on it. Without belief in the resurrection of Jesus, Christianity could not have come into being. The origin of Christianity hinges on the belief of these earliest disciples that God had raised Jesus from the dead. Now the question inevitably arises: "Where in the world did they come up with *that* belief?" As R. H. Fuller urges, even the most skeptical critic must posit some mysterious X to get the movement going.[10] But the question is, "What was that X?"

If one denies that Jesus really did rise from the dead, then one must explain the disciples' belief that he did rise in terms of either Jewish influences or Christian influences. Now obviously it couldn't have been the result of Christian influences, for the simple reason that there wasn't any Christianity yet.

But neither can the belief in the resurrection be explained as a result of Jewish influences, for the Jewish concept of resurrection from the dead differed in two important, fundamental respects from Jesus' resurrection. In Jewish thought the resurrection always (1) occurred after the end of the world, not within history, and (2) concerned all the people, not just an isolated individual. In contradistinction to this, Jesus' resurrection was both within history and of one individual person.

Joachim Jeremias writes,

> Ancient Judaism did not know of an anticipated resurrection as an event of history. Nowhere does one find in the literature anything comparable to the resurrection of Jesus. Certainly resurrections of the dead were known, but these always concerned resuscitations, the return to earthly life. In no place in the late Judaic literature does it concern a resurrection to [glory] as an event of history.[11]

The disciples, therefore, confronted with Jesus' crucifixion and death, would only have looked forward to the resurrection at the final day and would probably have kept their master's tomb as a shrine, where his bones could reside until the general resurrection. They would not have come up with the outlandish idea that he was already raised.

And remember: they were fishermen and tax collectors, not theologians. The mysterious X is still missing. According to C. F. D. Moule of Cambridge University, here is a belief nothing in terms of previous historical influences can plausibly account for.[12] He points out that we have a situation in which a large number of people held firmly to this belief, which cannot be explained in terms of the Old Testament or the Pharisees, and these people held on to this belief until the Jews finally threw them out of the synagogue. According to Professor Moule, the origin of this belief must have been the fact that Jesus really did rise from the dead. He writes:

> If the coming into existence of the Nazarenes, a phenomenon undeniably attested by the New Testament, rips a great hole in history, a hole the size and shape of the Resurrection, what does the secular historian propose to stop it up with? . . . The birth and rapid rise of the Christian Church . . . *remain an unsolved enigma for any historian who refuses to take seriously the only explanation offered by the church itself.*[13]

The resurrection of Jesus is therefore the best explanation for the origin of the Christian faith.

Taken together then, these three great historical facts—the resurrection appearances, the empty tomb, the very origin of the Christian Way—all seem to point to the resurrection of Jesus as the most plausible explanation.

Attempts to explain away these three great facts—like "The disciples stole the body" or "Jesus wasn't really dead"—have been universally rejected by contemporary scholarship. One might ask, "Well, then, how *do* skeptical New Testament critics explain the facts of the resurrection appearances, the empty tomb, and the origin of the Christian faith?" The fact of the matter is, they don't. There simply is no plausible explanatory alternative recognized today by modern scholarship as an explanation of these facts. Those who refuse to accept the resurrection as an event of history are self-confessedly left without an explanation.

These three great facts—the resurrection appearances, the empty tomb, and the origin of the Christian faith—all point, it seems to me, to the same conclusion: the resurrection of Jesus. The resurrection of Jesus supplies the key to answering the question before us this evening, for it confirms his radical claim to stand in the place of God. To quote Pannenberg again,

Jesus' claim to authority, through which he put himself in God's place, . . .was blasphemous for Jewish ears. . . . If Jesus really has been raised, this claim has been visibly and unambiguously confirmed by the God of Israel, who was allegedly blasphemed by Jesus.[14]

Jesus, then, was just who he claimed to be. In the words of the Apostle Paul, himself a Pharisee whose life was turned upside-down when he encountered the risen Lord on the Damascus road: "God was in Christ reconciling the world to Himself."

Chapter 3

Interactive Discussion

Peter Zaas and William Lane Craig

Zaas: I think it's fairly clear that we haven't been talking to each other up to this point, which is only understandable. Dr. Craig, in your publications, of which your talk is a wonderful summary on the question of the resurrection, I'm not entirely clear whom you're arguing against. As I tried to say before, the question of Jesus' resurrection seems to be a Christian question. As an outsider to the people who ask and answer Christian questions, I'm curious and would sure like to be instructed on the point: "With whom are you arguing?" It's not with me.

Craig: Very straightforwardly, I don't think of this argument as directed *against* anybody. I think of this as simply a positive justification for my own belief in the identity of Jesus and in general for the Christian view of Jesus. But this would not be something that is directed *against* anybody.

Zaas: Let me continue the inquiry then. Again, as an outsider, why is it that at this juncture in the history of Christianity you feel called to make such a vociferous case for the historicity of the resurrection? Those of us who read Paul's letters are familiar with asking the question, "He's making a case so strongly; who's making the opposite case?" "And what I'm saying to you," he says in Galatians, "before God I do not lie." Someone says he's lying.

Now you're making a strong case for the historicity of the resurrection. Who's denying it?

Craig: There are lots of people who deny it—modern secularists, for example. I'm not being disingenuous; I don't think of this as directed *against* somebody. My zeal and enthusiasm, rather, flow out of a belief that Jesus really was who he claimed to be. He really is God's gift to us; he is the means by which we can come to know God. He changed my life. I wasn't raised a Christian, but became a Christian as a teenager. It turned my life upside-down in the way that it did Paul's. And so this enthusiasm or "vociferousness" just flows out of a desire to share this with other people—not against somebody, but a genuine desire that others might also find this fantastic news. The word "gospel" means "good news," and so it's in this sense that someone wants to share this good news with people.

Zaas: Now let me deal with something you said toward the beginning of your remarks—this question of blasphemy. I think you referred to the Jews who rejected Jesus as a blasphemer. I wish you wouldn't have said it that way.

Craig: That was a quotation from Pannenberg, and I did feel a little bit uncomfortable myself with the quotation. But go ahead.

Zaas: It's at least worth pointing out that it's a dangerous problem to talk about "the Jews" doing anything.

Craig: Exactly. And that's why, if you noticed—I can show you the text with my remarks—I specifically said the Jewish *leadership*. But in the quotation from Pannenberg, he does say "the Jews." And I think that Pannenberg himself, if you would talk to him today, would also say that he wouldn't want to paint it with those wide brush strokes.

Zaas: Now let's talk about the question of blasphemy. This seems to me, as a reader of Mark's Gospel, to be an invention of the evangelist, that this was not the charge on which Jesus was condemned to be handed over to the Roman authorities for eventual execution. And I think that there is a reasonable case to be made from the text of the Gospel. Jewish legal historians have had a lot of trouble with the trial scene in Mark because it doesn't correspond to the correct procedure for how you do a trial of anybody.

Craig: The post-70 A.D. regulations.

Zaas: That's correct. And, of course, we don't have the pre-70 A.D. regulations. Nor do we, I believe, have the pre-70 A.D. rabbinic notion of how women ought to be treated in society.

Craig: True.

Zaas: And in Mark's Gospel, there are two charges brought against Jesus at his trial. One of them Mark explicitly puts into the mouth of false witnesses—that he threatened to destroy the Temple. (He made the claim, "Destroy this Temple, and in three days I will raise it up"—another not made by hands.) In John's Gospel, it's a true charge; that is, it's exactly what Jesus says in this scene in the Temple. And I actually believe that this was the charge—anti-Temple activities—which in fact resembles the superscription on the cross at least as much as it resembles some kind of blasphemy notion. What constitutes blasphemy is an area of Jewish law which is very vague. But an area of Roman law that is not very vague—

revolutionary activity—historically makes a lot more sense, it seems to me. This was the charge that the Romans were able, in their kangaroo court, to crucify Jesus by putting the superscription "King of the Jews," making a kind of claim of Jewish zealotry—a false claim, I think, but the claim nonetheless.

Mark, I think, however, is tremendously agitated about this kind of charge. Mark wants Jesus to look pretty good in a Roman kind of way and therefore has shifted the charge away from blasphemy. And I'm made uncomfortable by the notion of how, in your scheme, God has redeemed Jesus, the presumed blasphemer. I'm not sure any Jewish authority really ever did presume he was a blasphemer. I question that.

Craig: I certainly wouldn't deny that Jesus' actions in the Temple helped to precipitate his arrest and the charges against him. I think that's entirely true. But I think a real question that one needs to draw in here is whether or not Jesus' notion of the kingdom of God's coming in himself was not perceived as blasphemous precisely because it attempted to replace the Temple as the focus of Judaism with himself and the kingdom of God as the focus of belief. So I think the very perceived attack on the Temple itself was thought to be blasphemous in Jewish sight because Jesus arrogated to himself a type of authority that no person could have arrogated to himself. I would add to that, for example, the famous antitheses in the Sermon on the Mount, where Jesus would quote some portion of the Torah or tradition as having been delivered to the people; then he would say, "But *I* say to you." And he would oppose his authority to the Torah itself and to these traditions.

In my readings, I came across the statement by an orthodox Jewish scholar, whose name is Ahad ha'Am. He says this:

> Israel cannot accept as the word of God the utterances of a man who speaks in his own name. Not "thus saith the Lord," but "I say to you." This "I" is in itself sufficient to drive Judaism from the Gentiles forever.[1]

This "*I* say to you" involved Jesus' taking the place of God, arrogating to himself authority that belonged to God alone.

Zaas: I wouldn't see it that way at all. Ahad ha'Am is, what, a century old? I think you could find better evidence for your position than that. In the Sermon on the Mount specifically, Jesus makes a very typically Jewish legal exegesis. I think you could find this evidenced in lots of ways.

Craig: But not the opposition of his own authority by saying, "*I* say to you." For example, there's a recent book by Jacob Neusner, *A Rabbi Talks* *with Jesus*, and Neusner says exactly the same thing about these antitheses in the Sermon on the Mount.[2] I recently read an article in *Christianity Today* (an interview with Neusner) about this. The way Neusner would put it was: If he were with Jesus, he would say, "Who do you think you are, God?"[3] It's exactly that kind of thing that I think precipitated the reaction to Jesus.

Zaas: It's precisely stated that Jesus speaks as one with authority, not like the scribes—whoever they were.

Craig: Yes.

Zaas: But I'm not sure that it's blasphemy. It's speaking with authority. I think there's a theological motivation that I don't share in your claiming that Jesus is, though seemingly guilty of blasphemy from a Jewish point of view, vindicated by God in the resurrection. I don't think that Jews have so much concern as you seem to think they do for blasphemers—if this even constitutes blasphemy. Blasphemy typically is cursing God. And claiming the authority of God may be seen in Jewish quarters as odd—possibly even mad. I don't know that Jews typically have been so exercised about this.

Craig: I guess that's the impression that I've gotten from the reading that I've done—that this sort of authority could not be claimed by any sort of human being and that this, therefore, would be regarded as literally blasphemous. To claim to speak against the Torah in one's own authority, to claim that the kingdom of God had come in one's own person, to divert the worship from the Temple to focusing on oneself, to claim to forgive sins—these are only things that God can do. It seems to me that we can't get away from this sort of radical understanding that Jesus had.

Zaas: I think I would basically agree with you although I would really caution you to try to be sensitive to these kinds of things as they would sound in antiquity, not through the lens of millennia of Christian theologizing.

Craig: Yes, that's a good point. Now could I ask you a question?

Zaas: Just a minute. Does Jesus really speak against the Torah?

Craig: He revises it.

Zaas: True. I mean he argues for a particular interpretation of it.

Craig: What about, for example, Mark 7:15, where he declares all foods clean?

Zaas: Oh, that's a very interesting passage. He speaks as a Sadducee. He says that the things that come out of a person make him unclean, not the things that go in. And everyone who has ever read the Hebrew Bible knows that the things that come out of you make you unclean (e.g., urine, menstrual blood). And then he goes on to say, "But that's not what I mean, is it? I mean . . ."—and he lists out the vices. He moralizes the purity laws.

Craig: Right. Exactly. He's saying, "It's not the things that you ingest," but he seems to be overturning Old Testament dietary laws and regulations. He's saying that these aren't really what's important; what's important is, as you say, this moral dimension.

Zaas: I think he's entering into a contemporary legal dispute that hadn't been settled by that time—whether food could make you impure or not. Certain foods are impure, but they don't *make* you impure. Jesus characteristically moralizes the purity laws, in a way that really undercuts the authority of the priesthood, particularly. I mean the Pharisees were involved in a very similar enterprise in a very different direction. But here we have a historical situation in which all kinds of Jewish authorities—whatever kind of authority they're claiming for themselves—are trying to do something with the purity laws and trying to claim the authority of the priesthood for themselves.

Craig: But as far as I know, no Jew of antiquity ever simply claimed to overturn the dietary regulations of the Old Testament between clean and unclean the way that Jesus did.

Zaas: I just think you're pushing it too hard. Jesus has a unique approach to the Law; he claims it's fulfilled in his time and in his person; he claims not to be reducing it by a "jot or tittle" (isn't that a wonderful translation?).

Craig: Well, it's a cumulative case. It's not just one element. But when you put all these elements together, you have the emergence of a very radical self-understanding by this man.

Zaas: And a very radical understanding of the Torah, but not an overturning of it.

Craig: Let me ask you a question. Don't you think you're being a little bit disingenuous about Judaism's not having any beliefs? It seems to me that you've given us a definition of *ethnic* Judaism—that to be *ethnically* Jewish, it doesn't matter what you believe. But surely as a religion, Judaism affirms monotheism. And you make Judaism sound like modern-day Hinduism to me—that it has no beliefs, no doctrinal statements, no creeds. Surely, Judaism makes some religious claims; otherwise, why did they desert Shabbatai Zvi when he turned to Islam? And what about the extra curse added to the Twelfth Benediction to rule out the Nazarenes? It seems to me clearly that as a religion, if not as an ethnic group, Judaism has beliefs.

Zaas: You presuppose the answer by your question. "As a religion, doesn't Judaism have beliefs?" Of course it does; as a religion Judaism does have beliefs. But Judaism *isn't* a religion, it seems to me. Judaism is a sense of peoplehood, and Jews believe all kinds of things and still remain Jews. You can say that that's an ethnic definition, but it is the definition that Jews have inherited. Jews cannot be read out of Judaism for their beliefs, nor are they admitted into the community by their beliefs. It doesn't mean that there aren't some beliefs that large numbers of Jews share, and you can figure out what Jewish beliefs are by taking a survey at any particular time in history. "Jews believe in at most one God" is a typical thing to say. Jews affirm in their liturgy—a liturgy which is shared by all kinds of Jews whether they believe in what they're saying or not—any number of religious beliefs: the resurrection of the dead, the coming of the Messiah, etc. They read the "Nineteenth Benediction," which may or may not have been directed against Jewish Christians at the turn of the first century, the so-called *Birkat Haminim* (the Blessing against Separatists). There's a lot of dispute about that. I think you're right, though, that it was directed against Jews in synagogues who were separatists and, perhaps, who accepted the Christian doctrine.

Craig: There was a ruling a few years ago in Israel concerning ethnic Jews who wanted to come to Israel under the return-to-the-land law and become citizens,[4] but who believed in Jesus as Messiah, and the Israeli supreme court ruled that they weren't Jews and that they couldn't under this law come to Israel and become citizens. That seems to suggest to me that there's some kind of creedal belief system.

Zaas: There is a creedal belief system about the Law of Return in Israel, which is a highly politicized country. In fact, the Israeli law distinguished itself from the Jewish law about who is a Jew in 1962, in the Supreme Court ruling in the case of Oswald Rufeisen, aka "Brother Daniel," when a Carmelite brother who was born a Jew decided to express his Jewishness and return to Israel under the Law of Return (which, as you know, gives all Jews citizenship in the Jewish state). The court determined that because he was a Carmelite brother, he wasn't a Jew anymore. The Israeli Law of Return is scarcely Judaism. God forbid the Israeli courts should be identified with Judaism. It's a terrible mistake. That was a terrible error in the case of Israeli courts, and it's a terrible error for Jews to claim that Jews who express this particular belief can't be considered Jews anymore. Most Jews disagree with me on this question—or many do—that "messianic Jews" should somehow be excluded from the community. I think that's a terrible mistake and a terrible misreading by Jews about what Judaism stands for. A lot of people don't like this, but I think it's an error. If Judaism is going to be non-creedal on one side, it ought to be non-creedal on the other side too. If Jews are not going to be identified by their lack of belief in Jesus, then they ought not to be *un*identified by their belief in Jesus as the Messiah. Jewishness is something that transcends belief. It's possible in your value system that belief is a very high thing. For Jews, there's a historical consciousness that beliefs change over time, that Jews could be born without any consciousness of God and God's love, and then that their descendants recover it. Judaism has a historical continuity, and Jews have been guilty of all kinds of terrible, stupid beliefs at times, and other times not.

Chapter 4

Questions and Answers

Peter Zaas and William Lane Craig

Question 1: *"I would be very interested to hear you both comment on the concept of blood atonement for sin. As I understand it, God requires a blood atonement for sin, and I'd like to hear you both address that question from the perspective of the Scriptures."*

Craig: It seems to me that in Old Testament Judaism, the notion of the sacrificial system was an inherent part of that religious practice. And Christians typically think of Jesus, by his sacrificial death, as being the sacrifice, that is to say, the sin-bearer, that makes atonement. So that's why Jesus is referred to as the Lamb of God in the Gospels. He is the sacrificial lamb and is the fulfillment of Old Testament types, or prefiguring of this atonement. So the notion of the Old Testament sacrificial system finds its place in Christianity and the sacrifice of Jesus.

Zaas: This is Paul's notion first, I think, historically. Paul is the earliest source for Jesus as the paschal sacrifice. He's the Lamb of God, not because he's cute and wooly, but because he's the lamb sacrificed on the Passover. This is certainly an important aspect of the religious system of the Hebrew Bible, which I'm not sure I'd call Judaism. In Judaism, a faith, a culture, a people which develops and faces the loss of the sacrificial system following the destruction of the Temple no longer has the notion of a blood sacrifice except as a kind of memory of the way it was when there was a Temple. There are all kinds of ways of atoning for sin in Judaism, and mostly they involve saying "I'm sorry" to God or the person wronged. Of course, there is no more sacrificial system in Judaism although some Jews—a terribly small number (the smaller the better)—would like to start the sacrificial system up again, thinking they could rebuild the Temple, find the altar, recover the ark of the covenant, and do all these wonderful things in Jerusalem (first, by destroying all the Muslim holy places there). I hope this never happens, and I think that it's really intrinsically against what Judaism has come to stand for.

Question 2: *"A couple of quick questions. First, Dr. Zaas, as I understand it, the Romans didn't want to crucify Jesus. They found no reason to do it. I was under the impression that it was the Sanhedrin's charge of blasphemy that was the only way they could allow [the crucifixion] to happen under Roman law. Would you address that issue? Second, as a Jew, I would like to hear your scholarly perspective on why it is that the majority of Jews today do not believe that you can be a Jew and believe that Jesus is the Messiah."*

Zaas: I think the first question is pretty easy. The reason you think that the Romans didn't want to crucify Jesus and they found no crime in him is because you are informed by the Gospel of Mark. That's exactly what the Gospel of Mark wants you to think. The Romans were quite fond of crucifying people; it was a famous pastime. And Jesus, of course, was one of many victims of this tremendously cruel method. Nobody invented this method of execution who didn't enjoy it in a sadistic way, watching people die in this horrible, painful way. Mark, who writes for a Roman audience, wants Jesus to look good to them, and so he shifts the responsibility onto what you could call the Sanhedrin, if you want, but it's pretty unclear that that's the Sanhedrin. It's a gathering of Jewish priests and authorities who (in Mark) say, "He's guilty of blasphemy; let's turn him over to the Romans." It's not entirely clear to me that the Romans are all that concerned about executing Jewish blasphemers. They might give a medal to Jewish blasphemers, but they might consider it very irrelevant to their point of view. The Romans want to execute anti-Roman people, people who are a threat to Roman authority in this increasingly heated-up political atmosphere.

I don't believe the majority of Jews think that messianic Jews aren't Jews. I haven't seen any surveys on this, have you?

Questioner responds: *"Speaking as a son whose mother considers me not to be a Jew because I believe Jesus is the Messiah, I can speak firsthand. And I have a number of Jewish friends who also believe this. And even those who don't, say, 'Wait a second! You're a Christian now.' No, I'm a Jew who just happens to believe that Jesus is Messiah. I believe that the latter group's view is more pervasive than you are representing it to be."*

Zaas: I'm on *your* side in this, but I think you'll probably understand why Jews are uncomfortable with messianic Jews (if that's a comfortable term for you). One thing that Jews and Christians absolutely share is the notion that God works in history, and Jews' history with Christians has not been entirely comfortable. We live only two generations after the Holocaust, and you can understand how a people, which for much of its history has been vulnerable, may feel. You may be in the *avant garde*, and you may be facing something similar to what Jesus and his followers faced from *their* parents. How about the guy who couldn't even bury his father? What do you think his mother felt? You understand this.

Questioner responds: *"I do. I guess that that seemed to be half the draw, hearing a Jewish scholar discuss with a Christian scholar [the question], 'Who Was Jesus?' I'm just a little bit disappointed, maybe, that you're not coming from my mother's position and giving some of your reasons."*

Craig: I wanted to say something with respect to the crucifixion. If Jesus didn't make any radical claims about himself (as most New Testament scholars say he did), if he were just some Jewish rabbi or teacher as he is sometimes portrayed, then the whole reason he was crucified becomes a mystery. It would be a mystery why the Jewish leadership would have wanted him crucified, and it would be a mystery as well why the Romans would crucify him. The Romans apparently wanted him out of the way because, as Dr. Zaas says, they wanted to get rid of rebel influences. But the attempt to write Jesus off as some zealot or political revolutionary, I think, is largely discredited. So it seems to me that the fact that Jesus did make the radical claims I discussed, which were blasphemous to the Jewish leadership at that time, and that they then in turn interpreted these to the Roman authorities as rebellion—that is to say, Jesus is claiming to be a king and is a potential threat for Caesar—provides a plausible reason for why the crucifixion occurred.

Question 3: *"Dr. Zaas, I'm somewhat intrigued by your seeming indifference to Dr. Craig's defense of the resurrection because if it did happen and Jesus is who he says he was, this has profound implications for every single human being—especially in light of John 14:6, which says, 'I am the way, the truth, and the life. No one comes to the Father except through me.' That's a pretty radical claim, and I was wondering how you view him in view of that."*

Zaas: I don't know how to answer. I don't dispute the fact of the resurrection. It's not something I'm involved in, but it doesn't seem to be an event that's made much positive difference to Jewish history. I feel the weight of Jewish history. I hope even messianic Jews feel the weight of Jewish history. It's all I can say. Jews deal with the religious claims of other groups all the time. They make their judgments about other groups not based on their religious claims, it seems to me, but how they behave in the world. Jews judge themselves the way they behave in the world, and I think that's the criterion for how they look at other religious groups.

Jews in ancient times tried to establish lists of rules for what constitutes righteousness for non-Jews. Did they eat living flesh? (As far as I know, very few Christians eat living flesh.) They determined that Christians could be righteous.

It just seems to me that the Christian claim for the resurrection is a Christian claim. It doesn't seem to have much impact on me or my life. Christians have had a lot of impact; Christianity has had a lot of impact, and it seems that this is what I'm called to deal with. I can only say that that's my reaction. It may be intellectually absurd that I should pay so little attention to this miraculous event that should have happened two thousand years ago. Of course, "scoffers will come in the last days, saying, 'Where is the promise of his coming? For in all these generations things have stayed pretty much the same as they always have.'" But of course, that itself is a proof of Jesus' resurrection in 2 Peter. And I don't know what to make of it.

Craig: I'd like to respond to the idea that this hasn't made any impact for Jewish history. Pinchas Lapide, who is one of the most prominent Jewish theologians today, believes in the resurrection of Jesus on the basis of historical evidence such as I laid out. I heard Lapide lecture in Munich when I was there. I nearly fell off my chair when he got to the conclusion and said, "On the basis of the evidence, I conclude that the God of Israel raised Jesus from the dead." And what Lapide says about the impact of the resurrection is that through this event, the faith in the God of Israel has been spread throughout the entire world. He sees this as an event of incredible significance and moment for the Jewish faith, that belief in the God of Israel should through this event and its aftermath have become a universal faith around the world. And so that's not to be underestimated.

Question 4: *"I have a question for Dr. Craig and one for Dr. Zaas. Dr. Craig, Christianity obviously rests upon the resurrection. But Lazarus rose from the dead, and I don't know if there were others as well. Could you comment on that?"*

Craig: Yes. Remember what Jeremias said in the quotation that I read in my speech. Certainly the idea was known in Judaism of "revivifications"—the return to the earthly life. But Lazarus would die again; he was mortal. The little daughter of Jairus would die again. It was not a resurrection in the technical sense in which this word or concept was understood in Judaism, which involved a raising again of the dead to eternal life, to glory and immortality. It's in that sense that the resurrection of Christ stands apart and is singular from any of these revivifications to mortal life.

Same questioner: *"Thank you. And Dr. Zaas, the other gentleman quoted 'I am the way' from John's Gospel. Also in John, Jesus said, 'I and the Father are one.' As a New Testament scholar, how do you reconcile that with who he is?"*

Zaas: We could all list out New Testament Gospel claims of Jesus. "No one comes to the Father except through me"; "unless you confess Jesus with your lips" (Romans 10). These are books whose religious perspective I don't share. If that makes you uncomfortable that I continue not to share it, I'm sorry. But I don't. "Did Jesus claim to be divine?" I don't think that's quite as closed a question as you think it is. But perhaps he did. Did his followers claim that he was not only divine, but the only way that people could achieve some kind of notion of salvation? They certainly did. I don't agree with them. I think that the force of Jewish history suggests that for Jews, there is no reason to agree with them. You may see otherwise, and I appreciate your coming and saying so.

Question 5: "I'd like to address my question to both of you. Dr. Zaas, in the story of the paralytic in Mark, where the paralytic is let down through the roof, Jesus said to the paralytic, "Your sins are forgiven," and the scribes said that's blasphemy. Later on in that text, there is a verse that says that the healing was done so that you might know that the Son of Man has authority on earth to forgive sins. The implication seems to be that Jesus made some radical claims (from the Christian standpoint) to be God. I'd like to actually hear how you would interpret that passage and Jesus' claim from a Jewish standpoint. The implications there seem, from a Christian standpoint, to be clear to me, but if they're not, I'd like to hear from your standpoint why they're not."

Zaas: The implications are that Jesus himself could forgive sins and therefore was divine because only God can forgive sins. We have to go back to the text of Mark. (I'm not prepared to do that.) This is a typical belief of the early church. Jesus certainly had the power to forgive sins. Jesus was the Son of God, and Jesus was God. "In the beginning he was with God"— not to mention later! Why shouldn't he have the power to forgive sins?

As a New Testament scholar, my job is to try to figure out what Mark is saying to his audience, to figure out what he's talking about. It's not always to determine what exactly this is supposed to mean for me and the working out of my own plan for salvation. I don't feel that obligation all the time.

I think the Gospel of Mark is one of the great works of religious literature. This author is one of the most modern, sensitive, narratively sublime, blessed of authors, but I don't always feel obliged to determine whether I think he's right or wrong. I'm really concerned about how the Greek works out and what he's trying to say (For whom was he writing? What were his sources?)—the same kinds of questions *you* deal with. You have, perhaps, a different final purpose. Perhaps, but perhaps not.

Craig: I think it's important to see here (and perhaps some of the questioners don't understand this) that it's not enough to simply quote verses out of the New Testament because I think Dr. Zaas, like some New Testament critics, would say, "These don't reflect authentic traditions or words of the historical Jesus himself, but represent Mark's theology and John's theology." And therefore part of the task of the New Testament critic is to try to find those authentic traditions, those historical traditions, that come from Jesus of Nazareth himself. Now in this case from Mark 2, I think there are good grounds for holding that it represents good historical tradition; it enjoys a sort of multiple attestation in the sense that Jesus' parables, many of which are indisputably authentic, represent this claim to forgive sins. And his practice of table fellowship with social outcasts, prostitutes, and toll collectors was a lived-out parable for them of his opening the kingdom of God to them and forgiving sins.

So the fact that Jesus made the claim to forgive sins—which I agree would be blasphemous if he made it—can be plausibly established as belonging to the portrait of the historical Jesus of Nazareth.

Concluding remarks—Zaas: This is an untypical sort of Jewish-Christian dialogue—and very refreshing to me because when Jews and Christians meet in dialogue, they usually meet to discuss the things that they have in common—either theological things (which always turn out to be some aspect of the Old Testament) or the Jewishness of Jesus (which really wasn't the main topic here). Or they discuss items of common concern—what to do about the Muslims! It's easier for people to meet in dialogue when they agree in advance not to talk about things that they disagree about. This did not seem to be part of the plan tonight. We were going to discuss something that apparently there is some disagreement about, and historically there is serious disagreement about. I hope I didn't minimize the amount of disagreement that there has been historically.

Nonetheless, I'd like to end on a positive note. "Historically" is an important word. Jews and Christians share a notion that there is history, that history is a real force in human life. It's not just the sequence of events that seem to happen for whatever external cause. Jews and Christians share together this notion which, I guess, they get from the Hebrew prophets, but they continually reinforced it by whatever sources of reinforcement they get from their own worship. They believe that God (to the extent that they believe anything because Judaism is non-creedal) works in history. And I believe that this is right for Jews and Christians. And if you want to know what God is up to, you look in the newspapers; you observe God's actions in history. Of course, you don't always know how to deal with this revelation! But at least for Jews (and I'll only speak for Jews here), this is an ongoing revelation. For Jews, God's purpose is revealed in the Torah and in history. We can read the Torah and discuss it and have tremendously erudite scholarly discussion. But while we're having these, God is continuing to work in history. And we really ought to feel the force of this and to take this commonality with grave seriousness.

I just want to say how pleased I am to have had the opportunity to talk and to have you at Siena College. Thank you again.

Craig: I've read some of Dr. Zaas's dialogues with other Christian scholars, and he's certainly right that this has been different tonight. This has been so politically incorrect that it's incredible! But I personally find that very refreshing, too—that we don't have to try to affirm some sort of wishy-washy pluralism which becomes a sort of amalgam that blurs the distinctiveness of either of our belief systems (or lack thereof) but respects the distinctiveness of each separate tradition.

Tonight, I've tried to argue that the key to discovering who Jesus was and is lies in his resurrection from the dead. I think that there are good historical grounds for believing that in fact Jesus not only died on the cross but that he rose again three days later. And he left an empty tomb behind; he appeared to various witnesses; and the very origin of the Christian faith cries out for some explanation. And this suggests that God acts in history.

I want to close with a quotation from the German theologian, Horst Georg Pöhlmann. He writes,

> In summary, one can say that today there is virtually a consensus concerning that wherein the historical in Jesus is to be seen. It consists in the fact that Jesus came on the scene with an *unheard of authority*— namely, the authority of God—with *the claim of the authority to stand in God's place and speak to us and bring us to salvation.*[1]

Pöhlmann concludes,

> This unheard of claim to authority, as it comes to expression in the Sermon on the Mount, for example, . . . presupposes a unity of Jesus with God that is deeper than that of all men, namely, a unity of essence.
>
> This . . . claim to authority is explicable only from the side of his deity. This authority only God himself can claim. With regard to Jesus, there are only two possible modes of behavior: either to believe that in him God encounters us or nail him to the cross as a blasphemer. There is no third way.[2]

Part Two

Reflections

Chapter 5

Jesus: Bringer of Salvation to Jew and Gentile Alike

Donald A. Hagner

It is refreshing, as Peter Zaas points out, to encounter Jewish-Christian dialogue that does not sidestep the difficult questions of disagreement between Jews and Christians, but rather attempts to address them with frankness. And there is no point at which the difference of opinion is greater than on the question of the significance of Jesus of Nazareth. As in the Gospels, so too today, it is the question of Jesus, in particular the estimate of his person, that constitutes the deep chasm that divides Jews from his followers.

The obvious truth of this observation should caution us from the start about the correctness of Zaas's statement that there is no Jewish position on Jesus. Strictly speaking, of course, it is true that there is no official Jewish estimate concerning the person of Jesus. That is, there is no statement about who Jesus was, no description of his significance, that can be said to reflect universal Jewish opinion on the subject. The same was true in the time described by the Gospels: "Some say [you are] John the Baptist, but others Elijah, and still others Jeremiah or one of the prophets" (Matt. 16:14). But if there is no agreement today among Jews concerning who Jesus was, there clearly is agreement on *who he was not*. And the reason is clear. If Jews accept the significance of Jesus attributed to him in the New Testament, they are no longer Jews (so far as faith is concerned) but Christians. Jesus, in short, is defined by the Jewish community not positively, but negatively. There is universal agreement among Jews about what he cannot have been. He cannot have been what the church believes him to be. Again, this is no different than it was from the beginning. The Jews in the Gospels who do not follow Jesus at least agree that however he was to be categorized, he was not what he claimed to be.

It will be seen from the preceding paragraph that I am defining Jews religiously and not ethnically, as Zaas does. I realize, of course, that there is an ethnic dimension to Jewishness and that when Jews believe in Jesus as Messiah and Kyrios, they do not stop being Jews, but can well be regarded as "completed" or "fulfilled" Jews. This was indeed the case with all the first Christians of the Jerusalem church, and there is no reason why the same may not be true today. Indeed, one could even say that for Jews to become believers in Jesus is one of the most Jewish things they could do. And there is no reason to my mind why such individuals cannot retain many if not all their Jewish distinctives after believing in Jesus. But from the New Testament's point of view, ethnicity has become essentially unimportant. All of humanity, Jew and Gentile alike, are trapped in sin and are in the same dire need of salvation, a salvation that can be provided only through the death and resurrection of Jesus Christ. The very idea of Jewishness is redefined by Paul, indeed in dependence on the Scriptures of Israel, as a matter of spiritual, not literal, circumcision (Rom. 2:28–29), and Gentiles of faith who thereby fulfill the Abrahamic covenant are now designated the descendants of Abraham (Gal. 3:6–9). In Christ, Paul concludes, "there is no longer Jew or Greek" (Gal. 3:28). Ethnic Jewishness remains a relatively unimportant factor in the whole picture.

At one point, Zaas appears even to use the word "Christian" in an ethnic sense, (i.e., when he assigns responsibility for the Holocaust to people who were "all Christians"). Here "Christians" must mean "Gentiles" since most Nazis were Christians in name only, if that. This we must strongly protest. The perpetrators of the Holocaust were *not* Christians. At least the courtesy of the adjective "nominal" is required before the word is used in this way. Christians, who have been taught to love even their enemies (not that the Jews are to be regarded as such!), can have nothing to do with anti-Semitism, except to be the first to stand with the Jews against every manifestation of it.

The problems addressed in Jewish-Christian dialogue concern Jewishness not as a matter of mere ethnicity, but as a matter of religious faith. It is the differences between *Judaism* and Christianity that we must address, not differences between Jewish ethnicity and Christianity. It does not seem to me that one can justifiably reduce Judaism to Jewish ethnicity, as does Zaas, merely because there is no official Jewish theological orthodoxy. This matter is brought up by William Lane Craig, who insists, rightly in my opinion, that there are beliefs that matter very much to Judaism. For all of its emphasis on orthopraxy, Judaism does have beliefs that are of crucial importance.

Zaas correctly warns us about the dangers of an anachronistic approach wherein one makes statements about the time of Jesus based on information drawn from the present: "I would really caution you to try to be sensitive to these kinds of things as they would sound in antiquity, not through the lens of millennia of Christian theologizing." In my opinion, however, Zaas does something similar when he implies that the religious leadership of Israel in the time of Jesus would have exhibited the same broad-minded tolerance of viewpoints that we find in modern forms of Judaism. Without minimizing the great diversity we find in first-century Judaism, it is not hard to imagine that the Gospel reports of the reaction of the leadership to Jesus represent the truth and that the leaders regarded the self-claims of Jesus as blasphemous in character and his teaching as a threat both to the people as well as to their own privileged status.

It is true that the blasphemy spoken of in the trial narratives is not blasphemy in the technical sense. Jesus does not pronounce the divine Name. Nor would it have been blasphemy to claim to be the Messiah—Zaas is of course right on this. But if Jesus insulted God by arrogating to himself prerogatives that belong to God alone, this could well have been regarded as blasphemous. Jesus did not claim (i.e., accept the claim) that he was an ordinary messiah (i.e., a special person anointed for leadership) as did other messianic claimants. On the contrary, he redefined messiahship by his claim to be uniquely the Son of God ("David's Lord"; Matt. 22:41–46), "the Son of the Blessed One" (Mark 14:61–64), who was to be "seated at the right hand of Power [a circumlocution for "God," deliberately showing that he did not technically blaspheme]" and who would come "on the clouds of heaven" at the end of the age (Matt. 26:64–65), and this was an outrage to the Jewish leadership. It was, in effect, to make himself equal to God (cf. John 5:18). I find it difficult to believe that orthodox Jews today would not regard a man making such claims as guilty of blasphemy. I cannot imagine, furthermore, that these leaders in the first century would have endorsed a reduction of Judaism to merely a matter of Jewish ethnicity.

Having made these random remarks, I now want to address more directly some of the central issues before us in the discussion of the significance of Jesus. I will do this under three headings: the Gospels as historical sources, the aims of Jesus, and the birth of the church.

The Gospels as Historical Sources

I find it intriguing that in the discussion between Zaas and Craig the question of the reliability of the Gospels as historical sources finds such little place. It is Craig alone who raises the question explicitly. Zaas, as a New Testament scholar, might well have picked up on this and pushed it in his favor. Most Jewish scholars, indeed, make a frontal attack on the reliability of the statements in the Gospels that cannot be reconciled with the conclusion that Jesus was merely another Jewish teacher, calling people back to the righteousness of Torah, a prophet-like reformer of Judaism. In this rejection of the historical reliability of material that is consonant with the high Christology of the post-resurrection church, Jewish scholars are happy to follow the negative conclusions of radical Christian scholars. They are bound to find comfort these days in the views of the Jesus Seminar, which concludes that a meager 18 percent of the sayings of Jesus in the Gospels is authentic. The Jesus profiled by the Jesus Seminar is, not surprisingly, basically similar to the Jesus of twentieth-century Jewish scholarship, namely a teacher/prophet/healer who stands in considerable discontinuity with the Christ proclaimed by the church.

This is not the place to address this issue in the fullness it deserves, but at least a few observations may be made. It cannot be denied that the faith of the post-resurrection Christians has had an impact on the Gospel tradition and that the Gospels were written not as neutral historical documents but as theological documents designed to defend and promote the Christian faith. It is clear that they present *interpreted* history, and it must be admitted that sometimes the degree of interpretation is considerable, especially when we turn to the Fourth Gospel—which is thus seldom used in the discussion of the historical Jesus. Yet the truth of this observation should not be absolutized, for when all the above is conceded, it simply does not follow that the Gospels are therefore not basically historical documents or that they convey to us no reliable history.

There is something terribly wrong in an approach to this problem that concludes that 82 percent of the sayings of Jesus in the Gospels cannot be safely regarded as historical. There is also an extraordinary flaw in a methodology that assumes without discussion a historicist orientation to the Gospels that consistently rules out *a priori* that which is not acceptable to a naturalistic perspective on reality. Presuppositions are everything here, and if one's presuppositions go against the common statements of the Gospels, so much the worse for the Gospels! If our presuppositions will not allow otherwise, of course Jesus can have been only a teacher, an interpreter of the law, and a reformer of Judaism and nothing more. We may add charismatic healer, too, but only if the healing miracles are capable of psychosomatic (i.e., naturalistic) explanations. But how can we know with any confidence that such presuppositions are justified?

With a different starting point and different presuppositions, a more positive view of the Gospels emerges. Once it is admitted that the sayings of Jesus were exceptionally important to the disciples (is this not self-evident?) and indeed that they regarded it as their responsibility to preserve and guard those sayings by means of a carefully sustained oral tradition, the reliability of the sayings of Jesus in the Gospels takes on a high degree of probability. The situation has been set out illuminatingly by Birger Gerhardsson and Rainer Riesner, who have shown among other things that the context is one that favors the careful transmission of oral materials, that the tradition was held in the highest esteem, and that the tradition as it is actually found in the Gospels bears this out and is highly reliable. The fact that the Gospel accounts are accounts reflecting the faith of the evangelists does not mean they cannot also be historical.

Contrary to popular opinion, then, the transmission of the sayings of Jesus by oral tradition—in this case, what amounts to a holy or sacred tradition—is not a threat to the stability or reliability of the materials, but serves rather as a kind of guarantee of the integrity of the content of that tradition. To be sure, there were slight modifications of the sayings as they were transmitted in different contexts, and as the evangelists collected the materials and integrated them into their narratives, they received some interpretation and elaboration. But the degree to which this took place has been greatly exaggerated by scholars in the twentieth century. The idea of wholesale creation of sayings of Jesus or even of the radical alteration of them in the brief forty-year period of oral tradition before the writing of the Gospels is highly unlikely. The tradition maintained a relatively stable core. Because of this, any attempt to understand Jesus while dismissing from consideration great amounts of the sayings tradition is doomed to failure. Indeed, the more material in the Synoptic Gospels one regards as inauthentic, the greater the distortion of the resultant picture of Jesus will be, and the greater confusion there will be concerning what to make of Jesus.

The Aims of Jesus

No portrayal of Jesus as merely a teacher or healer can do justice to the New Testament record. He did teach and he did heal, but these activities were subordinate to his main calling and accomplishment.

But what was the purpose of Jesus' teaching? And how did it relate to Judaism and the law of Moses? This subject is given attention by both Zaas and Craig. Zaas records his impression that the teaching of Jesus is Jewish, and he concludes that "the Jesus of the Gospels is a Jewish teacher of righteousness, no matter how unrecognizable to Jews the church has made him," and that "Jesus offered a new way of looking at Judaism." For Zaas, then,

Jesus was simply a reformer of Judaism. With almost all other Jewish scholars—Neusner being a recent notable exception—Zaas concludes that Jesus was an upholder of the Torah, and he alludes to the "jot or tittle" of Matthew 5:18. Craig, on the other hand, rightly points to the antitheses of the Sermon on the Mount (Matt. 5:21–48) and to the editorial comment in Mark 7:19 ("thus he declared all foods clean") as indications of the fact that Jesus relates to the law as no other teacher did. In this regard, one might also point to Jesus' teaching concerning the Sabbath and divorce.

Both Zaas and Craig have valid points to make here. In my opinion, the question of Jesus and the law can be understood only as involving a paradox. This paradox is already apparent in Matthew 5, where Jesus' affirmation of the law is juxtaposed with the antitheses. The latter involve more than mere interpretation, Zaas notwithstanding. They involve a transcending of the law (see especially the third, fourth, and fifth antitheses) that immediately brings into focus the unique authority of Jesus. But for Matthew this transcending of the law by the Messiah is by no means to be understood as the overthrowing of the law. It is its authoritative interpretation. And the obedience to the teaching of Jesus is for Matthew (as for Paul!) the fulfillment of the Torah, and the very embodiment of the righteousness of the Torah. Thus it is true that Jesus is both the upholder of the righteousness of the Torah, as well as a sovereign interpreter of the Torah who can transcend it in favor of its ultimate meaning.

Craig is surely right that the key issue here is the authority of Jesus. This is a common and important motif in the Gospels, and it is hard to see how Zaas can minimize it in the way he does. We see that authority, of course, in the definitive way that Jesus interprets the Torah. He does not say "the law says" or "Moses says," but "*I* say to you." As the Messiah, he is the *only* teacher, the *one* tutor of his people (Matt. 23:8–10). But more than that, Jesus puts himself at the center of everything. He calls his disciples not so much to Torah as to himself: "Come to *me*," he says to the weary and burdened. "Take *my* yoke upon you," he says, rather than the yoke of the Torah (Matt. 11:28–30). It is he who is crucial in the relation between God and humanity. He talks about losing one's life for *his* sake (Mark 8:35; Matt. 10:39), not that of Torah or the kingdom, or being persecuted for *his* sake (Matt. 5:11). He says with all boldness: "Everyone therefore who acknowledges *me* before others, *I* also will acknowledge before my Father in heaven; but whoever denies *me* before others, *I* also will deny before my Father in heaven" (Matt. 10:32–33 = Luke 12:8–9). The love of Jesus is more important than all other human relationships, and "whoever does not take up the cross and follow *me* is not worthy of *me*" (Matt. 10:37–38). His relation with God is utterly unique: "All things have been handed over to me by my Father; and no one knows the Son except the Father, and no one knows the Father except the Son and anyone to whom the Son chooses to reveal him" (Matt. 11:27 = Luke 10:22).

Jesus is, in brief, the unique Agent of God, who takes upon himself nothing other than the prerogatives of God. He forgives sins, as Craig emphasizes, and not as an intermediary, but directly and on his own authority (thus the reaction of astonishment among the crowd in Mark 2:7). More than that, he identifies himself as the eschatological Judge. *He* will come on the clouds with power and great glory, he will send out *his* angels and gather *his* elect (Matt. 24:30–31). *He* "will sit on the throne of *his* glory" and "all the nations will be gathered before *him*, and *he* will separate people one from another as a shepherd separates the sheep from the goats" (Matt. 25:31–32). Furthermore, the final judgment is pronounced on the grounds of relationship to Jesus: "you did it to *me*"; "you did not do it to *me*" (Matt. 25:35–46). When reinforced by the disciples' encounter with the glorified, resurrected Jesus, this material leads readily to the high Christology of the early church, as articulated, for example, already by Paul a mere two decades later. This is the Jesus who could be identified as the "Emmanuel" ("God with us") of Isaiah 7:14 (Matt. 1:23), who could promise *his* presence to two or three who gather in *his* name (Matt. 18:20; cf. the presence of the Shekinah glory among two who study Torah), and who indeed promised *his* presence with his disciples "always, to the end of the age" (Matt. 28:20).

In the twentieth century, Jewish scholars have been engaged in what can be called the Jewish reclamation of Jesus. That is, they have been at work showing the full Jewishness of Jesus. The important corollary to their conclusion that Jesus was but a reformer of Judaism is that it was Paul, and not Jesus, who was the creator of Christianity. It is obvious that for such conclusions to be drawn, the material we have been considering in the last few paragraphs must simply be rejected outright. Jewish scholars have thus relied heavily on the negative results of radical scholarship applied to the Gospels. Their focus has accordingly been on the ethical teaching of Jesus, for it is here that they see the greatest possibility of bringing Jesus again into their ranks.

In a book that I have written on this subject, I attempted to show, however, that even the ethical teaching of Jesus cannot be successfully reclaimed for Judaism, for at a number of key points it does not fit into the normal framework of Jewish teaching, at least as we know it from the Jewish sources available to us. The reason for this is that the teaching of

Jesus is inseparable from his announcement of the dawning of the kingdom of God in his own person (see, e.g., Matt. 12:28; Luke 17:21).
Repeatedly the ethical teaching of Jesus has a strange ring to it when compared to typical Jewish ethical teaching. We have seen it in reference to
Jesus' authoritative stance in his interpretation of the law. We see it also
in such things as the command to love one's enemies, the teaching not to
resist an evildoer but to turn the other cheek, the "otherworldliness" of
Jesus with its self-renunciation and its negative view of wealth, the prohibition of divorce, the advocacy of voluntary celibacy, and finally the general tone of Jesus' ethical teaching (i.e., its absolute and idealistic
character). Again and again one encounters in Jesus' teaching material
that is not comfortable in a straightforward Jewish context. There is one
clear reason for this: *the teaching of Jesus is ultimately inseparable from his
personal claims*. More exactly, the ethical teaching assumes the new presence of the eschatological kingdom, which is in turn based on the person
and work of Jesus—namely, the presence and the death of God's Messiah,
the unique Son of God.

Although Jesus was a preacher of righteousness, he did not come to
reform Judaism. The full import of his work can be known only after the
cross and the resurrection, but it is clear already from the Gospel narratives that in his announcement of the kingdom Jesus sees his mission as a
turning point in the aeons. Quoting the prophecy of Isaiah 61:1–2a in the
sermon at Nazareth, Jesus announces that "Today this scripture has been
fulfilled in your hearing" (Luke 4:21). Elsewhere Jesus says: "The law and
the prophets were in effect until John came; since then the good news of
the kingdom of God is proclaimed" (Luke 16:16; Matt. 11:12–13). It is the
day of the bridegroom, of new cloth and new wine (Matt. 9:14–17; Luke
5:34–38). It is the day of messianic fulfillment (Matt. 11:2–6). Jesus calls
his disciples blessed, adding that "many prophets and righteous people
longed to see what you see, but did not see it, and to hear what you hear,
but did not hear it" (Matt. 13:16–17 = Luke 10:23–24).

We have thus moved into a new era of the history of salvation. Any
assessment of the significance of Jesus that ignores or denies this must
necessarily be fundamentally inadequate. The Jewish attempt to explain
Jesus quite apart from any forward movement in salvific time frames is
therefore bound to fall short. Jesus cannot be understood as "one messiah
among many," as Zaas puts it.

And this brings us to the cross. As has long been stressed, the heart of
the Gospels is the passion narratives. Indeed, in the absence of a passion
narrative, a document such as the so-called *Gospel of Thomas*—which con-

sists almost exclusively of sayings of Jesus—hardly qualifies to be designated a Gospel at all. It is very interesting to me that in almost all Jewish
discussion of the death of Jesus, the *meaning* of that death is neglected,
with the present dialogue being no exception. It comes up only briefly in
the first question of the question-and-answer session. There Zaas tips his
hat to the importance of sacrifice in the Hebrew Bible, but then indicates
that since the destruction of the Second Temple, atonement is accom-
plished by mere repentance. The logic underlying such a leap is not
explained, and the only apparent reason remains the mere nonexistence
of the literal Temple.

Jewish discussion of the death of Jesus focuses understandably on the
exceptionally sensitive matter of the determination of responsibility
(more on that below). My point here, however, is that the death itself is
apparently regarded as the tragic end of one who should really have been
honored as a loyal teacher of Israel. Jesus, however, seems to have interpreted his imminent death in terms of the servant of Isaiah 53 (especially
vv. 10–12). That is, his death was to be understood as a sacrifice that
atoned for the sins of the world: "For the Son of Man came not to be
served but to serve, and to give his life a ransom for many" (Mark 10:45
= Matt. 20:28). "Ransom" is used here metaphorically in reference to the
payment of the penalty of sin at the cost of the sacrificial death of Jesus.
Similarly, at the institution of the Lord's Supper, Jesus referred to the cup
as "my blood of the covenant, which is poured out for many for the forgiveness of sins" (Matt. 26:28; cf. Mark 14:24). This is the heart of the new
covenant that Jesus came to effect, and thus "this cup that is poured out
for you is the new covenant in my blood" (Luke 22:20). The death of Jesus
brings about a turn in the aeons and is itself the pivot of that turning.

The death of Jesus was therefore not merely a vital mission of Jesus; it
was his *central* mission. He came to die. The fulfillment he brings and the
kingdom he inaugurates depend squarely on his death. And therefore the
death of Jesus is not a tragic event wherein a great teacher and healer was
unfortunately put to death at a young age. It was, on the contrary, nothing less than the accomplishment of the will of God for the salvation of
humanity. The demeanor of Jesus all through the passion accounts of the
Gospels bears out this conclusion. Rather than being the helpless victim
of all that happens, he is strangely and quietly sovereign throughout, even
to the final moment.

By no means, however, did Jesus deserve to die. And by no means are
those who put him to death made into heroes for doing in ignorance what
ultimately was the will of God! To my mind, it is impossible to deny the

centrally important role of the Jewish leadership in the death of Jesus. As I indicated in my opening remarks, I accept the Gospels' record that Jesus was put to death for blasphemy, but a blasphemy involving a totally unacceptable self-aggrandizement. The old question, posed again by Craig, has never received an adequate answer: Why would the Jewish leaders—much less the Romans—desire the death of a charismatic teacher and healer who was fully loyal to Judaism? What was it about him, what threat did he pose, that the Jewish authorities were moved to such extreme measures against him?

The answer, as we have tried to say above, is that Jesus put himself at the center of God's purposes and made himself determinative and irreplaceable in the relationship of humanity and God. He calls humanity to himself, to follow him as their sole Master, to offer their lives in a pattern of discipleship modeled after him, to represent the good news of the gospel of God's free grace and forgiveness based on his cross. The Gospels from beginning to end thus call their readers to a decision concerning Jesus. The question posed in all three Synoptic Gospels—"Who do *you* say I am?"—is not meant as an academic exercise, but as an existential question of the greatest importance to all of humanity, Jews and Gentiles. If we are to judge by the Gospels, therefore, Zaas is completely off the mark when he argues that this question "remains as it has always been, entirely irrelevant to the Jewish enterprise."

From the point of view of the Gospels (and more clearly from the epistles), the death of Jesus was for sin. That is, Jesus died bearing the sin of the world—more precisely the sin of the myriads of individual sinners who make up humanity. Theologically, it is here that we should look for the cause of Jesus' death. The responsibility of the Jewish leaders and mob is ultimately one of a quite limited scope, namely one that could be designated as merely a responsibility of historical instrumentality. It should be regarded as of little consequence, and certainly as nothing that would warrant hatred or persecution of the Jews—or indeed as a sanction for any form of anti-Semitism. The substantive responsibility must be placed on each sinner's shoulders. If blame is to be placed, it is *I* who am guilty of crucifying Jesus. *My* sin put him on the cross.

The Birth of the Church

In my opinion, Craig is absolutely right, in discussing the significance of Jesus, to focus on the resurrection of Jesus. The reason the resurrection is so important is that, apart from its validation of the claims and identity of Jesus, we are left only with so many words and deeds, however unusual they may be. The resurrection serves as the vindication of Jesus' self-claims—indeed, of his whole mission. It is the determinative point in the Gospel tradition that brings meaning to the entirety.

The resurrection is both the key to the faith of the early church and the cornerstone of its proclamation. As the key to the faith of the early church, it is the single, indisputable fact that authenticated, made possible to assimilate, and brought understanding to all that the disciples had experienced through the words and works of Jesus. After the death of Jesus and prior to the resurrection, the disciples were confused, disillusioned, and disheartened. It is understandable that they were in this pitiable condition, for in light of what he said, a dead Jesus could leave them only with question upon question. The eschatological signs of the resurrection of Jesus and the outpouring of the Holy Spirit served as a demonstration of the truth of the dawning of a new era of salvation that was the fulfillment of the expectations of the prophets, albeit in a proleptic way, short of the consummation of the age. The resurrection and the outpouring of the Spirit were not only thereby the foreshadowing of the last day, but also its guarantee.

As the cornerstone of the church's proclamation, the reality of the resurrection is preeminently that to which the disciples were witnesses. In addition to the twelve disciples, the risen Jesus appeared to more than 500 people, as Paul testifies, adding the important point that most of these were still alive in the mid-50s when Paul wrote 1 Corinthians (1 Cor. 15:6). The church preaches the cross and the resurrection, not merely the former, not merely the latter. Either without the other is incomplete, for the new age owes its existence to the death of Jesus. But the resurrection is the powerful demonstration of the truth of the words, of the truth of the good news of a new era of fulfillment. It thus simultaneously underlines the high and mysterious significance of the death of one who is now seen as the glorified Son of God.

Craig sets forth the strength of the evidence for the resurrection of Jesus concisely and effectively: the witnesses, the empty tomb, the birth of the church. These are persuasive in themselves, but even more so when combined with one other fact. *Every other attempted explanation of the phenomena is plainly inadequate.* If historical sense is to be made of the facts of the witnesses, the tomb, and the rise of the church, then an adequate cause must be found. No naturalistic explanation has been offered that accounts for the facts. Indeed, the feeble attempts that *have* been made to explain away the resurrection are laughable and strain one's credulity far more than the resurrection itself.

It must be stressed, as Craig rightly does, that the resurrection of Jesus was *not* the resuscitation of a corpse followed by his return to life in this world. When Zaas says that he does not dispute the fact of the resurrection of Jesus, he means the resuscitation of Jesus. The same is clearly true of the claim of Jewish writer Pinchas Lapide when he says that he accepts the truth of the resurrection of Jesus. As Craig points out in his response to a question, there is a world of difference between revivification and resurrection. In the former instance, one comes back to life only to die again later. In the case of the latter, however, one enters into a new order of existence altogether. As Paul puts it in 1 Corinthians 15:35–55, the body that is "sown" is physical, perishable, and weak whereas the body that is raised is spiritual, imperishable, and glorious. Flesh and blood are transformed into a new "spiritual body" that is appropriate to eschatological existence. Such was the resurrection of Jesus, which Paul describes as "the first fruits of those who have died" (1 Cor. 15:20). In short, in resurrection we are talking about a new order—nothing less than dramatic reversal of the effects of sin on the world, the restoration of the perfection of the creation at the beginning. This transformation of the world is what the prophets spoke of when they foresaw a time when there would be no more evil, no more suffering or sorrow, no more death, when life would be filled with an extravagant abundance, and above all when men and women would be in unbroken fellowship with their Creator. It is all of this that the resurrection of Jesus symbolizes and points to. His resurrection is the beginning of that new creation and tangible evidence of its reality. It is furthermore a guarantee of the eventual realization of this hope in fullness at the final consummation. And the Holy Spirit in the life of the Christian provides a foretaste of the glory that shall be.

A resurrection of this kind—a true resurrection—has univeral consequences that necessarily touch on the existence of every human who has ever lived. Paul traces this out too when he writes in the same context: "For since death came through a human being, the resurrection of the dead has also come through a human being; for as all die in Adam, so all will be made alive in Christ" (1 Cor. 15:21–22). Therefore it is impossible to reduce the resurrection to a "Christian" question that is of no particular relevance to the Jews, as Zaas would do. This might be the case if we were dealing with a resuscitation, but not if we are dealing with a true resurrection. By its very nature the resurrection of Jesus impinges on every person, Jew or Gentile. And this is why the Christian wants to evangelize others—all others, including the Jews. This gospel became the driving force in the life of Paul, the Jew who had previously been a zealous Pharisee. He wrote of the gospel that "it is the power of God for salvation to everyone who has faith, to the Jew first and also to the Greek" (Rom. 1:16). The resurrection of Jesus is of the utmost importance to the Jew as well as the Gentile. In no way does the New Testament condone the idea that Christianity is a religion for the Gentiles only.

Concluding Remarks

There is a remarkable difference in the way Zaas and Craig approach the basic question before us. This, I suppose, is not particularly remarkable in itself, since after all, Craig believes in Jesus as proclaimed in the New Testament, while Zaas does not. But the difference does account for much of the discussion between them, as it does for the tone of my own response to the discussion.

As I see it, the difference is due to the way in which the central question is addressed. For Zaas, the question "Who is Jesus?" is merely an academic question. It is a question of some mild interest, but basically one for the intellect alone. Thus Zaas can be playful, open, provocative, stimulating. In the end nothing really significant is at stake, and Zaas is tolerant of a wide range of opinions (which is perhaps all they can be, in his view). To each his own. It matters not.

Craig, on the other hand, understands the question "Who is Jesus?" not merely as an intellectual challenge, but as involving a call to personal response. On this Craig follows the Gospels. When Jesus posed the question himself, the real issue was not correct information alone, but a response of the will that brought one into personal relationship with him. Thus for Craig there is a gravity to the question that is simply not there for Zaas. The answer one gives to the question matters vitally to Craig. There is only one correct answer to the question, and Craig wants to show as well as he can the strength of the evidence for that answer.

These comments should not be taken to mean that Craig is not or cannot be a good scholar. Nor do they imply that Zaas is a priori more objective than Craig. The fact is that no Christian can answer the question "Who is Jesus?" without becoming an evangelist! The question brings one close to the heart of a Christian as perhaps no other question can. But a faith commitment is not necessarily a hindrance to good scholarship. On the contrary, it may be an asset to be able to approach these matters from within.

It is right and good for these issues to be discussed openly, between persons of different opinions, in a friendly manner and with mutual respect.

We can continue to learn from one another, and we are in need of having our misunderstandings corrected. Differences will nevertheless remain. I am convinced, however, that it is possible to love others—i.e., to wish them well and to work for their well-being in every regard—even when one disagrees with them on matters of the deepest significance. It may well be my deepest wish and prayer that they might share the conclusion to which I have come. But that is not in my hands to accomplish. As a Christian, however, I must continue to share the truth as I have been led to see it. Like Craig, I am convinced of its cogency and that it is the authors of the New Testament who have the right answer to the question of the significance of Jesus.

Chapter 6

The Jesus of History and the Christ of Faith: Toward Jewish-Christian Dialogue

Craig A. Evans

The dialogue between Peter Zaas and William Craig illustrates well the religious and conceptual gulf that exists between Jews and Christians. Zaas, who is a Jew and a New Testament scholar, does not intend to be insulting or condescending toward Christians when he states matter-of-factly that Jesus is of no religious relevance for Jews: ". . . the question 'Who is Jesus?' remains as it has always been, entirely irrelevant to the Jewish enterprise, as most Jews, at least, have defined that enterprise." Craig responds, on the one hand, by arguing for the historicity of the resurrection of Jesus and by contending, on the other, that Jesus' remarkable claims of authority suggest that he was either God's Son or that he was delusional. Craig finds the second alternative implausible, because everything about Jesus' teaching and activities appears rational and because in his resurrection we should infer that his life and teaching met with God's approval.

This exchange illustrates the Jewish-Christian gulf because it is clear that the participants, like two ships passing in the night, have two very different agendas. Zaas wishes to explain what it means to be Jewish and how it matters little to Jews who Jesus was or what Jesus did. Craig thinks it is important to argue for Jesus' authority, which brought on his execution, and for his resurrection, which three days later followed his death. Zaas could, I suppose, respond to this in a Pinchas Lapide sort of way and say, "Yes, maybe Jesus did possess divine authority; maybe he really did speak for God and maybe he really was raised from the dead. All of that might make him a messiah and savior of the Gentiles, but that does not necessarily make him Israel's messiah."[1]

The issue of the *relevance* of Jesus and his resurrection revolves primarily around one's philosophical and religious interpretation. Lapide, a Jewish scholar who taught at the University of Göttingen, thought that Jesus' resurrection made him a messiah for Gentiles. Rabbi Peter Levinson, interviewed in the popular press, emphatically rejected Lapide's suggestion, stating: "If I believed in Jesus' resurrection I would be baptised tomorrow."[2] Lapide feels that Jesus' resurrection carries few or no implications for his personal faith, while this rabbi feels that his resurrection would necessitate conversion.

There emerge then two basic issues, each pertaining to a distinctive category: One issue has to do with history, and asks, "What happened?" The other issue has to with interpretation, and asks, "What does it mean?" Lapide and Rabbi Levinson, both Jews, disagree over both of these issues as they pertain to the resurrection of Jesus. Lapide thinks Jesus was resurrected; Levinson thinks not. Lapide thinks belief in the resurrection of Jesus would have little impact on being Jewish; Levinson thinks that such belief would have profound impact. The same divergence of opinion is found among Christians. Some Christians think the resurrection of Jesus is a fact of history; others think not.[3] Some believe that the historicity of the resurrection is essential to Christian faith; others think not.[4]

Zaas and Craig touch on topics that fall into these two categories. They differ at various points over the historical factors that led to Jesus' execution. They also differ over the ultimate significance of Jesus. Because my training is historical, I will speak to issues that pertain to the first category. I will leave to theologians and apologists the issue of what all of this means. But I am very concerned that we get the facts as straight as we can.

In a recent book in which a response is given to three much-publicized sensationalist books about Jesus, N. T. Wright raises five very important questions.[5] To these questions I shall add a sixth. All of these questions invite thoughtful persons to ponder issues of theology and philosophy, but the questions first and foremost are historical in nature. I shall address myself to Wright's questions and, along the way, will respond to various aspects of the Zaas-Craig dialogue. A few of their statements need qualification and even correction. I shall also bring into the discussion some of the important contributions made in recent years by the major scholarly participants.

What Was Jesus' Relationship with the Judaism of His Day?

It has been fashionable down through the centuries to view Jesus as opposed to Judaism in various ways. Christian theologians have assumed that Jesus criticized the religion of his people for being legalistic (or "Pharisaic"), for being caught up with externals, and for having little or no place for grace, mercy, and love. Jesus' action in the Temple, which has been traditionally referred to as the "cleansing of the Temple" (Mark

11:15–18 and parallels), was directed, we have been frequently told, against the system of sacrifice. Religion is supposed to be a matter of the heart, not rituals. Jesus understood this, but his Jewish peers did not.

Several scholars, both Jewish and Christian, have rightly complained against this caricature. Perhaps the most influential challenge in recent years has come from E. P. Sanders.[6] He rightly argues that there is no evidence that would suggest that Jesus opposed Judaism or criticized it as a religion of externals and rituals. Instead, there is substantial evidence that *Jesus accepted all of the major tenets of the Jewish faith*: the unity and sovereignty of God, the value and sanctity of the Temple of Jerusalem, the authority of the Jewish Scriptures, the election of the people of Israel, and the hope of Israel's redemption. Jesus, moreover, observed many of the practices associated with Jewish piety of his day: alms, prayer, and fasting (Matt. 6:1–18). Jesus fasted in the wilderness during his period of temptation (Mark 1:12–13); he prayed and taught his disciples to pray (Matt. 6:7–15; Luke 11:1–13; 22:39–46); he and his disciples gave alms, and he taught others to do likewise (Luke 11:41; 12:33; John 13:29). Jesus presupposed the validity of the Temple, the sacrifices, and Israel's holy days (Matt. 5:23–24; Mark 14:14). He read and quoted from the Jewish Scriptures and clearly regarded them as authoritative (Luke 4:16–22; 10:25–28; Mark 10:19; 12:24–34). Apparently he attended synagogue services regularly (Luke 4:16); his style and interpretive orientation toward Scripture reflect at many points the style and interpretive distinctives that emerged within the synagogue.[7] Predicting that Jerusalem faced disaster, Jesus wept over Israel's ancient city (Luke 19:41–44).

Jesus accepted the authority of Torah (i.e., the law, or Books of Moses); he did not reject it, as has sometimes been asserted. In his dialogue with Zaas, Craig suggests that Jesus set his own authority over against that of Torah. This claim needs to be carefully qualified. What Jesus opposed were certain interpretations and applications of the law. In the so-called "antitheses" of the Sermon on the Mount (Matt. 5:21–48), Jesus does not contradict the commands of Moses; he challenges conventional interpretations and applications. The antithetical "but I say to you" does not oppose the commandments themselves. For example, Jesus agrees that killing is wrong but adds that hatred is wrong too. He agrees that adultery is wrong but adds that pre-divorce lust (which often led to divorce and remarriage) is also sin. He agrees that swearing falsely is wrong but speaks against the practice of oath-taking in his time. Jesus does not oppose restitution ("an eye for an eye"), but he does oppose using this command as justification for revenge. He agrees that people should love their own people but adds that they should love other people as well, even enemies.

Jesus may very well have believed that his own authority, which derived from God's Spirit with which he had been anointed (Mark 1:10; Luke 4:18), equaled that of Torah. But his authority did not undermine the authority of Torah; it explained it and applied it in new ways conditioned by his strong sense of the dawning of the kingdom of God and the changes that it would bring. Jesus' innovative interpretation is consistent with parallel innovations articulated by Israel's classical prophets. As did theirs, Jesus' hermeneutic challenged conventional interpretations of Israel's sacred tradition. In Isaiah 28 the prophet declares that the "LORD will rise up as on Mount Perazim, he will rage as in the valley of Gibeon" (Isa. 28:21a). Isaiah alludes to stories of David's victory over the Philistines (cf. 2 Sam. 5:17–21; 5:22–25 = 1 Chron. 14:13–16), but he finds in this sacred story no guarantee of Israel's victory in his day. On the contrary, the Lord will do a "strange deed" and an "alien work" (Isa. 28:21b), by which the prophet means that God will give the victory to Israel's enemies.[8] Jesus also interpreted Israel's sacred story in this manner. In his Nazareth sermon (Luke 4:16–30) Jesus reads Isaiah 61:1–2, a passage understood to promise blessing for Israel and judgment for Israel's enemies,[9] and then appeals to the examples of Elijah and Elisha (Luke 4:25–27). From these examples, where these mighty figures of old ministered to Gentiles (1 Kings 17:1–16; 2 Kings 5:1–14), Jesus declares that his "anointed" task is to bless the marginalized and the suspect, not only the righteous of Israel.[10] This kind of interpretation may have been daring—and surely would have been opposed by many teachers—but it presupposed the authority of Israel's Scriptures; it did not attack it. Jesus' respect for Jewish Scripture places him squarely within first-century Judaism.

One may also ask, "In what way did Jesus' *ministry* fit into the Judaism of his day?" In his recent books, Geza Vermes, a Jewish scholar from Oxford, has concluded that Jesus was a Jewish holy man, much like Honi the Circle Drawer from the first century B.C. or Hanina ben Dosa from Jesus' own time.[11] E. P. Sanders thinks Jesus compares more closely to prophets of deliverance like Theudas or the anonymous Jewish prophet who hailed from Egypt.[12] Bruce Chilton thinks Jesus should be viewed as a rabbi who was very concerned with matters of purity and the proper way of offering sacrifices.[13] I tend to view Jesus more as the anointed, eschatological prophet who proclaims the kingdom (or, better, reign) of God.[14] Although disagreeing at various points, these diverse portraits of Jesus have in common the placement of Jesus squarely in a Palestinian, first-century Jewish context. All agree that Jesus was part of a broader Jewish concern to bring about the restoration of Israel. All agree that in comparing Jesus to his Jewish contemporaries, we can gain a clearer, more accurate picture of him.[15]

What Were Jesus' Claims?

Probably no feature of Jesus research has been more divisive than the question of the claims that Jesus made for himself. This topic is usually referred to as the question of Jesus' self-understanding. The main reason that this area of research has been so problematic is that Jesus says little about himself, at least directly (and again, the Gospel of John is best placed in reserve). But there are many indicators that he understood himself as a special agent in God's service.

He evidently claimed to be a prophet. Jesus himself complained: "Prophets are not without honor, except in their hometown" (Mark 6:4). This tradition is likely authentic, for it is hard to understand why early Christians would make up a saying implying that Jesus' relatives and acquaintances did not treat him with respect. Apparently the public also regarded him as a prophet: "Some say you are one of the prophets" (Mark 8:28); "A great prophet has arisen among us!" (Luke 7:16); "If this man were a prophet . . ." (Luke 7:39). This tradition is in all probability historical, for early Christians spoke of Jesus as Savior, Lord, and Son of God; they did not emphasize his identity as a (mere) prophet. And, of course, Jesus was remembered to have made predictions (Mark 13:2) and uttered what can probably be regarded as prophetic indictments against various persons, institutions, or groups (Mark 12:1–11; 14:58; Matt. 11:20–24 = Luke 10:13–15; Matt. 23:13–36 // Luke 11:39–52).

Jesus was frequently addressed as "rabbi" (Mark 9:5; 10:51; 11:21; 14:45). He taught as a rabbi, even if his admirers affirmed that he taught as one having much greater authority than did other teachers of his day (Mark 1:22, 27). Those outside of his following addressed him as "rabbi" (Mark 5:35; 10:17; 12:14).[16] Some scholars have asserted that the appearance of "rabbi" in the Gospels reflects an anachronistic usage of the epithet, since it did not become a title until after 70 A.D. But the use of "rabbi" in the Gospels is informal and evidently reflects Jewish usage in the first century, before its later, formalized usage.[17] Why would Christians writing after 70 apply a formal title to Jesus, a title used of religious teachers who were becoming increasingly critical of Christianity? If anything, the title would have been avoided.[18] That it is used so frequently suggests, in my judgment, that the Gospel tradition is primitive and authentic. Jesus is called "rabbi" in the Gospels because, like it or not, he was addressed as such during his public ministry.

Although there is not a hint that Jesus referred to himself as a priest or that any of his followers so regarded him, Jesus performed some actions usually understood as priestly functions. He declared persons "clean" (Mark 1:41; Matt. 11:5 = Luke 7:22) and "forgiven" (Mark 2:5; Luke 7:47–48). He also dared to challenge the Temple polity, a polity put in place by the ruling priests. The most provocative challenge was the so-called "cleansing of the Temple." (This incident will be taken up below.) It is only in the later theology of the church that Jesus' death and subsequent intercessory role in heaven came to be understood in sacrificial and priestly terms (as seen, for example, in the book of Hebrews).

Jesus regularly referred to himself as the "son of man," an epithet that has been hotly debated for many years. This is not the place to go into a detailed study of this complicated question, but I will hazard a few brief comments. In my judgment, this self-designation, which evidently was Jesus' favorite, alludes to the "son of man" of Daniel 7. Jesus saw himself as this figure,[19] to whom kingdom, power, and authority were to be given. This self-reference suggests that Jesus saw himself as God's vice-regent. In a saying that has good claim to authenticity Jesus assures his disciples: "I confer on you, just as my Father has conferred on me, a kingdom, so that you may eat and drink at my table in my kingdom, and you will sit on thrones judging the twelve tribes of Israel" (Luke 22:28–30). The disciples' self-interested request for the seats of honor when Jesus comes "in his glory" (Mark 10:35–45), which because of its embarrassing nature virtually guarantees its authenticity, in all probability arose out of the assumption that Jesus was indeed the "son of man" through whom Israel would be restored and the kingdom of God would be established.

Did Jesus regard himself as the Messiah? The evidence is ambiguous, but taken as a whole it seems that he did. He is confessed as such by his disciples, but they are silenced (Mark 8:29–30). When John the Baptist asks Jesus if he is "the one who is to come," he gives a reply that is full of allusions to Isaiah 35:5–6 and 61:1–2 (Matt. 11:2–6 = Luke 7:18–23). It is clear that by this Jesus intends to answer John in the affirmative. But did John ask Jesus if he was the *Messiah*? He probably did, judging by the recently published 4Q521. This text contains parallel allusions to the passages from Isaiah and understands them as the works of the Messiah.[20] In other words, Jesus has implied that yes, he is the coming one (i.e., the Messiah), as is evidenced by the fact that he is busy doing the works of the Messiah.

The blind son of Timaeus hails Jesus as the "son of David," which is probably a messianic designation, but he is hushed (Mark 10:47–48). However, when Jesus enters Jerusalem the crowd shouts for the coming of the kingdom of David (Mark 11:9–10). He rides the donkey (Mark 11:1–7), as did Solomon, the son of David (1 Kings 1:38–40; cf. Zech. 9:9). Jesus also presumes to have authority within the Temple precincts. This he could do only if he were a ruling priest or Israel's king. The first option is not likely, for reasons already mentioned. It has been pointed out that Jesus quotes and discusses Psalm 110:1 in such a way as possibly to distance himself from son of David tradition (Mark 12:35–37). But his exegesis may imply that he believed that the Messiah would be greater than David. Jesus is anointed (Mark 14:3–9), which was probably a messianic anointing by a devoted follower, though again Jesus speaks of his death. When asked by the high priest if he was the Messiah, Jesus said he was (Mark 14:61–62). And, probably most important, Jesus is crucified by the Romans as "king of the Jews" (Mark 15:26, 32). The early and widespread belief among Christians that Jesus was Israel's Messiah, or Christ, argues that Jesus was understood as such from the time of his public ministry and not simply from the time of the Easter proclamation.[21] All of this suggests that Jesus was regarded by at least some in his following as Israel's Messiah.

Did Jesus regard himself as God's "son"? The evidence here also is ambiguous (unless the Gospel of John is taken as pre-Easter, historical tradition, which few Jesus scholars are prepared to do), and it is tied to the question of Jesus' messianic self-understanding. David is called "son" in relation to God (cf. 2 Sam. 7:14; Ps. 2:7). The Messiah is therefore in some sense the "son of God." In 1 Chronicles 29:23 Solomon is said to have "sat on throne of the Lord"; so in a certain sense the son of David is expected to sit on the throne of God. This concept would add to the notion mentioned above that the Messiah would serve on earth as God's vice-regent.

The most dramatic utterance, and one that ties together the son-of-man imagery with the son-of-God identity, is found in Jesus' reply to Caiaphas. In the attempt to find incriminating evidence against Jesus, the high priest asks: "Are you the Messiah, the Son of the Blessed One?" Jesus answers: "I am; and 'you will see the Son of Man seated at the right hand of the Power' [i.e., God] and 'coming with the clouds of heaven'" (Mark 14:61–62). Because in this exchange Jesus confesses what Mark believes him to be (cf. Mark 1:1), some scholars doubt its authenticity. They wonder how the disciples would have learned of it, since they were not present but had fled (cf. Mark 14:50). Others have pointed out the apparent inconsistency in having Jesus "seated at the right hand," which is to be stationary, yet "coming with the clouds," which is to be moving.

These objections, however, carry little weight. To assert that Jesus did not regard himself as in some sense God's son makes the historian wonder why others did. From the earliest time Jesus was regarded by Christians as the son of God. Why not regard him as the great Prophet, if that is all that he had claimed or had accepted? Why not regard him as the great Teacher, if that had been all that he had ever pretended to be? Earliest Christianity regarded Jesus as Messiah and as son of God, I think, because that is how his disciples understood him and how Jesus permitted them to understand him.

The objection that the disciples were not present to hear the exchange between Jesus and Caiaphas and so could not have known what transpired is naive. Are we really to imagine that the disciples, who later became zealous proclaimers of their master and his teaching, never learned what happened, that they had no idea on what grounds the Jewish authorities condemned him? This defies common sense. Even if the rules later codified in the Mishnah were not in force in the early first century, it is likely that a capital verdict would have been made public (as the Mishnah in fact says was required). Jesus' claim to be Israel's Messiah would then account for the Roman crucifixion and for the posting of the *titulus* that read, "king of the Jews." For to claim to be Messiah is to claim to be the Jewish king. It is almost beyond belief that the disciples could have learned nothing of this. The fact that his disciples were not present probably does explain, however, why what is recorded of the exchange between Jesus and his accusers (Mark 14:55–65) is so brief and in places so vague.

Finally, the objection based on the apparently odd juxtaposition of being seated and of moving among the clouds is also without force when it is remembered that the throne on which God sits is a chariot. In fact, the very throne described in Daniel 7:9, on which the Ancient of Days takes his seat and to which the son of man approaches, is said to have wheels that "were burning fire." What apparently shocked Caiaphas was not only that Jesus boldly affirmed his messianic identity, but dared to assert that he would sit on God's throne.[22] Not only was Jesus' answer treason in the eyes of Rome, it was blasphemy in the eyes of devout Jews who did not hold to such messianic ideas—and the Sadducean high priesthood held to few messianic beliefs. Jesus has claimed that the day will come when Caiaphas and company will see Jesus, the "son of man," seated at God's right hand, on God's chariot throne, thundering through heaven and coming in judgment. That a man would dare claim such a thing was indeed blasphemous.[23]

What Were Jesus' Actual Aims?

Closely related to the question of Jesus' *claims* is the question of Jesus' *aims*. The old quest of the historical Jesus was launched when scholars began to question Jesus' intentions. H. S. Reimarus' posthumously published writings (1774–78) argued that Jesus attempted to have himself installed as Israel's earthly, political king.[24] This provocative thesis led to new, critical readings of the Gospels. The twists and turns of the old quest (sometimes called the nineteenth-century quest) have been eloquently reviewed and assessed by A. Schweitzer, in what has become a classic in its own right, *The Quest of the Historical Jesus*.[25] With the emergence of form criticism in the 1920s, whose early practitioners thought that most of the Gospel material originated in the church and did not derive from Jesus, many abandoned the quest. It was thought to be historically impossible (and theologically illegitimate, according to some theologians). But a new quest, seeking to find the link between the Jesus of history and the "Christ of faith," was initiated in the 1950s and then yet another phase, now called the "third quest," emerged in the 1980s.[26] It is from the perspective of this latter quest, which is not motivated or guided by the heavy theological and apologetical interests that motivated and guided the first two quests, that I write this essay.

What were Jesus' actual aims? The aims of Jesus are closely bound up with the question of what his proclamation of the kingdom of God meant. It is almost universally agreed that Jesus proclaimed the kingdom of God and that he recommended changes of thinking and behavior in view of its appearance.

Although it is disputed by some, it is probable that Jesus continued John the Baptist's call for repentance and that this call for repentance was preparatory for the appearance of the kingdom (cf. Mark 1:15; 6:12).[27] Jesus believed that his miracles were evidence of its appearance: "But if it is by the finger of God that I cast out the demons, then the kingdom of God has come to you" (Luke 11:20). Jesus urged his followers to have faith in God and to forgive one another (Mark 11:22–25; Matt. 6:14–15). These urgings in themselves do not mark Jesus off from Judaism, of course, but they take on a somewhat different nuance in light of Jesus' announcement of the kingdom. Jesus urged his followers to serve one another and not to be like the mighty or the rulers of their day, who lorded it over others and liked to be served (Mark 10:35–45).[28]

Jesus promised his disciples that they would sit on thrones judging the twelve tribes of Israel (Matt. 19:28 = Luke 22:28–30). This saying gives us a fairly clear insight into Jesus' aims. He and his disciples expected to set up a new administration. This expectation coheres with the judgmental parable of the wicked vineyard tenants (Mark 12:1–11), which threatened Jerusalem's Jewish authorities with the loss of their position. The "vineyard," that is, Israel, will be "given to others," that is, Jesus' disciples. This does not mean, contrary to some Christian and Jewish interpreters, that Gentiles or Christians are supposed to replace the Jewish people. Such an interpretation is anachronistic and inaccurate. Jesus evidently expected his own disciples to form a new government, to sit on thrones judging (in the sense of the judging done by the judges of the book of Judges, not in the sense of condemning) the twelve tribes. The reference to the "twelve tribes" also implies that Jesus fully expected the restoration of Israel, all Israel. This coheres with his call for repentance. If all Israel will repent, then all Israel will be restored.

One of the shocking and offensive features of Jesus' ministry was his association with "sinners," that is, with people who either were not or at least did not appear to be Torah-observant (Matt. 9:10–13; Mark 2:15–17; Luke 15:1–2). It seems that Jesus believed that forgiveness could be readily and quickly extended to those who violated or neglected the laws of Moses. But this forgiveness required repentance and faith (Matt. 11:20–24; Matt. 12:39–42 = Luke 11:29–32; Luke 7:47–50; 13:1–5; 15:7).

Jesus' rejection led to a new element in his preaching and teaching. He was not greeted by the high priest when he entered Jerusalem (Mark 11:1–11). He criticized some aspect of Temple polity and practice (Mark 11:15–19). Ruling priests challenged him and demanded to know by what authority he was doing these things (Mark 11:27–33). After his threatening parable of the wicked vineyard tenants, Jesus was challenged and questioned by various persons and religious parties (Mark 12:13–34). Jesus again went on the offensive warning his disciples to beware the scribes who devour the estates of widows (Mark 12:38–40). Then, as a living illustration of this warning, he lamented the widow, who gave her last penny to a wealthy and, in the opinion of some of his contemporaries, avaricious Temple establishment (Mark 12:41–44). When they had left the Temple precincts, Jesus told his disciples that the beautiful buildings of the Temple Mount would be leveled; not a stone would be left on another (Mark 13:1–2). His aims of national repentance (and restoration) frustrated, Jesus evidently began to speak of coming judgment upon the city of Jerusalem and her world-famous Temple (Luke 19:41–44; 21:20–24). It is in this context that Jesus probably uttered the words that were later used against him during his hearing before Caiaphas: "We heard him say, 'I will destroy this temple that is made with hands, and in three days I will build another, not made with hands'" (Mark 14:58).

Why Did Jesus Die?

The most probable reason that Jesus was put to death was because he made claims that his opponents understood as in some sense messianic. The *titulus* that the Romans placed over or near his cross, which read "The king of the Jews" (Mark 15:26), is the principal evidence for this view.[29] There is other evidence that Jesus held to messianic ideas, even if he did not assert his messiahship explicitly (which would have been inappropriate, according to Jewish expectations). This evidence, such as entering Jerusalem on a donkey and being anointed, has already been reviewed.

The Roman crucifixion of Jesus lends important support to the report that Jesus affirmed his messiahship in response to the high priest's question (Mark 14:61–64). Affirming messiahship in itself was probably not blasphemous,[30] but claiming to sit on the divine throne, next to God Himself, would surely have been regarded as blasphemous and would have added incentive to hand Jesus over to the Romans.

But another reason for desiring Jesus' death was his threat against the Temple establishment. He not only hinted in his parable of the wicked vineyard tenants that the ruling priests would lose their place, he also predicted that because of them the Temple would be destroyed. That the ruling priests could be deeply offended by such rhetoric is well illustrated in the experience of another Jesus, one son of Ananias, who some thirty years after the death of Jesus of Nazareth wandered around the city of Jerusalem, often near the Temple, uttering woes based on Jeremiah 7. (Remember that Jesus' criticism of Temple polity also had been based on Jeremiah 7.) According to Josephus (*J.W.* 6.300–309), this man was seized by the ruling priests, who interrogated him and beat him, and then was handed over to the Roman governor with demands that he be put to death. The governor interrogated him further, beat him further, and decided to release him as a harmless lunatic.

Jesus did not die because he quarreled with Pharisees over matters of legal interpretation. He did not die because he taught love, mercy, and forgiveness. Jesus did not die because he associated with "sinners." He did not die because he was a good man. Jesus died because he threatened the political establishment with the prospects of undesired change. His contemporaries foresaw the very real possibility of a serious riot, perhaps even a full-scale rebellion.[31] The Jewish leaders (who were principally the high priest and the ruling priests) were responsible to the Roman governor to maintain law and order, and the governor was in turn answerable to Rome. Jesus was viewed as a troublemaker by both of these authorities; he had to go. Because Jesus did not have an armed following, there was no need to seize any of his following (unless the two "insurrectionists"[32] who were crucified with him were his disciples). Hence, there was no battle and no bloodshed beyond the crucifixion of Jesus himself.

Why Did the Early Church Begin?

This question does not require a complicated or lengthy answer. The early church began because of its firm belief that Jesus had been resurrected and had appeared to dozens, even hundreds, of his followers. From its very inception, the early church proclaimed the resurrection of Jesus. Apart from the resurrection, there was no reason to develop and maintain a distinctive identity. Jesus' teaching had not condemned Judaism; so there would have been little reason for his following—which at the time of his death probably consisted entirely of Jewish people—to abandon or modify aspects of Judaism, especially something as controversial as the evangelization of non-Jews, without following the norms of Jewish proselytization.

It was their unshakable conviction that God had raised up Jesus, who had in turn commanded his followers to continue to preach his vision of the kingdom, that ultimately led to the emergence of the church. But I don't think that Jesus originally envisioned the "church," at least as it eventually came to be. Jesus spoke of a community and expected his followers to live and think in certain ways. But the church itself was a more or less ad hoc development of this community idea. The church took on the characteristics that it did in order to deal with the new challenges it faced in the years and decades following Jesus' death and resurrection.[33] The church believed that its Lord and Savior would return. But what should it do until he returned? How would it survive, especially in view of its growing estrangement from Judaism, the parent faith, and in view of increasing persecution at the hands of the pagan state?

Why Are the Gospels What They Are?

In my view, although the Gospels are written from a perspective of faith in Jesus and veneration of him, they are reliable. Criteria of authenticity, which are remarkably vigorous in their application to the Gospels, confirm the essential core of Jesus' teaching (as I have tried to summarize above).[34] It is not necessary to claim that the Gospels are inerrant, though for theological reasons many Christians accept them as such, and that every saying and deed attributed to Jesus is true to history. But claims that the Gospels are unreliable, full of myth and legend, and so tendentious that knowledge of what Jesus really said and did cannot be recovered are extreme and unwarranted. Even the Jesus Seminar—as extreme as its conclusions have been and as mistaken and wrongheaded as many of its assumptions and methods are—has "authenticated" a good portion of this essential core. The Seminar has presented the public with a skewed view of Jesus, to be sure, but its members have concluded, nonetheless, that Jesus proclaimed the kingdom of God and associated with sinners.[35]

It is true that the Gospels may very well tell us much about the concerns of their respective authors (the task of redaction criticism) and may even tell us something about early Christians who handed down the tradition (the task of form criticism), but their principal concern was to publish the teachings and deeds of Jesus. His words and example were considered normative. Indeed, there is evidence early on that the words of Jesus were considered on par with Scripture, which in a Jewish milieu is remarkable.[36] Given such a high regard for Jesus' words, it is not probable that early Christians would have freely invented sayings and then attributed them to Jesus. In fact, classical form criticism's assertion that many of the sayings were generated by questions and issues that the early church faced is called into doubt by the observation that many of the questions and issues that the early church faced (as seen in the New Testament epistles) are nowhere addressed by the sayings of Jesus. The early church was sharply divided over the question of circumcision, eating meat sacrificed to idols, spiritual gifts, Jew-Gentile relations, and qualifications for church office; yet, not a saying of Jesus speaks to any of these questions. There is every reason, then, to conclude (again, without invoking theological dogmas) that the Gospels have fairly and accurately reported the essential elements of Jesus' teaching, life, death, and resurrection.

I would like to conclude by expressing appreciation for Peter Zaas's helpful and fair comments. I was particularly pleased by his statement that although Jews may not consider Jesus *the* Messiah, Jews are not "prevented by reason of their Jewishness from accepting this Christian notion." In reading these words, I was reminded of a humorous question put to me by a Jewish woman some years ago. I had delivered a lecture about the origins of Christianity. Throughout the lecture I referred to "Jewish Christians." After the lecture she asked me, with a very perplexed look on her face, "Don't you realize that 'Jewish Christian' is a contradiction in terms?" To her way of thinking I might as well have referred to "Jewish Gentiles." This woman evidently did not know that the first Christians were Jews, Jews who came to believe that Jesus of Nazareth was the Lord's Messiah, Deliverer of Israel, and Savior of the world. It was these same Jews who proselytized Gentiles so successfully that the new expression of Jewish religion gradually evolved into a largely Gentile religion.

Zaas is quite correct. To be Jewish today is not necessarily to be religious. Likewise, to be Christian is not necessarily to be un-Jewish and, I hope, it is never to be anti-Jewish.[37] The earliest followers of Jesus were Jews. The church was predominantly Jewish until after the first major war with Rome (66–70 A.D.), and not until after the catastrophic Bar Kokhba war (132–135 A.D.) did the Jewish Church of Jerusalem come to an end and the Jewish bishop there was succeeded by a Gentile bishop. It would be many centuries before the Ebionites (Jewish Christians) would finally cease as a distinct and viable denomination within Christendom. Accordingly, for Jewish and Christian scholars today, the origins of Judaism and Christianity constitute a complex and interesting story whose interwoven threads should not be unraveled.

The story of Christian origins is a Jewish story. Indeed, many "Messianic Jews" today believe that Christianity remains a Jewish story. The original gospel proclamation—"Jesus is risen!"—was part of this Jewish story. Christianity was a Jewish movement rooted in the conviction that God had at last fulfilled his promises to Abraham and David, that he had at last fulfilled countless prophecies, and that he had at last inaugurated the kingdom of God. This new and energetic Jewish movement reached out to capture the Gentiles, to bring them into submission to the teachings of Jesus the Jew, the Messiah of Israel. Israel was now indeed the "light to the nations" (Isa. 49:6) and was engaged in a task that will redound to her glory (Luke 2:32). It is an ironic thought to consider: The mighty Roman Empire, which smashed the state of Israel in a series of punishing wars (from 66 to 135 A.D.), was itself overrun by a faith rooted in Israel's sacred Scriptures and her ancient belief in the God of Abraham. Those Gentiles who have been invited to play a part in this exciting story should never forget its Jewish authors and players.

Chapter 7

Jesus' New Vision within Judaism

Scot McKnight

Perhaps I will be forgiven if I strike a note of concordance between Judaism and Christianity by contending in this essay that Jesus fits comfortably within Judaism and, in so doing, explore a feature of this particular dialogue as yet uncharted. I do this, not as a slippery piece of apologetics that seeks in the end to come through the back door and then announce itself as a guest at what is surely a marvelous Jewish feast, but instead because I believe Jesus was thoroughly Jewish and that his first followers were too. Peter Zaas talks about Jesus in the same manner that many Christian scholars talk about the Teacher of Righteousness, who led a movement that eventually planted the scrolls around Khirbet Qumran, or about Bar Kokhba, who himself claimed to be a messianic figure. William Craig, on the other hand, speaks of Jesus as the Lord and finds the almost cavalier approach of Zaas to be inconsistent with the claims made by Jesus and about Jesus. The responses by my partners have taken each of these to task in a variety of ways, and such an approach could go on in the form of dialogue and debate for some time. While I am not adverse to such polemics, in this context I wish to toss another set of cards onto the table and ask how Jesus *fit into first-century Judaism in all its diversity.*[1]

Peter Zaas keenly observes that Judaism is non-creedal and by this I take him to mean that it is (today) *unlike Christianity*, which is fundamentally creedal. In other words, I take him to be talking more about the *respective distinctives of the two faiths* rather than about the gambit of Jewish faith. And I think I agree with him: the emphasis of Judaism is less orthodoxy and more orthopraxy. On the other hand, I take the criticism of Don Hagner to be important: within that emphasis on practice rather than specific creed, there remains a fundamental set of shared beliefs in both ancient and (in some cases) modern Judaism. Our concern can comfortably skip over modern worries and instead settle in the first century, where we find an incredible diversity. Take the Teacher of Righteousness, who may be behind the *Thanksgiving Hymns*, the *Damascus Document*, and later expressions of the community he founded, a community that shows some connections to the Essenes as described by Pliny and Josephus. Here is a fiercely loyal Jew who has a special view of the Torah and how it ought to be implemented in the Temple; here is a Jew who may have been put on trial and then exiled; here is a Jew who may have identified himself with the Servant of Isaiah, the Son of Man of Daniel 7, and the category of Messiah; here is a Jew who was put to death for his vision; here is also one whose teachings inspired a significant alternative movement within Judaism.[2] Or take Philo of Alexandria, a capable Jew who combined knowledge of Torah with neo-Platonic philosophy in order to demonstrate the compatibility of Judaism with, even superiority over, Greco-Roman philosophies. One could trot out more examples, but these two, taken from the Land of Israel and from the Diaspora, reveal the substantial variety within Judaism.

However, both of these examples operate within the categories of the Jewish story of the one God's covenantal relationship to Israel and Israel's obligation to live within the terms of that covenant (as each interpreted it!). Josephus, in what probably also reflects his ability to exaggerate, argued that Jews were united in belief and action: "Unity and identity of religious belief, perfect uniformity in habits and customs, produce a very beautiful concord in human character" (*Against Apion* 2.179). One recent study by a Christian scholar calls this pattern of similar faith "covenantal nomism," and his conclusion has withstood the test of scholarship.[3] All Jews believed in the One God, in the Torah, in the Temple, and in the election of Israel; most Jews saw this set of beliefs, which engendered Torah observance with a substantial variety, leading to a general separation from pagan society, beliefs, and practices. A variety of observance notwithstanding, these Jews observed the Sabbath, circumcision, and food laws, and they prohibited images. In other words, while I would affirm Judaism's essential diversity, that diversity emerges hermeneutically from its foundations.[4]

One issue on our table of discussion is confusing: at times my partners speak of "Christianity" and two assumptions are being made, neither of which is as obvious as they suggest, and those two assumptions are that (1) "Christianity" has a clear referent, and (2) Jesus is part of "Christianity." Let me explain. Christianity, as we now know it—as a post-Reformation set of beliefs, or as the Roman Catholic Church, or as an expression of faith within mainline American Christianity, or as a crystallization of faith by those committed to a non-state free church—as I say, this "Christianity" is far from clear in its referent, and it behooves scholars to define this sort of term when they are using it as a foil to compare with "Judaism." Are we, when it comes down to nuts and bolts, comparing modern Judaism (as practiced by believing, observant American Jews) to modern American mainline Protestant Christianity? Or is it Reform Judaism? Or is it Orthodox Judaism? Or is it Roman Catholicism? Or is it, as some would have it, a historical reconstruction of both, "ideal types," which find particular expression nowhere and among no particular group? Furthermore, it is simply a historical anachronism to place Jesus within Christianity. Jesus is before Christianity and, though Bultmann separated Jesus' teachings from New Testament theology (which itself is also an unhistorical approach to the evolution of the thinking of various early Christians), his person, mission, and teachings gave rise to various forms of Christianity. So, when we are talking about "Christianity," "Jesus," and "Judaism," we need to define our terms carefully enough that meaningful comparisons can be made.[5] Jesus and his followers, who can helpfully be called "the Jesus movement," are our concern, not "Christianity" as later expressed in the Pauline crystallization or even later in the Reformation revolution led by Luther, Calvin, and Zwingli. I shall understand "Judaism" to be a diverse set of Jewish beliefs, Jewish practices, Jewish ways of life, held by Jews in roughly the first century C.E. (Common Era) who set themselves within that story of God's covenant with Abraham, and I shall understand Jesus and his movement to be one or more of those sorts of Judaism, or as many would say today, "Judaisms."

In addition, we are not fair to those Judaisms if we explicate them in terms exclusively of a *religion*. That is, for most of these forms of Judaism we are dealing not so much with a "personal relationship to God" as with a "vision for Israel" in its full import: who a Jew is, who God is, how Jews are supposed to live before this God, how the nation is to conduct itself with outsiders—in short, a Jewish way of life in terms of God's covenant with Abraham, Moses, and David. In other words, we dare not separate "religion" and "politics" when we talk about ancient Judaisms and Jesus.[6] It is particularly a modern fallacy to describe ancient Judaisms in terms of a religion and to neglect that someone like the Teacher of Righteousness was not as much concerned with personal faith as he was with national vision. This simply picks up a theme that begins with Moses and finds further noble expressions in the pre-classical and classical prophets. Scholarship is making progress when it can see that the Sermon on the Mount of Jesus is best understood as "politics."[7] Thus, I shall attempt to explicate

Jesus within Judaism from the angle of his vision for the nation, for that is what "politics" is all about, understanding that his view of personal religion is included within and is a deduction of that vision for Israel.

Before I proceed, however, I need to make two comments about the presentations of Zaas and Craig. First, in contrast to Craig, the issue of Jesus and his relationship to Judaism as well as the larger topic of Christianity and Judaism is larger than whether or not Jesus was raised from among the dead. I doubt that Craig would disagree with me here, but the sole emphasis of his presentation is the issue of the resurrection. While I fundamentally agree with him that the facticity of the resurrection shapes not only the faith of the earliest Christians but also is involved in adjudicating debates between the two modern faiths, I shall not focus this essay on that issue. Long before Pinchas Lapide stated that he believed that God raised Jesus to give Gentiles grounds for Israel's faith, that view was articulated by Abraham Geiger, and, though surely in the minority, this voice with Judaism surely demonstrates that coming to affirmative terms with the issue of resurrection might not settle the whole debate.[8] But even more the dialogue between Christianity and Judaism should not be reduced to a debate about the resurrection for, as is the case with Enoch, Moses, and Elijah, a surprising ending does not tell the whole story or ultimately settle all the issues. I would argue, without denying the importance of the resurrection, that the "story" into which Jesus is set—the old, old story about God's covenant now finding its climactic expression in Jesus' kingdom message and mission—takes on a more fundamental value than even the resurrection. What Jesus said and offered to Israel in the terms of its story, its "myth-dream"—because his very mission was in the terms of Judaism and for Israel—provides for us the surest ground on which to stand in dialoguing with one another.[9]

Second, in contrast to Zaas and in agreement with Hagner and Evans, I believe that the debate about the relationship of Jesus and Christianity to Judaism quickly unfolds into a discussion about Jesus' self-consciousness or about his identity. At this point, I would like to interject a term that, though not often found in discussions about Jesus, remains helpful: egocentrism. Jesus was fundamentally egocentric. I do not mean by this that he was insufferably selfish or narcissistic. Instead, I think Jesus saw himself at the very epicenter of God's new work in Israel, and he had the robust conscience to think that how people responded to his mission determined their relationship to God in terms of Israel's covenant. Hagner is surely right in pointing to this issue as central to an objective debate about Jesus and Judaism. Both John and Jesus seriously engaged their contemporaries about the significance of what they thought God was now doing in ushering in the kingdom through them. The language is at times vituperative and caustic. But I want to contend even here that this debate is an *in-house debate and that neither Jesus nor the earliest Christians were fundamentally anti-Semitic.*[10]

In what follows, then, I shall seek to explicate *Jesus within Judaism* by focusing on two major events of his life (his baptism and his death) as the bookends to a discussion of a few themes in his teachings, and I shall show that each is an expression of his political plan for the nation, of his vision for Israel.[11] This vision of Jesus, if it is understood aright, needs to be set into the context of Jewish restoration movements, movements that (apart from the prophetic reforms or the attempt of Ezra to purge the nation) gained significant national attention and consideration after Alexander the Great and took on concrete shape and function in such movements as those connected with the Teacher of Righteousness, the Pharisees, the popular leadership prophets recounted by Josephus, John the Baptist, and even the Zealots.[12] In setting our course in this fashion, I become aware that the biggest obstacle confronting a Jewish-Christian dialogue is a "Christian" reading of Jesus which, however much a part of Christian theological development, is not anchored firmly in either history or, in particular, a historically nuanced understanding of Judaism. The so-called third quest, which seeks to understand Jesus as a prophet and within the categories of Judaism—even if eventually the picture of some third questers of Jesus invigorates a new religion—offers promise in the Jewish-Christian dialogue because its categories are enough of that time period to permit meaningful dialogue.

I avoid the term "Messiah," not because that title does not adequately describe who I believe Jesus was and is for my faith, but because I know from experience that far too frequently scholars *assume* a definition of what the Messiah was to be like and then ask if Jesus does not fit *that* definition. The term, in spite of centuries of debate about Jesus' status as Messiah, in and of itself says actually very little: "the Anointed One." Anointed by whom? For whom? For what mission? For how long? Under what conditions? These questions, to name but a few, immediately arise when we ask the meaning of the term "Messiah." But more important, I would say that the issue for the first followers of Jesus as well as their immediate successors was not "the Messiah is Jesus," which implies a set and well-defined job description to which Jesus dramatically corresponded, but was instead "Jesus is Messiah," which implies not so much a job description but a steadfast and unshakeable conviction about Jesus of

Nazareth. Recent scholarship confirms the variety, not to mention scarcity, of shapes and meanings given to the term "Messiah."[13]

My assumption in what follows is that Christianity is not "Jesus" enough—that is, it does not often enough anchor its faith in his mission and teachings, and, consequently, the original Jesus has been eclipsed too often by Christianity itself. Such a prevention of the light of Jesus affects the dialogue Christians today have with Jews. It is my belief that meaningful dialogue can take place at the forking of the paths—at the beginning point of the parting of the ways—with Jesus.

The Baptism of Jesus as Political Act

Although baptism is the "water that divides," both within modern Christianity as different denominations have formulated its doctrines differently but also within early Judaisms as some chose to enlist in Jesus' restoration movement, a careful examination of what John was doing reveals that his intentions were not so much to divide as to restore Judaism. John's perception of Israel and its corrupt leadership, his eschatological beliefs in an imminent judgment, as well as his call to radical obedience and repentance, each shares in the world associated with the Dead Sea Scrolls and the foundational leaders of that movement. His baptism shows no awareness of the Qumran daily purificatory rites, however, and neither do we have evidence that John's baptism derives from proselyte baptism.[14] John's baptism itself was an innovation, a "voice in the wilderness" as it were, and therefore we must look to its particularities in order to determine his intent.

First, John's mission is directed at Israel as a nation (cf. Luke 3:18: "the people"). In a prophetic form of his day,[15] John warns the crowds (Matt. 3:7: "the Pharisees and Sadducees") that Abrahamic descent forms no basis for a claim on God; instead, the judgment casts such an imminent shadow that repentance is the only option (Luke 3:7–18). Second, John's fundamental conception of his message centers around "kingdom" and, if that be a redactional reworking of the tradition (cf. Matt. 3:2 and 4:17), around the notion of a repentance that leads to redemption and a renewed fellowship (Luke 3:10–14). Third, John envisions an imminent judgment on those who do not respond to his call to repent (3:15–18). A messianic figure was about to arrive, and his message would be one of both fire and Spirit, judgment and redemption (3:16); this figure would clean up the winnowing floor, burning the chaff and storing the wheat (3:17–18).

In this context of a national call to repentance for redemption or a warning about imminent judgment, John's practice of immersing people finds its true significance. John's baptism does not find its context in personal salvation rituals or in personal piety; instead, it is a call for a national revival, and those who submit to his baptism are expressing their agreement with this mission to Israel. Those so baptized were making a "public statement." What we should notice, first of all, is that *water* surely evokes a message of purification, and John's baptism is in the first instance an expression of a purificatory repentance. We must cast aside any later Christian debates about the efficacy of baptism and set John's baptism in the ancient Jewish context of watery purifications. When uncleanness was contracted in ancient Israel, the individual underwent a process of purification, usually involving time and a cleansing agent, frequently water. The concern with purity and water is seen in the Jesus traditions (Mark 7:2–5; John 2:6).

The real world of Judaism at the time of Jesus was profoundly concerned with such matters as semen emission, menstruation, and dead carcasses—topics considered inappropriate for public discourse in our world. Whether a man's semen emission took place during a dream or in sexual intercourse with his wife, he was nonetheless in need of a bath, and, in the case of intercourse, they were both unclean until the next evening (Lev. 15:16–18). Archaeology has uncovered numerous *miqvaoth*, purificatory pools, sacred jacuzzis, throughout the Land of Israel (Jerusalem—at the Temple and in the Essene quarter, Qumran, Jericho, Gamla, and Sepphoris) in which the various required purifications of Leviticus 15 took place.[16] These pools were approximately twelve feet long, seven feet wide, and seven feet deep, but the descending steps consumed much of the space; one descended until one was immersed.[17]

When applied to John, we cannot think of a *water baptism* and not think of uncleanness and purification. That is, John's baptism is in some sense a purificatory rite (cf. John 3:25).[18]

Josephus tells us as much: John's baptism was, as he says, a "purification of the body" (*Ant.* 18.117), and the discoveries in the Judean desert have unearthed what may well be a baptismal liturgy with a central concern with purity (4Q414). And, because moral sin can cause impurity (cf. Lev. 18:24–29; 19:30; 20:1–3; Num. 35:33–34; Ezek. 5:11; 36:17, 18), it follows that physical acts of purification should concern themselves with moral impurities—it is, after all, a baptism of repentance to remove sins (Mark 1:4).[19]

Scholarship contends quite accurately that, if John believes this act of baptism removes sin, he must also think that the Temple is ineffective as a place of atonement, though we need not get into the details of why John might have come to that conclusion.[20] We have good reasons to think such a criticism led to the formation of the movement associated with the Teacher of Righteousness because the evidence for criticism of the priesthood is substantial.[21] Such a view, however probable, is implicit. What is explicit is that John's baptism took place in the *Jordan*. Instead of choosing some local *miqveh*, or even choosing to provoke the Temple authorities by utilizing the *miqvaoth* at the Temple, John chose to enact his baptisms at the river Jordan. It is likely this was in the southern regions of the Jordan, not far from Jericho (where archaeology has shown there were *miqvaoth*), since the crowds are from Jerusalem and the Judean countryside (Mark 1:5). Why here? It is not hard to answer this question. And this answer, I believe, shoves the evidence about the weight of John's baptism away from a purificatory emphasis to an eschatological one.

Two points can be made: the baptism took place in the *Jordan River*, and there is evidence that the baptisands *entered the water to be baptized from the other side of the Jordan*.[22] The Jordan, of course, is the boundary between *Eretz Israel* and the lands of the Gentiles, between Judea and Perea, the latter being part of Antipas's tetrarchy. More important, the Jordan is the point of entry into the Land for the wilderness generation led by Joshua. It was a place of solemn covenant and a place of God's miraculous intervention (Josh. 3:1–4:18). Notable, of course, is the protection granted through the presence of the ark of the covenant and the commitment on the part of the people to obey the Torah (1:1–9). It is not accidental, then, that the placement of twelve stones, one from each tribal leader, from the Jordan onto its banks as well as Joshua's placement of twelve stones in the Jordan corresponds to the number of Jesus' special followers (cf. 4:1–10 and Mark 3:13–19). Furthermore, in this case we have the formation of the "Land People of Israel," those who have entered into the covenant through Joshua to capture the Land for YHWH and who are now charged with a mission, as were the twelve apostles (Matt. 9:35–11:1), to take the Land under the control of the covenant with its Torah. No one who participated in John's baptism could fail to recognize either the oddity of this happening intentionally in the Jordan or of the significance of the Jordan for Israel's history and charge from YHWH.

A second observation clarifies John's baptism in the Jordan: it is that John's followers, including Jesus, must have crossed the Jordan to the Transjordan, reentered the Jordan, and then crossed back into the Land—

thus, reenacting the Entry into the Land as under Joshua. John, it will be recalled, exposed Herod Antipas, who was Tetrarch of Galilee and Perea but not of Judea, and it was Antipas who arrested him; Perea is on the east bank of the Jordan (Mark 6:8, 17–29; cf. Luke 13:31–33). Thus, John's ministry has a Perean, as opposed to Judean or Galilean, focus. In addition, we should recall that John was imprisoned east of the Jordan in Machaerus (Josephus, *Ant.* 18.116–119) and that imprisonment led to a questioning of Jesus in which his response alarmingly corresponds to substantive concerns of the Qumran community—located not too far from the southern Jordan area (cf. Matt. 11:2–6 and 4Q521, frag. 2, 4; 2.1, 6–8, 12–13). To confirm this, John's ministry is three times located in the Transjordanian area of Perea: at John 1:28 ("This took place in Bethany across the Jordan where John was baptizing"), John 3:26 ("the one who was with you across the Jordan"), and John 10:40 ("He went away again across the Jordan to the place where John had been baptizing earlier"). Two of these references clearly connect John's baptism with the Transjordanian Perea and, furthermore, inform us that John's baptisms took place there first. Thus, the evidence clearly supports the notion that John's ministry was Transjordanian and Perean.

We can now conclude that John baptized in the Jordan in order to reenact the foundational story of ancient Israel, the Entry into the Land. John asked his followers, and Jesus was one of them at this point, to leave Israel by crossing the Jordan, stand with him at the edge of the Transjordanian bank, confess the sin of Israel, enter into the water as a baptismal act of repentance, and then reenter the Land as a purified people ready to take the message of an eschatological repentance to the whole Land. If this interpretation comes anywhere near an accurate summary of what John, and Jesus, did when they were at the Jordan, we are led to the obvious conclusion that neither John nor Jesus was forming a new religion. Instead, they were calling the nation, Israel, to repentance in the same manner that Israel's prophets had done, and their "baptisms" of a variegated Judaism were as much vicarious repentance as they were individual conversions. Further, they were forming a remnant out of those who do exit the Land and reenter through a new solemn covenant ceremony of repentance and commitment. Very few have noted that this action of John is to be seen as a *prophetic action* more than a simple rite of redemption.[23]

It is to these actions of Jesus that I now turn in order to further the argument that Jesus was *within* Judaism and cannot be understood historically until he is seen as a Jewish prophet calling for the restoration of the nation through repentance, as he had learned from John, the baptizer and prophet.

Jesus' Vision and Israel

Jesus' Prophetic Actions: A New Moses

Some of the prophets of Israel acted out in a bizarre manner; at other times they just acted out. Prophetic actions are acts performed by a prophet that are (1) intentional, (2) conventional, and (3) designed specifically to embody God's purposes and mission of that prophet for the audience. The category of "conventional" distinguishes these actions from spontaneous actions which, however interesting, are not done with forethought in order to embody the mission of that prophet in a particular incident.[24]

One thinks, for example, of the following: (1) Saul tearing Samuel's robe in 1 Samuel 15:27–29, (2) Elijah casting his cloak over Elisha in 1 Kings 19:19–21, (3) Zedekiah making horns of iron in 1 Kings 22:1–12, (4) Elisha instructing Joash to shoot and strike arrows in 2 Kings 13:14–19, (5) Hosea taking a whore to be his wife (Hos. 1:2–3), (6) Isaiah walking about naked for three years in Isaiah 20:1–6, (7) Jeremiah breaking a pot in front of a select audience in Jeremiah 19:1–13, (8) Jeremiah purchasing a field in Anathoth in Jeremiah 32:1–15, (9) Ezekiel eating a honey-sweet scroll in Ezekiel 2:8–3:3, (10) Ezekiel lying on his left side for 390 days and on his right side for forty days in Ezekiel 4:4–6, 8, or (11) Ezekiel "acting out" an exile trip in Ezekiel 12:1–16. But these prophets gave rise to singular prophets called either "Jewish sign prophets" or "popular leadership prophets," who, according to Josephus in various ways, promised to reveal Mosaic vessels on Mount Gerizim (*Ant.* 18.85–87), or gathered his followers to the Jordan River to see it part again (20.97–99), or seduced his followers into the desert to see signs and wonders (20.167–168), or gathers followers at Mount Olivet to see the walls collapse (20.169–172), or coaxed his followers into the desert to find liberation (20.188), or finally who declared his followers would find tokens of deliverance (*J. W.* 6.285–286).

A close examination of these prophets reveals that Jesus is more like the second group than the first group. Although Jesus refused to participate, much like Jeremiah and Ezekiel, in public religious ceremonies, his actions (mentioned below) are significantly different from the classical prophets and much more in tune with the actions of the popular leadership prophets recorded for history by Josephus. In particular, these prophetic actions embody acts of redemption in an eschatological context.

The prophetic actions of the ancient prophets of Israel were consistently acts of judgment, and these form a substantive contrast to the popular leadership prophets and Jesus. More important, the actions of the popular leadership prophets evoke the actions of *Moses and Joshua*, and these draw out certain motifs of the actions of Jesus so much that one is driven to examine the "prophetic actions" of Moses.

Here we need to mention (1) the sign-acts of Moses and Aaron before Pharaoh, climaxing as they do in the Passover event, all recorded in Exodus 5:1–12:51, (2) the deliverance at the Red Sea in 14:1–15:12, (3) Moses' tossing of the tree into the water to make it sweet in 15:23–26, (4) the provision of manna in 16:1–36 and (5) water at Rephidim in 17:1–7, (6) the enactment of covenant ritual in 24:1–8, (7) Moses' transference of his spirit to seventy others in Numbers 16:1–50, and (8) his investiture of Joshua at Numbers 27:12–23. Moses, who is in the deuteronomic tradition the Prophet *par excellence* (Deut. 13:1–5; 18:15–22; 34:9–12), here enacts redemptive signs for his people as he leads his people to receive the Torah and then on to the banks of the Jordan, where they prepare to take the Land. A comparison of the prophetic actions of Moses, the preclassical and classical prophets, and the popular leadership prophets reveals that Jesus fits more with the popular leadership prophets and with Moses. Even more, the actions of Jesus most like the popular leadership prophets are those that have Mosaic and Joshuaic dimensions, and this leads me to the conclusion that Jesus' prophetic actions are *intentionally designed to evoke the redemptive acts of Moses and Joshua and that Jesus self-consciously saw himself in terms of these two figures.*

Thus, Jesus (1) exorcises demons by the "finger of God" in Luke 11:20, an expression that emerges from Mosaic tradition at Exodus 8:19, (2) he heals abundantly, as seen in Luke 7:18–23, (3) he chooses twelve to further his mission and judge Israel, according to Mark 3:13–19 and Luke 22:28–30, a number which evokes Joshua 3–4, (4) he embodies a new table fellowship that is inclusive, eschatologically anticipatory, and covenantal in Mark 2:13–17, (5) he instructs his disciples to shake the dust off their feet when they meet the unresponsive in Mark 6:11, (6) he enters Jerusalem, cleanses the Temple, and curses a barren fig tree in one big event that casts doubt on the integrity of Jewish leadership while it also establishes his own role in leading a new people into Jerusalem in Mark 11:1–19, (7) he tops these actions off with a newly enacted effective form of atonement in his last meal with the disciples in Mark 14:22–25, (8) he feeds 5,000 men in a manner intended to evoke the manna miracle of

Moses (Mark 6:30–44), and (9) he joins John in a Jordan-crossing evocation of God's sending Israel into the Land to conquer it for his name's sake (Mark 1:1–13).

Lots of things could be said about these actions in particular, and though some events would be disputed by critical scholarship, my point is simply that Jesus' actions intentionally evoke, over and over but not in each instance (and I have given but a sampling), the acts of Moses in particular with some bleeding over into the acts of Joshua—who is the successor and completer of Moses. In other words, the image of Jesus implied by these actions is much less "Son of God" and "Messiah" and "Servant of YHWH" and "Son of Man" and "Word of God"; instead, the Christology of Jesus' actions is Mosaic through and through. Jesus presents himself in these actions before Israel as a New Moses. While this theme of Jesus as New Moses is not pervasive in the New Testament (cf. Mark 9:4, 7; Acts 3:22–24; 7:37; John 6:14; Rev. 11:3–13), it is certain that early Christians and more especially later Christians found this shape of Christology less than what was desired, and it was quickly jettisoned in favor of other shapes. I am suggesting, then, that the actions of Jesus evoke a New Moses figure and that this evocation shows once again that Jesus was within Judaism.

Jesus and the Name of God

At no place have Christians been more insensitive to Judaism than when it comes to what Jesus believes and teaches about God.[25] In particular, the concept that Jesus was the first to teach about God as *Abba* and that this innovation revealed that Jesus thought of God in terms of love while Jews thought of God in terms of holiness, wrath, and distance are intolerably inaccurate in the realm of historical study and, to be quite frank, simple pieces of bad polemics. I need not develop the personal insensitivity it expresses for those who are Jews who experience God quite differently than Christians suppose.[26]

The God of Jesus was the God of Israel, and there is nothing in Jesus' vision of God that is not fully formed in the Bible he inherited from his ancestors and learned from his father and mother. I shall focus here on that dimension of "holiness" in Jesus' vision of God.

Countless Christians repeat the Lord's Prayer daily. But when Jesus urges his followers to "hallow" or "sanctify" the Name of God (Matt. 6:9), many are simply unaware what such a command might have meant in Jesus' day—in part because Christianity has lost sight of God's awesome, splendorous holiness. A good angle on the meaning of reverencing the Name of God can be found by focusing on the meaning of "profane," and one thinks of a text like Amos 2:6–8 (italics added):

Thus says the LORD:
For three transgressions of Israel,
    and for four, I will not revoke the punishment;
because they sell the righteous for silver,
    and the needy for a pair of sandals—
they who trample the head of the poor into the dust of the earth,
    and push the afflicted out of the way;
father and son go in to the same girl,
    so that my holy name is profaned;
they lay themselves down beside every altar on garments taken in pledge;
    and in the house of their God they drink wine bought
    with fines they imposed.

A very noticeable feature of the meaning of reverence is brought out in this text: "reverencing the Name of God" is not just how Israel speaks about God—that it does not take the Name of God in vain when it utters oaths or when someone stubs a toe or hits a finger with an instrument— but that God's name is profaned when Israel lives outside the covenant and by defiling the name of God in its behavior (cf. Jer. 34:15–16; Ezek. 20:39; Mal. 1:6–14). God's Name is attached to the covenant people, and when that covenant people lives in sin, God's Name is dragged into that sin along with His people. So, it can be inferred that when Jesus urges his followers to "reverence" the Name, to "sanctify" it, he is thinking of *how his disciples are to live in the context of the covenant: they are to live obediently as Israelites.*

    This means, in the context of Jesus' prayer in terms of the covenant, that his followers will long for the kingdom and for God's will to be realized in the Land. God's name is honored when God's kingdom comes. Further, this prayer invokes God's Name to be honored by scattering his enemies, in particular for Jesus, Rome. This is the natural implication of the concepts of profanation and sanctification when they come into play with the term "Name of God." God's Name is disgraced when God's people are displaced and when foreigners rule in his Holy City, Jerusalem. For Jesus, "kingdom" is not just spiritual relationship with God; it is a vision for Israel as a nation, for his people. Finally, this means that the followers of Jesus, those who have been baptized into the Jordan and into that vision for Israel, will use the term "Abba" specially for God (Matt. 23:9). The debate about whether children should call their father "father" misses the point and trivializes Jesus' vision for God. What Jesus has in mind here is the first commandment of the Decalogue: "you shall have no other gods before me" (Exod. 20:3).

But I do not want to suppose that Jesus did not also include *God-talk* in his prescription to "hallow the Name of God" (Matt. 6:9). A fundamental interpretation of Exodus 20:7, the prohibition of taking God's Name in vain (and its disobedience carries its own punishment) was a delineation of appropriate speaking about God when using his Name (cf. e.g., 4Q380 frag. 1.5–8; 11Q5 19.6, 12; 11Q6 frags. 4–5 line 8). Even today many Jews never pronounce the Name of God, YHWH, or speak any term that identifies God. Instead, they write "G-d" or "L-rd" and so, by never pronouncing the Name of God, they can never use it in vain. I have friends and former (Jewish Christian) students who, in their letters and emails to me, write this way. While I am not attempting to resurrect the first-century practice today, I have many times wished and prayed that Christians would recapture a sense of God's holiness with the effect that it would lead to a chaste form of speaking about God! Jesus surely was not on the side of Christians when it comes to this matter. So much were Jews captured by this holiness and reverence of God that they substituted phrases for God and so avoided mentioning God. Thus, the psalmist prays to "O Most High" (9:2) and Isaiah speaks of "the Holy One of Israel" (41:14). While such a practice might become compulsive in a later form of Judaism, Jesus himself spoke of God frequently in substitutionary phrases. For instance, I believe Matthew's practice of editing Mark's "God" with "heaven" has its anchor in Jesus' own language (cf. Matt. 4:17); the sinful son returns to his father saying he has sinned against "heaven" (read: God; Luke 15:21). This may be best illustrated in Mark 14:60–62 (NASB) where we find several substitutions of God in an exchange between a Jewish high priest and the Jewish Jesus: "Son of the Blessed One," "Son of Man," "right hand of the Powerful One," and "clouds of heaven."

The God of Jesus, then, is the God of Israel, and he adopts and inherits all that he believes about God. It is simply inaccurate for Christians to maintain that Jesus' God is somehow different from the God of Judaism. I would be willing to say that the God of Christians today is frequently at odds with the God of Judaism, and by that I mean the God of the Old Testament and the God of Jesus! When it comes then to the matter of God, Jesus is comfortably *within* Judaism. Adolf Schlatter said it right: "The first and final thought of Jesus was thought about God."[27] If this is so, the first and final thought of Jesus was thoroughly Jewish and found its home within Judaism.

The Ethics of Jesus

I turn now to three terms that emerge from Jesus' ethics that evince a similar conclusion: that Jesus is to be situated within Judaism as a covenant member who, as God's Prophet at the end of the age, is calling Israel to repent in light of the coming judgment.[28]

Those who don't respond to this call will be swept away in that judgment. These terms—righteousness, love, and peace—have been classically understood to express the genius of Jesus as well as the essence of the Christian tradition. In what follows, I hope to demonstrate that they are each expressions of Jewish piety without denying their importance to the Christian ethic.

Righteousness

I begin with the term "righteousness."[29] When most Christians think of this term, they are faced with two immediate problems: first, that the apostle Paul used this term so much in the sense of "imputed" righteousness and did so in an innovative, however effective, manner; and second, that what is cognate in Hebrew, Aramaic, and Greek is not so in English. That is, the following terms are all cognate in the ancient languages: righteous, righteousness, justice, justify, justification, and almsgiving. I shall try to point out the significance of this system of cognates in what follows. But, before I do that, we need to address the issue of Paul's influence on Jesus—it should be the other way round! Instead, Christians, trained to think theologically as they are through Paul's wonderful letter to the Romans, have learned to define "righteousness" (read: justification) as something that humans cannot do for themselves but something God must do for them (declare them sinful but nonetheless acceptable in his presence for an enduring covenant relationship).[30]

So, when they see Jesus claiming that his followers must have a "righteousness" that greatly (really now!) surpasses the righteousness of the scribes and Pharisees (who seemed to be fully committed to the Torah and all its details!), they immediately think he can't really mean what it appears he is saying. He must be tricking the Jewish audience by using their term while his own followers already know they have to trust instead of trying to obey God. Or, he is speaking before the cross/resurrection when the Torah was in full control but that now, since he has died and been raised, he would not be urging the church to have such a righteousness. Wrong twice!

We need to look at this term more honestly and more historically because, after all, Paul came after Jesus. Fundamentally, the term "righteousness," along with its cognates, describes an Israelite's relationship to God and his Torah, and that relationship is conceived in behavioral categories: the righteous Israelite is one who does the Torah as a covenant member (cf. Deut. 6:25; Job 22:6–9, 23; Ps. 1:4–6; Ezek. 45:9; *Ps. Sol.* 15:1–3; 1QS 1:5–6; 3:1). Thus, this term describes conformity to God's will in the context of covenant faithfulness and a relationship to the God of that covenant. Jesus teaches about such righteousness as did his Jewish ancestors, as well as John (Luke 3:7–14; Matt. 21:28–32), to describe those Jewish followers of his who wholeheartedly conformed their obedience to the Torah, as taught by him (Matt. 5:17–48; cf. the similar usage at CD 4:7; 20:20–21; 1QpHab 2:2; 7:3–5), in the context of the renewal of the covenant taking place through his offer of the kingdom. This "righteousness" of Jesus "greatly surpasses" that of the scribes and Pharisees, not because it is imputed but because it is a righteousness that conforms to the newly arriving kingdom of God. Thus, he calls his followers to conform their lives to his teachings (Matt. 5:20) and to practice their righteous deeds humbly (6:1–18). In an instance that anticipates the later Pauline emphasis, Luke 18:9–14 declares that the tax collector "went down to his home *justified* rather than the other" (18:14)—and here the term describes the person's approved relationship with God.

Christianity has found the Torah of Moses to be a stumbling block because, so it seems to me, its theologians have overemphasized certain portions of Pauline theology (notably texts like Gal. 3:10–14, 19–25; 5:1, 3, 4, 18) and, to aggravate the situation, have also misunderstood Judaism's perception of the Torah. When Christians read the Torah properly, when they learn what Judaism was all about, they more accurately place both Jesus and Paul within Judaism. Jesus' emphasis on "righteousness" as the necessary virtue of his followers, all understood within the covenant, illustrates not only how Jewish Jesus was but also how inaccurate Christian exegesis has become. A firmly anchored historical understanding of Jesus' ethic of righteousness affirms that Jesus demanded his followers to obey him as part of their covenant relationship to God and, when they did, they would be fulfilling the Torah itself.

Love

Protestant liberalism, as seen in the massively influential study of Adolf von Harnack,[31] correctly emphasized love as central to the message of

Jesus. But if there is anything more Jewish about Jesus than his message of love, I don't what it would be.[32]

When the scribe asks Jesus which commandment is the greatest (Mark 12:28), a thoroughly Jewish/rabbinic question (cf. *b. Mak.* 24a), Jesus essentially answers: "Love God and love others" (12:29–31). We need to emphasize that Jesus' answer is not an innovation but instead is a quotation of Israel's age-old central affirmation: the Shema, found in Deuteronomy 6:4–5, as combined with Leviticus 19:18, a summary of the Two Tables of the Law (cf. Ex. 20:1–17; Deut. 5:6–21).[33]

Nothing is more central to Judaism and, at the same time, nothing can shake this from the bedrock tradition about Jesus: he affirmed love of God and love of others as the two central obligations of the covenant for his disciples. And, of course, just as Jewish is the "Golden Rule," which is a reaffirmation of love as the central commandment of God (Matt. 7:12).[34]

Accordingly, Jesus taught that his followers should love others and in so doing they would imitate God, who provides natural blessings for the whole world (Matt. 5:44). Such an imitation of God extends to love all neighbors, and, to make his point provocatively clear, Jesus utilized in almost humorous fashion a Samaritan as the embodiment of what neighborly love is all about (Luke 10:29–37). Jesus' teaching here intends to cut into the grain of a love directed one-sidedly toward covenant members alone, as can be seen, for instance, in the exclusiveness of the Qumran community (e.g., 1QM). One does not ask, in any restrictive sense, "Whom do I love?" but, in an inclusive sense, "To whom can I behave in a loving, neighborly manner?" In fact, Jesus' emphasis on love as central and on an inclusive definition of those who were to be loved leads him to contend for "enemy love" (Matt. 5:43–48). Instead of restricting their love to fellow covenant members, Jesus utters the extreme command that his followers were to love their enemies, and that can mean only one thing: love the Romans who now occupy *Eretz Israel* and who now prevent us from realizing the fullness of the end of the exile.[35]

Without denying the emphasis Jesus gives to the love-command, however, we must back up and notice once again that this foundational ethical norm of Jesus emerges straight out of the daily confession of the Jews who heard Jesus talk about love: the Shema (Deut. 6:4–5) and Leviticus 19:18.

So, to understand what Jesus meant by love, we are compelled to return to two principle texts of Jesus' Bible: Deuteronomy 6:4–5; 10:2–12, as well as Leviticus 19. From the Deuteronomy texts, four points can be gleaned about how Jews understood "love." First, love was *elective* in that it was God's choice to love Israel by calling and establishing the covenant with

Abraham, as well as calling, enabling deliverance, and promulgating the law through Moses. In all this, God is stubbornly and wooingly loving (cf. Hos. 11:1–2). Second, when Israel loves God and others it is because this is the *response to God's elective love*. Israel does not so much choose to love God and love others as it responds back to God's love by loving God and others. Third, love for God is expressed *in obedience within the covenant*. While in Christian circles love and obedience are too easily separated, not so with ancient Israel and the Jewish context of Jesus: to love God was to live joyously and obediently within the covenant. Fourth, Jesus learned from his ancestral faith that love was *central to the covenant relationship with God*. Finally, when it comes to manifesting love toward others, Jesus learned that love was *concrete action for others*. Thus, Leviticus 19:18, which extends God's elective love to others from the Shema (Deut. 6:4–5), finds expression in respect for parents (19:3), provision for the poor (19:9–10), respect for the property of others (19:11), care for the physically challenged (19:14), justice for the powerless (19:15), kindness in language about others (19:16), as well as a prohibition of hate and vengeance (19:17–18). In other words, this levitical tradition emerges in Jesus' ethical tradition as the response to God's elective love: as Israel was to act lovingly toward others, so especially the followers of Jesus. We are thus led once again to the same conclusion: Jesus' teaching on love is fundamentally and thoroughly Jewish. He may have given love a centrality not otherwise attested in Judaism, but what he says about love is from Judaism, and because of this emphasis we have a table round which practitioners of Judaism and Christianity can sit to discuss our mutual past.

Peace

Instead of finding in "peace" a placid state for the individual, the traditions Jesus inherited and the understanding his audience assumed emerge from a conception of nation and eschatology: peace describes Israel's standing before God in the context of the surrounding nations. Dispersed and punished because of unfaithfulness to the covenant, Israel found itself in exile and at enmity with its enemies. Consequently, the prophets revealed that a day would come when peace would reign in the land for the covenant people who were faithful. This finds beautiful expression in Isaiah 60:17–18:

> I will appoint *Peace* as your overseer
> and Righteousness as your taskmaster.

> Violence shall no more be heard in your land,
>   devastation or destruction within your borders;
> you shall call your walls Salvation,
>   and your gates Praise.

One could cite numerous examples (e.g., Isa. 9:5–6; 11:6–9; Ezek. 34:25; Zech. 8:16; 9:10). This sense of national well-being lies at the heart of Jesus' message about peace, for he envisioned himself as a messianic figure who would bring peace (e.g., Isa. 9:6)—what else does a national deliverer envision?

Jesus blesses the "peacemakers" (Matt. 5:9), which in the context of Jesus almost certainly blesses the nonviolent (Luke 9:51–56; 22:38) and those who seek instead reconciliation (Matt. 5:23–24). The frequently misinterpreted parable of the wheat and weeds (13:24–30, 36–43) is about the (peaceful) coexistence of wheat and weeds until the end. As an injunction, it denies to the followers of Jesus any permission to strike their fellow (unbelieving) Jews or Gentiles with violence in an attempt to bring about the kingdom, justice, and peace.[36] And, when Jesus entered Jerusalem, the expectations of those who saw in him salvation expressed their hopes in graphically national categories: peace (Luke 19:38). Jesus, tragically, informs them that instead of experiencing such a peace at his hand they will experience war (19:41–44). He opines that, had they seen him for what he was, they would experience that peace (19:42). In other words, Jesus' concept of peace once again draws us back into the ambit of Judaism: national deliverance from Rome, the end of exile, and the restoration of the nation.

These three themes, drawn from the ethics of Jesus, demonstrate that Jesus' teachings are to be understood as "Jewish ethics" and not as a form of ethics outside Judaism. He calls his followers to be conformed to the Torah, albeit in his distinctive manner but which does not make him anything other than a visionary within Judaism, to make love central in their covenant relation with God and others, and to pursue peace within the context of a national expectation for deliverance and restoration. Jesus got his public start from John's public baptism as an entry into the Land to restore Israel. Did the end of his life conform to the same pattern?

The Death of Jesus as Political Act

Because the evidence for the death of Jesus is so complex and Christian interpretation of that death so theologically intricate, I can but sketch out here what I take to be Jesus' perception of his death. I begin with the obvious: Jesus was tried—and the complex and at times uncooperative evidence suggests it was carried out at least somewhat surreptitiously (cf. John 11:45–57)—and then put to death on a charge of blasphemy as part no doubt of a belief about his supposed claim to be King of the Jews, so the *titulus* affirms (cf. Mark 15:12, 18, 26).[37]

To be crucified, which itself was a humiliating act of savagery that fueled human desires for the sadistic,[38] was to be publicly vilified as a criminal, and Jesus no doubt was seen as a national seditionist. One was not crucified for predicting the destruction of the city or the Temple, or for teaching parables, or for criticizing the morality of fellow Jews or the purity practices of the reigning priests, or for consorting at table with sinners, or for healing the needy—even if doing so on the Sabbath—or for any of the noteworthy things that characterized so much of Jesus' public ministry. Instead, crucifixion indicates Jesus threatened national peace, and this means that Jesus' death is directly related to his public mission of calling the nation to repent in the context of his very offensive action of causing a disturbance in the Temple (Mark 11:1–19)—an act of "cleansing" or "occupation" or "destruction," which brought down the leaders on him.

I cannot be alone in thinking that Jesus knew what he was doing and did it purposefully; nor can I be alone in thinking that he knew it would bring down the authorities and get him in serious trouble. Therefore, I cannot be alone in thinking that this action *culminates his very mission.* I cannot believe for a minute that Jesus would do something stupid and rash at the end of his life that would endanger his life; *instead, it is more reasonable to think he wanted to get in trouble with the leaders.* He didn't wake up the next morning under guard saying, "What did I get myself into? How could have I been so foolish?" Instead, he was saying, "Father, I have committed myself to your will and I am now in the thick of my mission—take me, use me, and heal your people, Israel!" And, if I am right in these suppositions, then it follows that Jesus' death is the inevitable implication of his very mission—to protest what is going on in the Judaism of his day, especially as embodied in its leadership in the Temple, and to call that nation to repent in light of a coming judgment at the hands of Rome. In other words, at the heart of Jesus' death is *the same idea of politics that we have seen so far: his mission is to restore the nation, the political body of his people.* Consequently, the *death of Jesus is his personal national sacrifice to bring about the completion of the story of Israel, to restore the fortunes of Israel, to end the exile, and to bring forgiveness, peace, and righteousness.*

Three further points about his death need to be made that contribute to this discussion that Jesus' death is to be understood as part of his larger mission. First, a fairly widespread perception of the end of history in Judaism, though quite flexible in interpretation and expression, is that the climax of history would involve *an ordeal or a tribulation*.[39]

While many Jewish writers of our period envisioned a tribulation at the end of history, not all believed Jews would experience its hardships or that it was primarily purgative. Instead, for some it was God's meting out of punishment against wicked sinners and Gentiles. Nonetheless, for many Jews the kingdom/Age to Come could not arrive until there was a tribulation (e.g., *1 Enoch* 91–105; 1QM). Jesus expected a time of tribulation soon (Mark 13:9–13, 21–23, 24–27). If Jesus saw his death as suffering (Mark 8:31; cf. 8:34–9:1), and suffering is an integral part of that tribulation, it is not surprising that Jesus might have seen his death as the onset of the tribulation, and texts like Luke 12:49–50, 51–53; Matthew 11:12–13, and Mark 10:38–39 clearly connect Jesus' ministry and mission to the time of tribulation. And, that Jesus assumed that he embodied the Son of Man figure of Daniel 7, which figure undergoes suffering prior to vindication before the Ancient of Days, also suggests that Jesus saw his own mission as one which would find its climax in a suffering-then-vindication scheme.[40]

Thus, it is reasonable to think Jesus purposefully threw himself into suffering because he knew that such was God's plan for the redemption and vindication of his people. He sacrificed himself for his mission, for his people, and unto God.

A second line of thought clarifies why he might have thrown himself into suffering as he did. Jesus, in a saying that many scholars today think finds its origin in Jesus himself, sees his mission as one of serving others so unselfishly that he envisions a self-sacrificial death for others (Mark 10:45). Scholarship fights today over most of the features of the important expressions in the last part of this saying, and, if we learn to read it more historically and less in light of the Christian understanding of atonement, we can settle on firm ground: Jesus envisioned his own death, he envisioned that it would be for "the many"—a term for Israel (i.e., a contrast of the one with the many), and that he saw himself in some sense as atoning for the many.[41] He may have seen his mission in terms of Daniel 7, but he combined that tradition with others, notably Psalm 22 and Isaiah 40–55. Thus, we have reason to think that Jesus saw his own imminent suffering as the onset, or at least an embodiment, of the great tribulation and that he undertook such intentionally for the benefit of Israel, "the many" (cf. 1QS 6:1, 7–25).[42] Here we should not find Jesus' theory of atonement, nor should we attribute to him a position in the debate between substitution and representation, but instead we should find here Jesus' *theory of history coming to a climactic moment as he offers himself to God for his people—at the hands of his enemies.*

Finally, we need to note the connection that runs from Jesus' entry to the incident in the Temple to the Last Supper he celebrated—rather ominously, one suspects—with his disciples. In this context, not everything can be explained adequately, but this much is clear: just as John's baptism was implicitly a critique of the effectiveness of the Temple, so we may reasonably argue that Jesus' words over the Passover meal he celebrated with his disciples reveal that he, too, finds the atoning work of the Temple to be ineffective. His celebrated Temple incident, staged undoubtedly to fit in with his public entry into Jerusalem, significantly demonstrates that we are on a sure path when we connect the three events together and understand the Last Supper to be Jesus' "alternative" form of atonement. As Bruce Chilton has put it: "After Jesus' occupation of the temple, and his failure to change arrangements in the cult, he presented his 'blood' and 'body'—his meals in anticipation of the kingdom—as a replacement of conventional sacrifice."[43]

That is, Jesus' acts here were of a piece of those sorts of acts found in the Essenes of the Qumran scrolls—criticism, alternative form of atonement (perhaps even in anticipation of a new covenant and a new Temple!), and restoration of Israel as embodied in the people around their charismatic leader.[44]

Putting these three lines of argument yields the following: Jesus intentionally and self-consciously embodied the expectation of the great tribulation by throwing himself into a situation in Jerusalem that he knew would produce suffering. He did this, so it seems, because he wanted to offer himself to his Father as a sacrifice for his people as the Son of Man and, in the Last Supper, he symbolically offered himself, again as sacrifice, to his followers and promised that if they partook in his meal they would find an atonement more effective than the Temple. While the records that survive of his last few days squarely blame corrupt leaders, it can also be firmly espoused that his death was not an accident of history: he willed it as a sacrifice for his people. Thus, in his death *we find how he understood history; no, how he understood himself.*

Conclusion

There are moments when I wish I had been born Jewish, nurtured in the Torah and trained to read Talmud—moments, I say. Not because I am unhappy with the Christian faith or with Jesus as Messiah. But this won't happen because it can't. I am a Gentile, of Scottish-American extraction. No, I wish this only to eliminate what I think are Christian obfuscations which prevent Christians from seeing Jesus as he really was, from seeing Jesus in interaction with his Jewish world. I can't alter my upbringing in the Christian faith, but I can erase, largely as a result of the growth and development in the Jewish-Christian dialogue, some of the secondary readings of the Christian palimpsest. I can repent from the bad scholarship that has driven far too much Christian theology,[45] I can urge my students to learn what Judaism was (and is) and in light of that knowledge come to terms with their faith more truthfully, and I can pledge to continue in a search for the beginnings of the Christian movement. For this discussion to move forward, and so much has taken place to give one substantial hope, we need to listen to one another, to evaluate our own sets of beliefs and conclusions in light of that hearing, to give unconditional respect to the other side, and to work together to gain light as we travel this road together.

To be sure, the road parts—and that parting takes place with Jesus, and even that parting took place over time and in different ways and over different presenting causes.[46] Jacob Neusner, in an insightful discussion, states this eloquently:[47]

> What matters is that Jesus Christ for Christianity uniquely is the Messiah, uniquely is God incarnate, uniquely reveals Torah against which all other Torah falls short. . . . Christianity stands or falls on the claim of the uniqueness of Jesus Christ. . . . After all, everyone knows, when it comes to mere mortal sages, we of holy Israel have hundreds who compare in wisdom and piety and supernatural insight; and prophets, priests, and martyrs to compare as well. What we do not have is God incarnate in one person only, and what we have not known is the Messiah in any one person—at least, not yet.

He is surely right: what forks the road is Jesus as Messiah, Lord, and God incarnate. Some have followed in the direction he points; others have not. Jimmy Dunn, in a magnificent book on the development of earliest Christianity, turns this confession of Jesus in a helpful manner when he claims: "The more divine significance we Christians recognize in Jesus, God's self-revelation in fullest form possible within humanity, the more we need also to recall that this incarnation took place precisely in a Jew—Jesus the Jew."[48]

This Jesus may have worn *tzitzit* (cf. Mark 6:56), gathered faithfully with others in synagogue, attended the feasts in Jerusalem, and evidently was an observant Jew. But not all roads charted by Christians can take a direct path from this Jewish Jesus. The central issues and pillars at his time were God, Torah, Temple, Land, Israel—not the expected Messiah and who might fit that job description, not incarnation, and not the need of a new atoning method. And so, in light of these central issues, I have attempted in this essay to point out that there is a better way to debate the issues, a way that seeks to describe Jesus as much as we can as he really was—and he was a Jew within that Judaism who was faithful to the covenant. It is in that covenant, within the terms set by the God of Israel and Jesus as emerging from that Israel, that we find common ground, common hope and love, and the salvation of God for those faithful to that covenant.

Chapter 8

Early Christianity and the Synagogue: A Parting of the Ways

Carsten Claussen

Christianity was born in the middle of Judaism.[1] Jesus was born as a Jewish child into a Jewish family and society. His early followers were Jews. Jesus himself obviously saw his mission as being primarily directed toward his fellow Jews (cf. Matt. 10:6, 23; 15:24). However, his later followers left the synagogues and started defining their own religious convictions against the background of their mainly Jewish origins. What did his early followers experience that made them set up their own meetings? Why did they finally have to leave the framework of Judaism? The following essay will draw a picture of the development that set Jesus and his followers apart from the environment of ancient Judaism and will thus face the question: "Who was Jesus?"

Jesus and the Kingdom of God

William Lane Craig argues that "the key to answering the question of who Jesus was lies in our assessment of the historicity of the resurrection of Jesus." Craig is certainly right to emphasize that the belief in the resurrection is a vital and indispensable point for nascent Christianity. The end of the original text of Mark's Gospel in 16:8 provides good evidence for the atmosphere preceding the first resurrection appearances. Some of Jesus' female followers who had already been watching the death of Jesus from a distance (Mark 15:40) are now "trembling and bewildered"[2] (Mark 16:8) after being informed about the resurrection (Mark 16:6). Consequently, they flee from the tomb. The male disciples—apart from Peter (Mark 14:66–72)—had left the whole scene already when Jesus was arrested (Mark 14:50).

Between Jesus' death on the cross and the resurrection appearances, the followers of Jesus could hardly have believed that Jesus' mission would go on. This makes the belief in the resurrection of Jesus on the part of his early followers an indispensable link, to say the least. Although the resurrection of Jesus must be distinguished from any concept of revivification or resuscitation, as Donald Hagner has rightly emphasized, this does not yet entail a split between Judaism and Christianity.

The parting of ways between nascent Christianity and ancient Judaism seems to be a far more complex phenomenon and begins, as we shall see below, already in Jesus' own proclamation of the kingdom of God in his own ministry (Matt. 11:5).

It is widely accepted that Jesus did not found a new institution. His message was not just about minor or even major changes of society. He proclaimed a new world order that should soon expand to a new world. The central term of his preaching is the "kingdom of God" (Mark 1:15).

Jesus' preaching stands within the historical context of Jewish apocalypticism. Thus, it may be helpful to compare the worldview of Jesus and his followers with what we know about Jews with an apocalyptic worldview like the Pharisees. First of all, what both groups had in common is that they showed complete commitment to a new world order and tried to live accordingly. But at the same time, their different perspectives on eschatology set them completely apart. The Pharisees tried to live according to the Torah. Although they tried to adapt some of it to their contemporary situation and interpreted the Law accordingly, they did not dare to change it. While Jesus criticizes Pharisaic ethics as "heavy loads" (Matt. 23:4), he promises rest to the "weary and burdened" and defines his "yoke" as "easy" and his "burden" as "light" (Matt. 11:28–30). Accordingly, for the disciples of Jesus his presence in their midst brought major changes amounting to a new life: "How can the guests of the bridegroom fast while he is with them?" (Mark 2:19). Should they starve on a Sabbath "when one greater than the temple is here?" (Matt. 12:6). Therefore, it is no surprise that, compared with some of the Pharisees, Jesus and his followers were viewed as gluttons and drunkards (Matt. 11:19). This is, of course, an exaggeration, but it shows that Jesus and his disciples' attitude to the Law changed completely in the light of the presence and power of the kingdom of God (cf. Luke 11:20 = Matt. 12:28).[3] The main difference between the Pharisaic teaching and Jesus is rooted in two different eschatological perspectives: Jesus is the only Jew in classical antiquity we know of who did not just proclaim that one was on the threshold of the last days, but at the same time that the new time of salvation has already begun in himself.[4]

In the time of Jesus, the kingdom of God was a current topic in the liturgy of the Jerusalem Temple.[5] It denotes God's reign, which is already present in heaven and will finally also lead to a world without war and suffering. This conviction already had considerable impact on the day-to-day life of pious Jews. The difference for Jesus and his disciples was, however, that Jesus proclaimed the beginning of the kingdom of God on earth in his very own words and deeds: replying to John the Baptist's question from prison: "Are you the one who was to come" (Matt. 11:3), Jesus answers: "The blind receive sight, the lame walk, those who have leprosy are cured, the deaf hear, the dead are raised, and the good news is preached to the poor" (Matt. 11:5). Thus the kingdom of God begins with Jesus himself. The presence and the future of salvation come together in his eschatological existence.

Jesus and the Spirit

The early followers of Jesus became a distinctive group because they shared certain beliefs and experiences. Peter Zaas stresses the point that "Judaism is non-creedal." He even pushes the argument a bit further and says that "Jewishness expresses itself most significantly as a consciousness of peoplehood, of belonging (with whatever degree of strain) to the Jewish nation." Although I dare to disagree with Zaas' definition of a merely ethnic Judaism that ignores the doctrinal dimensions, his argument certainly helps to sharpen the focus. From a Christian point of view, Judaism may indeed too often be reduced to a religion similar to the Christian concept of a personal and creedal faith. Thus Christians must be disturbed by the possibility of someone claiming to be an atheistic Jew. However, if one ignores the doctrinal dimensions of being Jewish, the picture becomes equally one-sided and unbalanced. Even somebody who argues in favor of an ethnic definition must face the question of how any sense of belonging may be described. Defining Jewishness is far from being a question only for non-Jews. Jews define themselves by being born as children of a Jewish mother or, for many of them, in a more specific sense as belonging to Orthodox, Conservative, Reform, or other groups within contemporary Judaism. And the belonging to certain groups also has to do with the acceptance of certain beliefs and the rejection of others. In a similar way, we know about certain groups within ancient Judaism. Pharisees, Sadducees, Essenes, Zealots, Therapeutae, and probably many more defined themselves not just by being Jews ethnically but by expressing certain beliefs. However, all of these groups somehow remained within the framework of Judaism even if they set themselves apart, as the Essenes did, or claimed to be the true Judaism. This brings

us back to the question why another Jewish group whose members proclaimed Jesus to be the Messiah did not remain within the boundaries of
ancient Judaism.

The early followers of Jesus began as a movement of renewal within
first-century Judaism. Luke-Acts portrays them as follows (Acts 2:42–47):

> They devoted themselves to the apostles' teaching and to the fellow-
> ship [*koinonia*], to the breaking of bread and to prayer. Everyone was
> filled with awe, and many wonders and miraculous signs were done
> by the apostles. All the believers were together and had everything in
> common. Selling their possessions and goods, they gave to anyone as
> he had need. Every day they continued to meet together in the tem-
> ple courts. They broke bread in their homes and ate together with
> glad and sincere hearts, praising God and enjoying the favor of all the
> people. And the Lord added to their number daily those who were
> being saved.

However stereotyped this description may be, there can be no doubt
that this new fellowship is a Jewish group. What we find here is Christianity within the Temple courts—and that is more than a metaphor. The
so-called primitive church—certainly an anachronistic term—is defined
by the apostles' teaching and by concrete meetings in private houses and
in the Temple. But what made them special? As James Dunn stresses:

> It is this shared experience of the Spirit which is the source of what
> we now more usually think of as 'fellowship.' That is why the word
> *koinōnia* first occurs in the description of the Christian congregation
> after Pentecost—a new experience of community was the conse-
> quence of this foundational experience of the Spirit which they had
> shared (Acts 2:42).[6]

Later Dunn goes on to say that "at the heart of the fundamental unity of
the NT is not just a *doctrine* of Christ's resurrection but the *experience* of
God's acceptance through his Spirit."[7]

Sometimes Christian theology seems to become a bit nervous of talking about experience. However, this is essentially what Luke-Acts wants
to say: The first fellowship of the followers of Jesus came into being as a
result of a shared experience of God's Spirit. And even if one should raise
the problems of the historicity of Acts,[8] the apostle Paul allows us to
appeal to experience even more directly: "Because you are sons, God sent
the Spirit of his Son into our hearts, the Spirit who calls out 'Abba,

Father'" (Gal. 4:6 cf. 3:2–5; Rom. 8:15–16). But this first stage did not exclude the followers of Jesus from Judaism. There is good reason to think that the early believers in Jerusalem continued to observe the Torah. Peter's own testimony that he had never eaten "anything impure or unclean" (Acts 10:14; cf. 11:8) until the changes mentioned in Acts 11:3 and Galatians 2:11–14 is not to be doubted. Especially the circumcised believers in Jerusalem insisted on not having table-fellowship with Gentiles (Acts 11:2f.; cf. 10:28). The new movement obviously continued to be faithful with regard to food laws and table-fellowship, and thus remained very much within the matrix of Second Temple Judaism. Only the shared experience of the Spirit and the apostles' teaching set them apart "in the temple courts" (Acts 2:46; 5:42). However, these exceptional features led Jews and Gentiles alike to call the followers of Jesus by distinctive names.

Jesus and the Names of His Followers

If a certain group of people can be identified from outside or if members of a group want to identify their social grouping, the need for a name arises. The names of the early Jesus movement provide evidence as to what insiders and outsiders noticed as most typical concerning the identity of this group.

In Acts 24:5 Paul is accused of being a "ringleader of the Nazarene sect." According to Luke-Acts, the case is put forward by an orator named Tertullus. We hardly know anything about him. His speech (Acts 24:2–8) shows him as well-trained in forensic rhetoric. His name does not identify him as a Jew. However, as he serves the high priest Ananias and some of the elders, we may assume that he is a Hellenistic Jew familiar with the procedures of Roman courts. The Greek term for "sect" used to define this group—*hairesis*—has, in contrast to its modern translation, no derogatory tone in it. Josephus uses the same word to describe the four "sects" within Judaism: Pharisees, Sadducees, Essenes, and Zealots (*Ant.* 13.171; *J. W.* 2.118). As we have already seen, Second Temple Judaism consisted of a range of different schools or, as one might say, interest groups. It may even be correct to speak of "Judaisms" as Jacob Neusner and Alan F. Segal have argued.[9] Among these Jewish sects the followers of Jesus of Nazareth formed just another one. The title *nazōraios* or *nazarēnos* was already given to Jesus and is widely attested in the Gospels (Matt. 2:23; 26:71; Luke 18:37; John 18:5, 7; 19:19; Acts 2:22; 3:6;

4:10; 6:14; 22:8; 24:5; Mark 1:24; 10:47; 14:67; 16:6; Luke 4:34; 24:19). This name was most likely an inner-Jewish designation of the followers of the man from Nazareth. Although it may not have sounded all that positive (cf. John 1:46: "Nazareth! Can anything good come from there?"), it did not serve to exclude the Nazarenes from Judaism. It just helped to mark yet another Jewish "sect."

The more important name, however, is the name "Christ-ians"—*christianoi*—as the disciples were first called in Antioch (Acts 11:26). The prevalence of this name in the subsequent history of the church stands in surprising contrast to the observation that the term appears only thrice in the whole New Testament (Acts 11:26; 26:28; 1 Peter 4:16). This rareness strongly suggests that the name was hardly used by the early followers of Jesus to designate themselves but was invented and at first used only by non-Christians.[10] This accords with Agrippa II's use of the term (Acts 26:28) and with its use in the context of hostility (1 Pet. 4:16) and trials against Christians by Roman authorities (Pliny, *Ep.* 10.96). As a direct parallel to other groups that were named after persons like, for example, *herōdianoi*,[11] the Hellenists in Antioch were linked to a person: Even if one did not listen too carefully to the missionary preaching of those people, one could hardly fail to observe that it was all about somebody called "Christ." Their proclamation of Jesus as the "Christ" led to this nickname.[12]

Thus it becomes apparent that these people were, even from the outside, no longer just identified simply as "Jews" (*Ioudaioi*). It is difficult to say what else may have been recognized regarding their new identity. However, it is most likely that they were known as those who welcomed great numbers of non-Jewish sympathizers and granted them full membership even without circumcision (cf. Acts 21:21). Since the time of Julius Caesar, Jewish synagogues were protected by Roman law. However, now, as new designations appeared, the Roman authorities were on the way to recognizing that these people were not simply Jews. The Neronian persecution in 64 C.E. shows that Christians in Rome were no longer protected by those generous Jewish privileges (Tacitus, *Annals* 15.44.2). In Antioch the meeting of the "Hellenists" may have been regarded officially as some kind of "synagogue of the Christians." We do not have any evidence of persecutions there. However, 1 Peter 4:16 gives the impression that the name Christian had to do with slander and reckless name-calling (cf. Pliny, *Ep.* 10.96). Even for outsiders, the differences became more and more visible and marked the growing distance between Christians and Judaism. Nevertheless, in Palestine prior to 70 C.E. Jews were able to believe that Jesus was Messiah and yet remain largely undisturbed (Acts 21:20–26).

Jesus, Paul, and the Law

Like Jesus, Paul saw his own mission within the framework of eschatology (cf. Rom. 11:13–32; 15:14–24).[13] However, he made little use of the term "kingdom of God," except in 1 Corinthians.[14] He rather stressed "God's righteousness" as something given to us by God. Ernst Käsemann has insisted that in this case gift and giver are inseparable.[15] So God's kingdom and God's righteousness can be seen as two different aspects of God's dealing with his creation.[16] Or as A. J. M. Wedderburn notes, both are linked: "(R)ighteousness was expected to characterize the king's rule and it was his business to establish righteousness in his land.[17] And this was equally true of God."[18]

According to Luke-Acts, Paul usually started his missionary preaching in the context of a Jewish synagogue. This is reported for quite a few places on his missionary journeys like Salamis (Acts 13:5), Pisidian Antioch (13:14), Iconium (14:1), Thessalonica (17:1f.), Berea (17:10), Corinth (18:4), and Ephesus (18:19; 19:8). What follows seems to be rather stereotyped: After a period of time, some members of the synagogue refuse his teaching and expel him from their meetings (e.g., Acts 14:1–6; 17:1–15; 18:4–7) or even from the whole region (Acts 13:50).

If this picture is historically credible, what were the issues that upset the members of the synagogue so much that they expelled Paul? A good summary of the reasons can be found in Acts 21 when Paul finally arrives in Jerusalem. James and the elders address Paul:

> You see, brother, how many thousands of Jews have believed, and all of them are zealous for the Law. They have been informed that you teach all the Jews who live among the Gentiles to turn away from Moses, telling them not to circumcise their children or live according to our customs (Acts 21:20c–21).

Although the reader of Acts has already been informed (cf. Acts 16:3–4; 18:18; 20:6) that Paul still lives according to Jewish customs, these accusations reflect the early conflicts between Jewish and Gentile Christians. For outsiders, these conflicts were seen as intramural-Jewish ones (Acts 18:15).

Zaas is definitely right to protest against an all too narrow concept of ancient Judaism and thus to question the concept of any orthodox or normative Judaism for the period prior to 70 C.E. However, this does not mean that there is no common and unifying core for Second Temple Judaism at all. James Dunn has outlined what he calls a "fourfold foundation on which all these more diverse forms of Judaism built, a common heritage which they all interpreted in their own ways."[19] According to Dunn, these were:

> Monotheism: God is one;
> Election—a covenant people, a promised land;
> Covenant focused in Torah;
> Land focused in Temple.[20]

We cannot go into detail here. However, it is certainly worthwhile to have a quick look at these four pillars. This will also show how nascent Christianity no longer rested on these pillars.[21]

In postexilic Judaism or even earlier, monotheism had become a fundamental dogma. Texts like the first commandment (Exod. 20:3) or the Shema—"Hear, O Israel: The Lord our God, the Lord is one" (Deut. 6:4)—provide the strongest evidence for Jewish monotheism.

The fundamental belief in the special election of God, who is self-bound to covenant, is equally crucial to Israel's self-understanding. Already in Genesis, the initial choice of Abraham (Gen. 12:1–3; 15:1–6) is filled out with the explicit promise of the land (Gen. 15:17–21; 17:1–8). This is also the backbone of the whole Exodus tradition (Deut. 6:20–25; 26:5–10). Among other texts Second Isaiah shows the re-establishment of this conviction in the post-exilic period (Isa. 41:8–9; 44:1).

Crucial for the self-understanding of Second Temple Judaism is the centrality of the Torah for Israel's consciousness of being God's chosen people (Deut. 5:2–3; 29:1). This led Israel to a sense of separateness from the surrounding nations (*Jub.* 22.16; *Ep. Arist.* 139, 142).

The Jews' reaction to Caligula's plan to have a statue with his effigy set up in the Temple in 40/41 C.E. (Josephus, *Ant.* 18.261; Philo, *Legatio ad Gaium* 203) indicates clearly the importance of the Temple as the center of Israel's national and religious life. "Tens of thousands" of Jews met the Syrian legate Petronius asking that he slay them first (*Ant.* 18.264).

From these four topics, it is mainly the Torah and the issue of monotheism that are decisive matters of dispute between Jews and Christians. The Torah led to dispute particularly in the areas of food laws, circumcision, and the observance of the Sabbath. James Dunn describes these three topics under the sociological heading of "boundary markers."[22] Although it would be too schematic to reduce the whole issue of Torah to these three aspects, it is nevertheless helpful to look at these major areas of conflict.

From the Maccabean period onward, these laws gained increasing significance. For Jews they became points of particular sensitivity, which were especially important in the mixed environment of Diaspora Judaism. People outside Judaism recognized them as particularly and distinctively characteristic for Jews. In Asia Minor as in other areas, Jews sought at every opportunity to acquire rights identical with those of non-Jewish citizens. In doing so, however, they had to make sure that they could nevertheless live according to their customs and keep their sacred rights. It is therefore not surprising to find the rights to keep the Sabbath and to have their "ancestral food" mentioned quite frequently in the decrees in favor of Jews in the Diaspora.[23] Circumcision belonged more to the private and inner-Jewish sphere and was thus not a matter of Roman decrees.

We have already seen some of the opposition against Paul from Jews and Jewish Christians in Acts. The same areas of conflict can be found in his own letters. He felt persecuted because of his stance on circumcision (Gal. 5:11; cf. Gal. 4:29; 6:12–13; Acts 21:21). Even fellow Jewish Christians were opposed to his policy of eating with Gentiles (Gal. 2:11ff.). His teaching was viewed as an encouragement to libertinism (Rom. 3:8; cf. Acts 21:21). This makes it easy to imagine why he received the synagogue punishment of the thirty-nine lashes on five occasions (2 Cor. 11:24). His treatment of the Law provides enough reason to argue that his expulsion from one synagogue after the other (e.g., Acts 14:1–6; 17:1–15; 18:4–7) is not just a Lukan stereotype.

Thus the question of keeping or abandoning the Torah can be seen as a very important factor resulting in a growing distance between Jews and Christians. It was not just important for the Pauline churches but for all early Christian communities (cf. Matthew 5–7 or the letters of James and Barnabas). But the bigger issue is certainly the one that is addressed in the present collection of essays: "Who was Jesus?" From a Christian standpoint, this question inevitably has to do with the relationship between Jesus as Lord and God the Father. Already Jesus himself prays to God, addressing God with the Aramaic "*abba*" ("Father"; Mark 14:36; cf. Rom. 8:15; Gal. 4:6). We cannot enter at this point into the whole discussion about Jesus' self-consciousness. However, it seems perfectly clear to the early Christians that Jesus did indeed see himself as God's Son in an exclusive sense. As a consequence, the early followers of Jesus started addressing prayer to Jesus (Luke 24:52f.; Acts 7:59; Rom. 10:12; 1 Cor. 1:2; 16:22). It is therefore no surprise that the conflict between Christians and Jews was growing precisely in the area of prayer, as we shall see below. Jesus himself stresses the importance of the Shema

(Mark 12:29). Christians from a Jewish background very likely continued to pray as Jesus did. In addition to this, Paul gives an example of how Hellenistic Jewish Christianity may have combined faith in one God with faith in Jesus: "Yet for us there is but one God, the Father, from whom all things came and for whom we live; and there is but one Lord, Jesus Christ, through whom all things came and through whom we live" (1 Cor. 8:6; cf. Gal. 3:20; Rom. 3:29–30; 1 Tim. 2:5).

The earliest confessions of Jesus as "both Lord and Christ" (Acts 2:36) arose in Jewish Christian communities. The Aramaic (probably eucharistic) prayer formula *marana tha* ("Come, O Lord"; 1 Cor. 16:22 NIV; *Did.* 10:6; cf. Rev. 22:20) gives evidence that already the pre-Pauline communities called the risen Jesus "our Lord." By the time of Paul, the title *kyrios* (Lord) had become the usual Greek rendering of the Hebrew divine name. Within the Pauline letters, *kyrios* is used about 230 times for Jesus. Paul does not feel any tension between the affirmation of monotheism and a clear distinction between the two persons of the Father as creator and the Son Jesus Christ as the divine mediator. For the early Christians, Jesus' resurrection and glorification were interpreted in the light of Psalm 110:1: "The Lord says to my Lord: 'Sit at my right hand until I make your enemies a footstool for your feet.' "[24] According to this verse Jesus is installed at the right hand of God (Acts 2:34–35; Rom. 8:34; Eph. 1:20; Col. 3:1; Heb. 1:3,13). The honor that originally belonged to the God of Israel *only* is now also directed to Jesus as the *kyrios* (cf. Phil. 2:10–11, with Isa. 45:23; Rom. 10:13, with Joel 3:5). This extension of divine prerogatives to the risen Jesus was a threat to the Jewish understanding of monotheistic faith. The confession of Jesus as Lord in worship and especially in prayer and Eucharist made joint worship of Jews and Christians practically impossible.

The picture would not be complete without coming back to Paul's apocalyptic worldview. He makes use of apocalyptic categories while describing Christ's death and resurrection (1 Cor. 15:20–28) and the redemption of Israel (Rom. 11:1–36). God had "put everything under Christ" (1 Cor. 15:27) already in Paul's present. Finally, Christ will hand over his kingdom (1 Cor. 15:24–25) to God the Father in order that "God may be all in all" (1 Cor. 15:28). The death of Christ creates already a new relationship of the Christians to the Torah (Gal. 2:21; Rom. 8:1ff.) for the present time.

As we have seen, the Pauline letters in the middle of the first century show a rather careful attempt to integrate monotheism and the confession of Jesus as Lord. The Gospel of John at the end of the century presents a further developed picture.

Jesus As God

By the end of the first century, Johannine Christians had been expelled or separated themselves from Jewish synagogues (John 9:22; 12:42; 16:2). The degree of polemic in the Fourth Gospel makes it clear that these Christians have been engaged in harsh disputes with Jewish authorities, which brought about separation. The Temple (John 2:18–22) and the observance of the Sabbath (John 5:16; 7:19–24) have probably been among the disputed issues. However, the main conflict with the synagogue was the question of who Jesus was. The affirmation of Jesus as the Christ inevitably led to expulsion from the synagogue (John 9:22; cf. 1:41; 20:31) because the sort of Messiahship involved here was more than the human leadership of a Bar Kokhba. What is at stake here is the rejection of Jesus as Messiah, Son of God and king of Israel (John 1:41, 49; 20:21). Nowhere else in the New Testament is the relation of Jesus and the Father as close as here (John 10:30; 17:11, 21–23). Consequently, the Jewish reaction is far stronger. On a chronological scale, Paul's and John's theology show different stages of the growing distance.

There is one ancient source that has very frequently been regarded as the central text showing the schism between Judaism and Christianity: The twelfth *berakah* in the Jewish so-called "Eighteen Benedictions" (*Shemoneh Esreh*), which is usually called the "blessing of the heretics" (*Birkat ha-minim*):[25]

> And for the apostates let there be no hope; and may the insolent kingdom be quickly uprooted, in our days. And may the *noṣrim* and the *minim* perish quickly; and may they be erased from the Book of Life and may they not be inscribed with the righteous. Blessed art thou, Lord, who humblest the insolent. (Palestinian recension)

This addition to the original prayer is remembered in rabbinic tradition as stemming from the time of Rabban Gamaliel II at the end of the first century (*b. Ber.* 28b). This fits nicely with the expulsion of Johannine Christians from synagogues (John 9:22; 12:42; 16:2), although the precise circumstances are somehow obscure.[26]

The term *noṣrim* may refer to the Nazarenes. However, it is not clear whether it belonged already to the original version of the prayer. The other heretics (*minim*) who are cursed are quite frequently interpreted as Jewish sectarians, including Jewish Christians. William Horbury even supposes that "Christians, both Jewish and Gentile, were cursed in synagogue."[27] This view has been supported by the witness of some ancient

Christian texts. Justin Martyr shortly after the middle of the second century, for example, repeatedly states in his *Dialogue with Trypho the Jew* (16.4; 93.4; 95.4; 96.2; 108.3; 123.6; 133.6; 137.2) that Jews curse in their synagogues those who believe in Christ.

What we recognize here is the attempt to narrow down the legitimate self-definition of the broad heritage of pre-70 Judaisms. Those who may be viewed as the first proponents of rabbinic Judaism take a stand against those regarded as Jewish sectarians—now in a pejorative sense. This must be seen as a sign of growing distance. The reason for this politics of separation is, however, that contacts between those different groups were continuing more widely than one might expect. Justin speaks of Christians who adopted Judaism (*Dial.* 47.4) and says that Jewish authorities had to prohibit Jews from conversing with Christians (*Dial.* 38.112).

What lies behind this must also be viewed in the light of "membership statistics." By the end of the first century, the numbers of Gentile Christians had grown heavily. Most of them—apart from some former proselytes and one may add with caution the God-fearers—had never been members in Jewish synagogues. Compared to them, the number of Jewish Christians was now quite small. Although the importance of their Jewish theological background can hardly be overestimated, they were absorbed into what became the church.

In addition to theological and statistical reasons, political events played an important role. The Jewish War (66–73 C.E.), and to an even greater extent the Bar Kokhba rebellion (132–135 C.E.), had dramatic effects on Jewish-Christian relations. Jewish Christians did not assist the Jewish side in their struggle. However, these developments cannot serve as definite dates for a final parting between synagogue and the Jesus movement.

The whole process is far longer and more complex than can be shown in this article. A first sign of a definite distinction was reached when the Gentile Christian and martyr Ignatius distinguished *christianismos* and *ioudaismos* early in the second century.[28] Not much later, too, pagan authors like Pliny, Tacitus, or Suetonius recognized the new movement as separate from Judaism. Martin Hengel has drawn attention to the fact that on the Jewish side the split becomes visible in the avoidance of the erstwhile popular name Jeshua in tannaitic literature from about the beginning of the second century.[29] However, for a few more centuries we find not just distance or hostility but still ongoing interaction and sometimes even friendship between Christians and Jews.

So, for instance, Origen (d. 253/254) is well aware that some of his congregants in Palestine attend synagogue worship on the Sabbath.[30] He attacks the observance by Christians of the Jewish fasts and feasts.[31] However, Origen does not make clear whether he refers to Jews who embraced Christianity or Christians who were attracted by Judaism.

Even as late as in the fourth century C.E., John Chrysostom in his *Homilies Against the Jews*, held at Antioch in Syria in 386/87 C.E., gives strong witness that large numbers of Christians still frequented Jewish synagogues,[32] went there to take oaths,[33] and participated in a number of festivals[34]—practices that he strongly opposed. However, he had to concede that "many have high regard for the Jews and think that their present way of life is holy."[35]

Conclusions

From this discussion, I think we may draw the following five conclusions:

1. Already in Jesus' own preaching the soon forthcoming kingdom of God is a contentious issue. And even more conflict arose when Jesus proclaimed God's new world beginning already in his own ministry. Thus the separation of Jesus' followers from their fellow Jews started already very early—long before the dispute regarding the resurrection.

2. The early followers of Jesus were linked together by their shared experience of the Spirit of God. As we have seen above, they accepted certain beliefs and rejected others. The apostolic teaching became their creedal foundation. However, in the earliest days in Jerusalem, they still worshiped at the Temple. Thus they became a new group *inside* Judaism.

3. In the middle of the first century, the question of Torah observance was the main point of conflict between Christians and Judaism. Nicknames like *christianoi* or *nazarenoi* show that the new messianic movement was identifiable from inside and outside Judaism. There were local expulsions of Jesus' followers from synagogues but no definite split yet.

4. By the end of the first century C.E., the main issue of conflict arose with regard to the question who Jesus was. Christological confessions and titles like Lord, Messiah, or Christ, and Son of God were a growing threat to the Jewish belief in one God. For Jews, though not for Christians, monotheism was at stake. As conflict and polemic grew, more and more Jewish Christians were expelled from synagogues.

5. Early in the second century, Christian authors started defining Christianity in contrast to its Jewish background. The split also became

more and more obvious to people outside the Jewish and Christian tradition. What neither Jews nor early Christians had expected occurred: two separate branches developed which are, however, related in many ways up to the present day.

Although Christianity had started in the synagogue, by the second century C.E. Jews and Christians became related strangers. Far too often, hostility was the dangerous framework of their interaction. Thus it is valuable to (re-) discover Jesus as the bringer of peace and salvation to both Jews and Gentiles alike.

Chapter 9

The Gospels Would Have Been Greek to Jesus

Herbert W. Basser

My reaction to the views of Zaas and Craig is tinted by my own studies, which I hold in high esteem. I hope personal offense is not taken at my criticisms of views I cannot espouse; none is intended. My position is as follows.

A central goal of the Gospel writers was to instill contempt, an odium, against Judaism: Jews were children of hell, their leaders a brood of vipers. To this end, we see Jesus is supposed to have given some kind of message to the Jews, which by and large they rejected. We have no idea what this message might have been save that the book of John's apologetics and Jewish polemics tell us that Jesus claimed some kind of divine stature for himself. Jesus' death and resurrection are in some way good news for the Gentiles.

Noting now what has been taken as the correct interpretation for 1,700 years, I introduce one new feature. The debates between Jesus and the scribes are framed as hostile encounters. If we strip away the nasty rhetoric of Jesus from these encounters, we can find traces of the sources embedded in the Gospels which show us little controversy. The Pharisees merely ask about some general principle, and Jesus correctly informs them of the specific detail which Pharisees find operative in such cases. The debates in the Synoptic Gospels are framed by literary rhetoric; in point of fact, one can argue that the prior sources have no hint of Jesus' rejecting anything in Pharisaic law. Why these pre-Gospel legal questions (the present formulations indicate the evangelists did not really comprehend them) form part of the early Christian corpus I cannot say. Perhaps they were at one time meant to establish Jesus as knowledgeable and worthy of everyone's attention. I simply do not know this with any degree of certainty, but I do know the exchanges in and of themselves, in their early formulations, could not at all have been confrontational.

William Craig's claims to know about Judaism and historical method are unfounded. His use of Jewish sources is confused. Let us begin and end with one glaring example. When making a historical observation about the accounts in some Gospels concerning the witnesses of the risen body of Jesus, Craig leads us to believe something concerning the status of women in Jewish Palestine that is not so.[1] He tells us no Gospel writer would invent women's testifying to Jesus' resurrection unless it had really happened that way. After all, he alleges, women were not acceptable witnesses in Jewish law and had low status. Toward this end he lumps together all rabbis as certifying his words. But in fact rabbinic law says Jewish women (indeed even one woman under urgent circumstances) should testify in order to identify a corpse.[2]

If we look more closely, we will find that many women of high standing (including the Queen of Adiabene) in first-century Roman society were attracted to Judaism. This must indicate that the status of women was higher in Jewish society than in Roman society and that women were prime candidates for conversion. The numbers of women converts in the early church were also substantial. That women play an important part in the Gospels in recognizing Jesus would likely have more to do with the desire to appeal to them as converts, rather than proving anything historical about women's relationship with Jesus. Craig's hypothesis cannot be sustained.

Craig alleges that New Testament scholarship has reached a consensus that the historical Jesus came to speak in God's place. There is no such consensus. The book of John alone makes this claim, and it hardly represents anything that all New Testament scholars accept as a historical picture. Craig persists in telling us that the Gospel and Pauline accounts about Jesus are accurate representations known from eyewitnesses. He alleges that Jesus died in 30 A.D. and that Paul converted in 33, in time to know the real facts, but he does not tell us how he knows any of this. Furthermore, he says the canonical Gospels were written in the first generation after the crucifixion while the apocryphal Gospels were written later. He asserts that all New Testament scholars agree on this. They do not. What he argues to be indisputable facts about Jesus are not only disputable, but few historians would even care to consider matters for which we have no evidence at all. We have not a shred of writing describing Jesus from anyone who claimed to have known Jesus. Some have only imagined we have.

Myth and legends about living people are so widespread in antiquity, the Middle Ages, and modern times that were one to accept them uncritically and on that basis accept a religion as true, one would have to change religions daily. Indeed, in the latter part of 1995, the news media announced a report from India claiming that a Hindu idol of Ganesh astonished many who watched while it actually consumed its offerings ("It's a Miracle!" *Hinduism Today* 17 [November 1995]; at www.himalayanacademy.com/ht/.)

Craig's treatment of the empty-tomb story in Matthew does not lead us anywhere. All religious debates in Jewish contexts allow the opponent to have noted the facts accurately. It is how debate works. A historical conclusion based on the facts is another matter entirely. We have none. In Matthew's account the Jewish debater simply says, "Here is what really happened." The Christian opponent says, "Well, okay, you are right too, but then this other thing happened after that." Now when people hear the Jewish debater's claims, they will think that they know the final piece of evidence that discredits the debater. No one says the opponent's facts are wrong, just that the salient features were omitted. That was the accepted convention of debate. The background of Matthew's story goes like this: The Christian says that the tomb was empty; hence Jesus rose. The Jew says, "Yes, the tomb was empty; hence the disciples stole the body, and the proof is that the Roman guards admitted that." The Christian says, "Yes, it is true they admitted it, but they were bribed to admit it; hence Jesus rose from the dead." That is the literary style of debate, and we might even assume that such debates were real. That does not mean there was an empty tomb at all—just that Christians claimed there was. The debate after that is simply familiar apologetic and polemic, which proves nothing except that the issue was debated. Matthew 28:11–15 simply provides the bottom line of the debate. It is not hard to see the layers behind it. Matthew maintains the Christian side of the debate by filling in the story the Jews omitted. He tells us so—namely, "This story has been spread among the Jews to this day." But clearly he means only half the story was. The other half is the Christian rebuttal. There is nothing at all to learn from this conventional debate as to whether or not there was ever any missing body.

Craig asks how Jesus got to be the Christ of the cross. It is likely that in his lifetime Jesus was thought by some to be a Messianic figure. He had attracted some following among Jews. These Jews were dismissed by the official voices of Judaism as having no validity. The title "Jesus the Messiah" became a name after his death; the idea of Messiah was not the Jewish idea anymore. He was now Jesus Christ, superstar.

Why did he die? Was he teaching people to worship idols as some Jewish texts claim? Was he a revolutionary bent on the destruction of Rome as some Christian scholars believe? We simply do not know. We can only assume he really was put to death. Otherwise, the movement would not have needed to create an elaborate theology of salvation for its believers to go on believing. The various Gospel accounts of the trial do not tell us a great deal about the charges. The life of Jesus in the Gospels shows us no reason for Jew or Roman to want to kill him through due process.

It stands to reason that some believers, not willing to accept that their hopes had ended in his death, needed to find him still living among them. Though they had to admit historical failure, they could still have theological victory. In this vein, Paul asserts time and time again that the Christian's faith succeeds while the Jew stumbles because of the crucifixion on the cross. It is to this theological success that Craig testifies in his assertion that his zeal and enthusiasm flow out of a belief that Jesus really was who he claimed to be. Craig overlooks the possibility that maybe Jesus was just a healer who came to be acclaimed as a Messiah. The sources that Craig uses as putative normative scholarship to claim historical bases for Jesus' sonship, not only for New Testament but also for Jewish positions, are not viable. Pinchas Lapide's views that Jesus rose from the dead are not shared by any reputable, recognized rabbi or Jewish religious scholar. I was shocked to see Ahad ha'Am (the pen name of Asher Ginsberg) characterized as an "orthodox Jewish" spokesman, as I would have been to see Luther called "a traditional Catholic spokesman." Nevertheless, Ginsberg's assertion that no Jew can accept the idea of the Incarnation (a human speaking as if he were God) is far more typical than that of Pinchas Lapide's. Most correct is Zaas's view that Jews do not at all think about Jesus. I should think they do so less than Christians think about the Buddha.

Peter Zaas's views deserve a careful hearing. I would take exception to a few issues. Unlike Zaas, I affirm that Jewish belief exists as an essential part of all Judaic systems and is important for Jewish self-definition.[3] Throughout their long history, Jews have spoken of those who rejected "principles of faith" as *kofer ba-ikar* (denying a tenet). They spoke of correcting heresies by "removing improper matters of the mind" as *lehotsi et hadavar melibam*. They defined the one who may be called a Jew.[4] The Bible prescribes severe punishments for those who would lead Israel astray and for those who would prophesy falsely.[5] It is true, as Zaas asserts, that membership in the Jewish people can be defined by parentage alone, but biology or conversion does not characterize the essence of Judaism.

Jews, long after the first century and into the eighteenth, saw their peoplehood in terms of duties to a divine covenant. They were a people characterized by that one commitment. If they erred, they were errant Jews, but the obligations to the covenant remained. In trying to override that so-called "old" covenant in favor of the "new," Christians attempted to override Judaism. That "old" covenant dictated a relationship of the Jew to God. To redefine that God, to redefine that relationship, to redefine that Jew was to obliterate any possible Jewish belief system of integrity. Zaas is certainly correct in saying that belief does not define who is a Jew, but it does determine the culture of the community. Any prayer, any ceremonial act, any study of a text that betrays the God of a living covenant is invalid for the community. Any person who rebelled against the Jewish system, by breaking the Sabbath, for example, could not be entertained as a member in good standing in Jewish society. Having said that, I can agree with Zaas that any claim made by Christianity is irrelevant to Judaism. Judaism does not define itself by what others do or think. Furthermore, historical events are simply things that happen and are different from interpretations of events that are part of theological commitments. Events, in and of themselves, have no meaning beyond raw data and cannot be used to prove matters of faith. The Christian appeal to the Christ-event cannot expect any privileged hearing except from the already-converted. One must not lose sight that for the Jew, central to the covenant was the promise of land and security, divine protection, and other things, none of which came to pass after the death of Jesus. What the Jew meant by salvation and what the Christian thought the Jew meant are totally separate issues.

The Jewish response to Christianity's empire and its supersessionist claims is varied. That history has been laid out by James Parkes and Jacob Katz in great detail.[6] Here I shall note only the widespread texts of *Toldot Yeshu*[7] that served as a popular Jewish tract to ridicule the claims of the Gospels and also the texts of the medieval disputations that served to ridicule Christian interpretation of Jewish Scriptures. I might also note the profuse efforts of Jewish leaders to calm tensions that could have, and sometimes did, result in the obliteration of their communities.

As for the idea of sacrifice, I am not as confident as Zaas that a redeemed Israel should not reestablish cultic rituals. After all, the sheer volume that Temple rituals occupy in the sacred Jewish texts would seem to require these rituals be instituted. The redemption of Jews might well mean the reversing of the great destruction suffered in the year 70 when the Temple was destroyed. Covenant and Temple, while not completely interdependent, are not completely independent categories either. It is entirely understandable why the Catholic bureaucracy could find that a renewed Temple might put theological burdens on the belief in a Christ who was to be the sole road to salvation. It is understandable that in the future Jews might seek a fuller involvement with their sacred heritage. The traditional liturgy certainly acknowledges such seeking.

Let us move on now to consider some ancient Jewish views of Jesus. These views were censored out of the current editions but remain in older texts. A second-century tradition (*b. Sanh.* 43b) says:

> On Passover eve they hung the body of Jesus [for display]. A herald had gone out 40 days prior to it: "He is to be stoned for sorcery and leading Israel astray. Anyone able to show his innocence should come and do so." No one was able to find him innocent and he was hung on Passover eve.

Here we see the claim that Jesus was a renegade who was tried as a magician who misled Jews into worshipping foreign gods. That was an early view which later became mitigated as the church became dominated by Gentiles.

We find *Yalkut Balak* 766 (Salonika edition, 1521) preserves what looks like an authentically old tradition:

I.   "He blesses his fellow with a powerful voice," (Prov 27:14). How far did the voice of Balaam travel?

II. Rabbi Yohanan says, "Sixty miles." (His warning went only to the Israelite Camp, i.e. Gentile Christianity is permissible.)

III. Rabbi Joshua ben Levi said, "The seventy nations of the world heard the voice of Balaam." (His warning went to the whole world, i.e. Gentile Christianity is forbidden.)

IV. Rabbi Elazar HaQappar says:

    1. God endowed his voice with the power to travel from one end of world to the other . . .

      a) He gazed and saw that the nations would bow down to the sun, to the moon, to the stars, to trees, and to stones.

      b) He gazed and saw that a man, born of woman, would arise in the future seeking to lead astray the entire world by making himself a god.

      c) It was for this reason He endowed his voice with the power (to go from end of the earth to the other)—

    2. . . . that all the nations of the world might hear.

The passage goes on, but we have enough for our purposes here. One statement had been to the effect that even Gentiles were forbidden to practice Christianity, and in IV this view is elaborated upon. Rabbi Yohanan argued that the prohibition concerned Jews only. Hence Balaam's warning was heard by all the Jews at the time but by no one else.

We now turn to the Yerushalmi, the ancient Palestinian Talmud:

> Rabbi Abbahu said: If a man says to you, "I am a god" he is lying (**a man cannot be a god; so he is lying**); "I am the son of man [here the title reflects the Son of Man sayings in the NT]," at the end he will regret it (**and the son of man so he will regret**); "I will go up to the heavens," **this he has said but will not do it; he spoke but will not accomplish it**. (*y. Ta'anit* 2.1 [end])

This tradition is based on the verse in Numbers 23:19, Balaam's prophecy, but only the last part cites it. I have supplied in bold print those parts of the verse which are interpreted to yield the final results. From this passage alone we do not know if Rabbi Abbahu's objections were only to Jewish Christianity or to Gentile Christianity as well. We have already seen that close to the time that Christianity became a state religion, we find some positive sentiment toward it. Some Jews saw it as an advance over Roman paganism for the world Gentile community.

Zaas and Craig mentioned the antitheses in Matthew 5. My space allotment does not permit me room for any discussion of this beyond noting there is no instance in the so-called antitheses where Jesus would permit things the Pharisees would forbid. To get an idea of the material that Gospel writers inherited about Jesus, let us consider the debates in the Synoptic Gospels between Jesus and the Pharisees concerning the Sabbath. In not a single case will it be clear that Jesus does not simply end up teaching the Pharisees their own law. At no point will Jesus deny either biblical law or even scribal law in regards to the Sabbath.

Matthew

Matthew 12:10–12: Apologetic for Curing on the Sabbath a Man with a Shriveled Hand

> And behold, there was a man with a withered hand. And they asked him, "Is it lawful to heal on the Sabbath?" so that they might accuse him. He said to them, "What man of you, if he has one sheep and it falls into a pit on the Sabbath, will not lay hold of it and lift it out? Of how much more value is a man than a sheep! So it is lawful to do good on the Sabbath."

Animals are categorized as "non-Sabbath items" and thus not to be moved.[8] Since the New Testament uses the expression "lay hold of and lift," we see the problem is one of scribal *muktseh*—"animals are not set aside for Sabbath use"—and so must not be taken and lifted. The scribes prescribed that *muktseh* items are not to be taken and lifted. In the need to justify a teaching, the Babylonian Talmud reveals there could be a rule of *hefsed meruba* (substantial loss).[9] The Talmud posited that if something was of small value it could not be rescued by overriding scribal law.[10] This is said to be the idea behind *m. Shab.* 24:1. We now infer that where something was of great value it could be rescued and, if necessary, even at the expense of scribal law.[11] The passages dealing with alleviating animal pain can be found in *b. Shab.* 128b. That scribal prohibitions are overridden in cases of doing important good deeds is discussed in *m. Shab.* 18:1 and the commentaries of the Talmuds on it. Jesus is not saying anything very radical here.

Luke

2.1 Luke 13:14–16: Apologetic for Curing a Woman on the Sabbath Who Was Crippled for Eighteen Years

But the ruler of the synagogue, indignant because Jesus had healed on the Sabbath, said to the people, "There are six days on which work ought to be done; come on those days and be healed, and not on the Sabbath day." Then the Lord answered him, "You hypocrites! Does not each of you on the Sabbath untie his ox or his ass from the manger, and lead it away to water it? And ought not this woman, a daughter of Abraham whom Satan bound for eighteen years, be loosed from this bond on the Sabbath day?"

The Talmud allows tying[12] common knots for the welfare of animals—even to both the collar or nose ring on the animal and to the hitching post.[13] Normally tight knots could not be tied or untied by rabbinic prohibition, even if untied daily. This was so because strong, permanent knots were considered forbidden by Torah law. The rabbis relaxed their own ruling in the case of welfare for animals.[14]

2.2 Luke 14:3–5: Apologetic for Curing a Man on the Sabbath Who Was Swollen with Fluids

And Jesus spoke to the lawyers and Pharisees, saying, "Is it lawful to heal on the Sabbath, or not? . . . Which of you, having a son or an ox that has fallen into a well, will not immediately pull him out on a Sabbath day?"

The earliest extant specific teachings concerning an animal stuck in a pit on the Sabbath[15] are found in the Damascus Document[16] and may well relate to the problem of scribal decrees which are found in the Tosephta. The Tosephta[17] says that if an animal falls into a place where there is water from which it cannot get out on its own, then one should feed it food there but not extricate it. The Babylonian Amoraim thought that this meant if the animal could stay comfortably, then one should feed it in its place, but if it would cause the animal pain to stay put, then it could be removed even though this would entail infringing upon a minor scribal decree.[18] The Babylonians[19] apparently followed the reasoning that animal pain had to be absolutely relieved by Torah decree,[20] and this Torah injunction could override some scribal prohibitions of the Sabbath. Although we have no tannaitic statements like this, the force of Babylonian Amoraic tradition is borne out by the New Testament. The practice of alleviating pain for animals stuck in pits dates to Second Temple times although the written Jewish sources are attested relatively late.

All Three Synoptic Gospels

Matthew 12:1–8; Mark 2:23–28; Luke 6:1–5: Picking Sheaves

At that time Jesus went through the grainfields on the Sabbath; his disciples were hungry, and they began to pluck heads of grain and to eat [rubbing them in their hands (Luke's version)]. But when the Pharisees saw it, they said to him, "Look, your disciples are doing what is not lawful to do on the Sabbath." He said to them, "Have you not read what David did, when he was hungry, and those who were with him: how he entered the house of God and ate the bread of the Presence, which it was not lawful for him to eat nor for those who were with him, but only for the priests? [Or have you not read in the law how on the Sabbath the priests in the temple profane the Sabbath, and are guiltless? I tell you, something greater than the Temple is here. And if you had known what this means, "I desire mercy, and not sacrifice, [Hos. 6:6][21] you would not have condemned the guiltless (Matthew's version)]. And he said to them, ["The Sabbath was made for man, not man for the Sabbath (Mark's version)]. For the Son of Man is lord of the Sabbath."

All the problems, textual and conceptual, inherent in unraveling Jesus/Pharisee debates can be found in this one example. It seems that the evangelists had little idea about the details of Jewish laws, and only by careful analysis can we establish what lay behind their words. We must note that in all cases in legal debates about Sabbath in the Synoptics, the question of dispute revolves around scribal laws and whether or not the questioning Pharisees know these laws as well as they thought they did. The debate about eating in the fields is of this order too.[22] When people pluck out grain, then push out the kernel of wheat which is an unusual or rare circumstance (normally wheat is harvested in large amounts with an instrument), they do not violate biblical Sabbath rules.[23] The scribes, to protect the spirit of Mosaic laws, banned biblically allowed "abnormal" Sabbath acts. Ears of grain were not usually plucked one by one from fields as against the more common harvesting, threshing methods in use at the time. In *b. Shab.* 103a,[24] we find a very early tradition that specifies the types of plants that are forbidden by biblical law to be plucked (by hand), and ears of grain are not mentioned (since they are normally harvested with a sickle). Deuteronomy 23:25 specifically mentions a method of plucking off the tops of the wheat to get to the kernels by hand in an unusual way when eating another's field. The normal processes of reaping and threshing are bypassed. The activity in this New Testament passage mirrors the activity in Deuteronomy. Furthermore, this tradition notes that in fields not belonging to the plucker one would not transgress the prohibition of clearing fields. Another source, *b. Bezah* 13b, contains examples of the rabbinic rules of *shinui* (change from regular manner) to show specifically that rubbing kernels of ripened grain to eat was unusual (as we find in Luke's version). It is not considered a biblical prohibition in regards to the Sabbath. It follows that what is described in the Gospels would be forbidden by a scribal prohibition and not a biblical one. Thus room for leniency might be available as the scribes left loopholes in their rulings for various circumstances when their rulings would not apply.

Matthew has provided his own understanding by prefacing his point with the notice that priests may profane the Sabbath in the Temple; thus the disciples may also profane it since they are in the presence of the Son of Man. Matthew claims the Torah commands Temple sacrifices on the Sabbath. No other Gospel claims this, and it seems likely that Matthew's version was simply contrived to be parallel to "have you not read (i.e., in Scripture) what David did . . ."

Let us examine the details. The defense of Jesus is precisely to the point: we know David properly overrode biblical law, and so we know biblical law can be superseded.[25] It is a talmudic principle that whatever the scribes enact usually follows biblical models, and, indeed, the model for overriding laws is to be found in the Scriptures. Furthermore, in Matthew's addition, the scribes allowed that in the Temple the Torah made the offering of the daily and musaf sacrifices mandatory on the Sabbath. Consequently, much scribal law could be suspended in the Temple because the scribes assumed the Temple authorities would be careful and watchful that no biblical ones would be infringed upon.[26] So this shows that indeed scribal laws can be infringed upon where there is watchfulness (the awe of the Temple itself provides such). Jesus argues the Son of Man is greater than the Temple, which must mean his own presence on the scene provides more watchfulness than the presence of Temple authorities in the Temple would—and so the scribal infringement would not apply in this case either.

It is not clear the Pharisees were thrilled by this answer,[27] but they would have been assured by the type of argument that the infringement was of a scribal nature and that there was supervision to see that no biblical laws were violated. Again, there would be little warrant here for any condemnation save that the Pharisees would not have accepted Jesus' claim that his presence would guarantee no laws would be broken. Similarly, *b. Shab.* 29b refers to the upper chamber of the house of Nithza in Lod (noted in many places, e.g., *b. Sanh.* 74a) to be the chamber where the supreme court of elders decided many problematic issues. Here the elders did not protest Rabbi Yehuda's trespass of a rabbinic enactment as the Sabbath approached. The circumstances somehow obviated the law. Maimonides, in his commentary to *m. Shab.* 2, explains that the sages of the court who met here were alert, watchful, and vigilant so as to guarantee no biblical laws would be broken in those Sabbath sessions (probably lectures) that were held under their auspices in this particular place.[28] Therefore the reason for the enactment (i.e., suspected negligence) did not apply, and they said nothing about the laxity.[29] In sum, there is nothing at all to learn from these Jesus/Pharisee debates, if seen out of their later literary contexts. Originally, they might have been preserved to show Jesus' mastery of Jewish law and humane application of it.

Now we come to the crucial exchange between Zaas and Craig. Jesus is said to have annulled biblical laws concerning pure and impure foods. In my opinion neither Zaas nor Craig sees the origin of this statement. The notice to this effect in Mark 7:19 must be taken as original to that Gospel and not a later insertion. It is the more difficult reading and has support from *Gospel of Thomas* 14. Jesus' answer in Mark fits eating carrion (food not ritually killed) more than it does questions of purity, for *Thomas* 14 takes the notice that the "things that enter the body do not defile" to mean that carrion is permitted to missionaries. Mark 7:19 notes that Jesus permitted carrion by these words: "things that enter the body do not defile."

It would thus seem that the riddle "Not what enters defiles but what comes out" was originally meant to deal with the eating of carrion by Jewish-Christian missionaries. It has been borrowed here to serve another purpose, that of scribal purity laws. But we cannot ascribe these words to Jesus, for in his lifetime there were no such missionaries.

Conclusion

We can now respond to the basic questions:

1. *Who was Jesus?* The Jesus of history who lived in the first century may have been a Jew who considered himself (or was proclaimed by others) to be the Jewish Messiah who would free them from Roman oppression. The Christ of faith is another figure entirely. *What can we know about him from history?* Nothing. We have not a single document from his time period that mentions him.

2. *Can a Jew remain a Jew in good religious standing if he has become a follower of Jesus?* Absolutely not. The idea is preposterous. The two are mutually exclusive. In stark terms of present theological realities, following the Christ of faith for a Jew is what following a Hindu idol is for a Christian. That does not mean that Christianity is idolatrous for a Christian in Jewish terms, although for a Jew it is. This has to do with legal intricacies that cannot be discussed here. I have dealt with some sources in my Introduction (xxi) to *Pseudo Rabad: Commentary to Sifre Deuteronomy.*[30] The division between Jewish ethnicity and religion is not simply a problem that developed in modern times. In early Maccabean times we find Jews who wanted to worship Zeus. While nominally Jews, they were judged by Jewish tradition to be traitors. We might then say that an ignorant Jew is very much a Jew who cannot be held directly responsible for breaching covenant while a Jew who converts to Christianity out of conviction has lost any right in being part of a Jewish community. Such a person is called *meshumad* (one whose soul has been obliterated). That person cannot be counted in a prayer quorum and is not even entitled to a proper Jewish burial. The person will not be mourned. This, of course, does not mean the person will not be held completely responsible for breaching covenant since the person indeed is a Jew, even if deemed a traitor. In short, difficult as it may be for Christians to understand, in Jewish law the worship of Jesus constitutes a defection from Jewish monotheism.

3. *What was Jesus' relationship with the Judaism of his day?* We do not have access to the Jesus of history in any way that can help us deal with this question. We have nothing but the literary portrayal of the evangelists.

They present a Jesus who taught the ultimate understanding of what God wanted but who was spurned by his own people, who had him crucified. Jesus rose as Christ for the Gentiles and not for the Jews, who remain blind to his blessings. Thus Jesus is pictured in conflict with the authorities of his day. In point of fact, only the framing of the evangelists portrays this picture. Detailed source analysis tends to show that these debates, if historical, would have been very superficial. Jesus, for the most part, does not argue against scribal authority.

The one place where this does appear to happen has to do with oaths and presents Jesus as champion of the law. I have discussed this passage at length elsewhere and hope to publish my account of it shortly in a book dedicated to legal exposition of the New Testament. One must assume some tension existed between Jesus and the Jewish authorities, but only in the literary colorings can we find the pitting of the Jesus of compassion against the Pharisees of ritual. In the actual dialogues themselves, there is no acute tension—only rhetorically so, and when we look at Jewish tradition (i.e., Talmud and Midrash), late as it may seem to us, there is hardly any tension at all. Jesus wins the debates by showing a finer grasp of the principles than do his opponents. On the other hand, the literary tension shown in the fierce rhetoric gives us the view of Jesus as an intolerant scrapper. We do not know why he was condemned, but we may accept that he was. The Gospels do not shed much light on this.

4. *What were Jesus' actual aims?* Whether he was a reformer, a rebel, both, or neither is beside the point now. If he was a teacher of righteousness as Zaas would have it, then that was his aim. If he was a healer, that was his aim. I do not know that people have but one aim in life. One would suspect that as a Jew he cared for his people and the continuation of his religion and wanted to know how best to serve God.

5. *Why did Jesus die?* Teleological questions are for philosophers and theologians to debate. There is no historical answer. The better question is whether there is any significance to his death beyond that of the thousands of Jewish martyrs who likewise perished in those days. The still-better question is for the theologian—what can be made of the risen Christ for the churches? Creating meaning, seeing here the passion and not just death, was the genius of some enthused follower who managed to snatch victory from the jaws of defeat.

6. *Why did the early church begin?* The early churches certainly began as communities, each with its own peculiar views, to partake in some way in the salvation offered by Christian missionaries. The hegemony of the Apostolic church in Jerusalem was not total, and the forces that shaped

doctrines and beliefs (including what the Fathers would brand heretical) were dictated by the kinds of religious beliefs the members held before their conversion. Christianity was not Judaism and did not function within the synagogue. That recognition of separateness necessitated hierarchies of authority in the church. Almost immediately mere membership in the church came to be seen as salvific in itself.

7. *Why are the Gospels what they are?* There is no question that the writers of the Gospels were theologians who inherited theological traditions. Within these traditions they shaped a story for the purpose of separating Jew from Gentile, synagogue from church. The Jews are the doomed, who rejected Jesus. The Christians are the saved, who accepted him. That is the shaping motif and motive of the writers. Are there historical truths here? There may be, but they do not show us anything unique about Jesus. An examination of the parables will yield only normative Jewish ideas or normative Christian theology. If there is anything at all to learn about Jesus, it must be that he was not a very extraordinary teacher, for we have no extraordinary teachings in his name in the Synoptic Gospels. That picture changes dramatically with the Gospel of John. Were we to accept the picture of Jesus in John as a total rebel claiming to be the divine messenger and voice, lashing out at the Jews whose father he says is the devil, we would not be so hard put to see his ministry and death portrayed as it is. This is not a Jesus who accommodates Pharisaic law at all. Given that picture, we could understand Jesus more readily.

However, the historian finds it easier to account for the claims of this Gospel as a Christian reaction to Judaism rather than a historical portrayal of a living person. Namely, the Gospel writers operated under a single premise: "If Jesus is the risen Christ, Jewish teachings are wrong; if not, Gospel teachings are wrong. But he is the Christ, and thus the Jews are wrong. If so, why do they not know it? Because they are evil and hate truth." That is the design of the Gospels and the book of Acts. For Paul, the law is no longer viable. His approach meshes with the views of the Gospel writers.

While we can isolate traditions to periods prior to the Gospel writers' times (by noting they inherited materials they did not fully grasp), we cannot say what Jesus in fact proclaimed. We can only know what people *thought* he proclaimed.

Chapter 10

At What Points Do Judaisms and Christianities Meet?

Jacob Neusner

Judaisms and Christianities never meet anywhere. That is because at no
point do Judaism, defined by the Torah, and Christianity, defined by
the Bible, intersect. The Torah and the Bible form two utterly distinct
statements of the knowledge of God. The Torah defines Judaism—all
Judaisms—and the Bible defines Christianity—all Christianities. The differences between the Torah and the Bible cannot be negotiated, and those
shaped by the one can never know God as do those educated by the other.
That is why the faithful of Judaism can never concede the truth of Christianity: at its foundations it rests on a basis other than the Torah of Sinai.
Once God has made himself known in the Torah, the Torah must stand
in judgment on all other claims to know God. And that judgment, for
Christianity and for Islam, takes the form of the persistence of Israel, the
holy community of the Torah. That is why, when Jews adopt Christianity
or Islam, they can no longer claim a portion in the God of Jacob. That
implacable judgment, broadly shared among Jews, will never change and
is beyond negotiation.

Recognizing the diversity of Judaic and Christian religious systems in
the formative age, we may still speak of Judaism and Christianity as distinct religious traditions, incompatible from the beginning. That is
because all Judaic religious systems of antiquity privilege the Pentateuch,
within the larger canon of ancient Israelite Scripture, and affirm that
through the Torah Israel knows God. All Christian religious systems of
antiquity concur that through Jesus Christ Christianity knows God. So far
as the two large families of kindred religions intersect, it is at Scripture.
Judaisms read forward from Scripture, Christianities read backward from
Christ to Scripture. The reason that Judaism can never formulate a Judaic
theology of Christianity that Christian faithful can comprehend then is
simple. Judaism—all Judaisms—begin in the Torah and find there the criterion of theological truth. And Christianity, for its part, from important

teachings of Jesus forward violates the teachings of the Torah. By that criterion Judaisms and Christianities can never meet. The faithful of Judaism and the faithful of Christianity pray to the same God, the God who spoke to Abraham and at Sinai. But they cannot say the same prayers because, from the perspective of Judaism, we know God through the Torah and judge all truth by the criterion of the Torah. Much that Jesus taught, and still more that his disciples taught, does not meet that criterion but violates the teaching of Moses our rabbi.

Since at issue is living Judaism—meaning, the Judaic religious tradition that carries forward the rabbinic teachings of the Torah, oral and written, and that is expressed in the canonical liturgy of the synagogue—let us dispense with the notion that many Judaisms compete and deal with the normative one, while recognizing diversity in the setting of the norms. That is for a simple reason. The theology of the Oral Torah in its union with the Written Torah, on the one side, and with the liturgy of synagogue and home life, on the other, defines Judaism's worldview, the details in context of its way of life, its explanation of what, and who, Israel is. In their distinctive language and idiom, which in no way copied the language and reproduced the modes of discourse of Scripture, the sages of the Oral Torah retold the story of the Written Torah. The liturgy of the synagogue and home, for its part, would rework modes of thought characteristic of the sages of the Oral Torah and re-frame clusters of categories that sages had formed to make their statement. That is why anyone who wishes to describe the principal characteristics of the religious worldview of that Judaism, in proportion and balance, will find the prescription in the canonical prayer book (Siddur and Mahzor and related canonical collections of prayers). It is the simple fact that Judaism and Christianity—any Judaism, any Christianity—cannot say in common a single prayer—excluding only Psalms, and that tells the whole story.

This theological structure and system hold together both received teaching and contemporary and future liturgical expression and elaboration. Sages claimed through the oral tradition formulated in the documents of the Oral Torah to complement the written tradition and so to set forth for all time the one whole Torah of Moses, our rabbi, and past and future join to prove them right. That claim to state the Torah—in secular language, "here is Judaism, pure and simple"—constitutes sages' theological apologetics, an integral, logical component of their entire statement. And that fact shows us where—by their word, at least—to situate the Oral Torah in the cartography of Judaism. On that map all roads but dead ends coming from one side lead into the Oral Torah; all roads indicated for public use coming from the other side emerge from the Oral

Torah. Diverse Judaisms of antiquity passed from the scene. Only the Torah, oral and written, endured.

Speaking descriptively, standing back and seeing things whole, can we concur? The answers to two questions place that theology into the context of the history of the Judaism continuous with the Oral Torah, fore and aft, and validate sages' claim to stand at the vital center of the Torah.

Before: Are sages right about the written part of the Torah, meaning, is what they say the Written Torah says actually what the ancient Israelite Scriptures say? Will those who put forth the books of Genesis through Kings as a sustained narrative and those who in that same context selected and organized the writings of the prophets, Isaiah, Jeremiah, Ezekiel, and the twelve, in the aggregate have concurred in sages' structure and system? Certainly others who lay claim to these same Scriptures did not concur. At the time the sages did their greatest theological work, in the fourth and fifth century c.e., their Christian counterparts, in the Latin-, Greek-, and Syriac-speaking sectors of Christianity alike, not only read Scripture in a very different way but also accused the rabbis of falsifying the Torah. How would the sages have responded to the charge?

After: In the ages that have passed since the conclusion of the documents of the Oral Torah, has holy Israel's encounter with God in synagogue worship found its shape and principal expression in sages' re-presentation of the one whole Torah of Moses? How—on the basis of what evidence—do we know that it was, in particular, the sages' theology that animated the soul of faithful Israel in the prayerful encounter with God?

Accordingly, the question, framed merely descriptively, presses: did the sages get the past right, and did they effectively define the future? These two questions, the one concerning the written Torah or Scripture, therefore the *before* of the Oral Torah, the other, the one concerning synagogue liturgy and piety that flow around and from the Oral Torah, therefore its *after*, respond to the mediating situation of the Oral Torah. But what is that situation, meaning, where and how, in what context, do I propose to situate or locate (borrowing the Spanish, *localizar*) the Oral Torah?

My answer must appeal not to sequence ("history") and circumstance (sages' legislation concerning, and well-attested participation in, synagogue life) but to the persistent point of insistence. Nor can the question concern what came first and what then followed, purporting to account for matters by appeal to temporal-causative sequences.[1] And the question further is raised not for the merely adventitious fact that, in temporal sequence, the Oral Torah reached written form in documents that together come after the Written Torah had come to its ultimate statement but before the closure and systematization of the liturgy, from the ninth century C.E. Any of these approaches to explanation would provide a plausible answer to the question of the future: why did the course of the Torah realized in address to God take the route that it did? The sequential facts of history—first came this, then that, and finally, the other thing—do not explain the realities of faith.

My exposition of the theology of the Oral Torah[2] claims to set forth normative theology; what represents sages' views is (1) an integrating logic on the one side, and (2) a ubiquitous principle on the other. Consistent with the intellectual discipline that governs, I maintain that these realities too—the integral relationship between the two Torahs, on the one side, between the Torah and synagogue liturgy on the other—unfold in accord with their own inner logic, their own dialectic and its tensions. That is to say, relationships fore and aft spin out their potentialities in the dialectic defined by the deep logic of theology that is built into the most profound levels of structure; the dynamics find motivation in the system's inexorable inertial forces. So I frame the question in my terms in this language: crossroads and meeting place, the Oral Torah forms the gateway to the Written Torah, Scripture, in the one direction, the highway opening outward into the long future of practiced piety, in the other—by what logic, by what admissible evidence?

Let me therefore spell out the localizing circumstances in which we address the matter. The faithful of Judaism through the ages reach Scripture through oral tradition recorded here, never encountering an unmediated Scripture (whether historically or philologically or archaeologically, for example). Moses is always *rabbenu*, "our rabbi," and Isaiah, "Rabbi Isaiah." Jacob looked into the present and described the future, and Abraham, Moses, and the prophets met God on the afternoon of the ninth of Ab in the year we now number as 70 and rebuked him for what he had done through the Romans. These realizations do not draw upon easy sentimentality or resort to figurative conceits. People acted upon them every day, built their lives around them, met God in them. Their concrete actions, the deprivations they accepted and humiliations they turned into validation—these attest to the palpable reality, for holy Israel, of the vision of the dual Torah. Have they been, and are they today, right in reaching the Written Torah through the path set out by the oral one?

For their part, those who practice Judaism found their liturgy upon the theology set forth in that same oral tradition of Sinai. When holy Israel prays, people assume, it expresses in practical terms of "we" and "you" the relationship that is posited by the theology of the Oral Torah. That liturgy moreover takes place within the timeless world of enduring paradigms formulated by the Oral Torah. How people situated themselves to face, to speak to God uncovers the deepest corners of their soul. So the theology of the Oral Torah—further encompassing its realization in normative law—for Judaism compares with the brain and heart of humans. For holy Israel, the Oral Torah defines the point of consciousness and cognition, the source of life, respectively. Is that so?

That is certainly how sages want us to see matters, for that is how they present them. Implicit in the apologetics that forms an integral part of the theology of the Oral Torah, two judgments take up a constant presence.

First—so this apologetics goes—sages are right about Scripture. That is to say, nearly every proposition they set forth, the main beams of the structure of faith they construct—all sets securely and symmetrically upon the Written Torah. Proof texts constantly take the measure of the structure. That is why sages speak of the one whole Torah in two media, correlative and complementary.

Second, sages' formulation of the Torah, the one whole Torah of Moses, our rabbi, defines holy Israel's relationship with God for all time to come. The very character of the prayers that holy Israel offers up in place of Temple sacrifices attests to that fact: the theology of the oral Torah is recapitulated in the liturgy of the synagogue. Sages teach Israel how to pray and what to say.

Accordingly—that is now sages' view—if we take up the Oral Torah and explore its theological structure and system, we meet Judaism, pure and simple. There we find its learning and its piety, what it knows about and hears from God, what it has to say to God. So much for the claim of theological apologetics.

The facts support it. Sages have not only history—the pivotal position of their writings in the sequence from *before* to *after*—but also hermeneutics on their side. In their reading of the Written Torah whole, in canonical context, as a record of life with God, they are right to say their story goes over the Written Torah's story. Start to finish, creation through Sinai to the fall of Jerusalem, all perceived in the light of the prophets' rebuke, consolation, and hope for restoration, Scripture's account is rehearsed in the Oral Torah. All is in proportion and balance. Viewed as a systematic hermeneutics, the sages' theology accurately sets forth the principal possibility of the theology that is implicit in the written part of the Torah— to be sure, in a more systematic and cogent manner than does Scripture.[3]

And, at the other end of the story, piety has certainly proved sages correct in their claim to define holy Israel's encounter with God for all time. The character of the liturgical life of the synagogue proves that sages' theology in particular—which is Scripture's theology—in important indicative traits of mind and of message defines holy Israel's approach to God in prayer. So when Israel hears God's message in the Oral Torah, it is listening to God's message in the Written Torah. And when Israel speaks to God in the liturgy of the synagogue and the private life as well, Israel addresses God as the Oral Torah's theology shapes that address, to be sure in language that accommodates the circumstance of worship.

First, why do I maintain that the sages are right about Scripture? It is because, start to finish, the Oral Torah builds its structure out of a reading of the Written Torah. Sages read from the Written Torah forward to the Oral Torah. That is attested not only by the superficial character of proof texting, but by the profound congruence of the theology of the Oral Torah with the course of the Scriptural exposition. Any outline of Scripture's account begins with creation and tells about the passage from Eden via Sinai and Jerusalem to Babylon—and back. It speaks of the patriarchal founders of Israel, the Exodus, Sinai, the Torah, covenants, Israel, the people of God, the priesthood and the tabernacle, the possession of the Land, exile and restoration. And so too has this outline of the Oral Torah's theology focused on all of these same matters. True, sages proportion matters within their own logic, laying heaviest emphasis on perfection, imperfection, and restoration of perfection to creation, focusing on Israel, God's stake in humanity.

The theological structure and system appeal to the perfection of creation and account for imperfection by reference to the fall of humankind into sin by reason of arrogant rebellion and into death in consequence. They tell the story of the formation of holy Israel as God's party in humanity, signified by access to knowledge of God through God's self-manifestation in the Torah. They then present the exile Israel from and to the Land of Israel as the counterpart to the exile of Adam from Eden and the return of Israel to the Land. Therefore, main beams of the Hebrew Scripture's account of matters define the structure of the Oral Torah's theology. The generative tensions of the Hebrew Scripture's narrative empower the dynamics of that theology.

A few obvious facts suffice. Take the principal propositions of Scripture read in sequence and systematically, meaning, as exemplary, from Genesis through Kings (the Authorized History, in the language of some scholars of Scripture). Consider the story of the exile from Eden and the counterpart exile of Israel from the Land. Sages did not invent that paradigm. Scripture's framers did. Translate into propositional form the prophetic messages of admonition, rebuke, and consolation, the promise that as punishment follows sin, so consolation will come in consequence of repentance. Sages did not fabricate those categories and make up the rules that govern the sequence of events. The prophets said them all. Sages only recapitulated the prophetic propositions with little variation except in formulation. All sages did was to interpret within the received paradigm the exemplary events of their own day, the destruction of Jerusalem and Israel's subjugation in particular. But even at that they simply asked Scripture's question of events that conformed to Scripture's pattern. Identify as the dynamics of human history the engagement of God with people, especially through Israel, and what do you have, if not the heart of sages' doctrine of the origins and destiny of humankind. Review what Scripture intimates about the meaning and end of time, and how much do you miss of sages' eschatology of restoration? Details, amplifications, clarifications, an unsuccessful effort at systematization—these do not obscure the basic confluence of sages' and Scripture's account of last things (even though the word "last" has its own meaning for sages).

Nor do I have to stress the form that sages impart to their propositions, nearly everything they say being joined to a verse of Scripture. That is not a formality. Constant citations of scriptural texts cited as authority serve merely to signal the presence of a profound identity of viewpoint. The cited verses are not solely pretexts or formal proof texts. A hermeneutics governs, dictating the course of exegesis. Sages cite and interpret verses of Scripture to show where and how the Written Torah guides the oral one, supplying the specificities of the process of recapitulation. And what sages say about those verses originates not in the small details of those verses (such as Aqiba was able to interpret to Moses's stupefaction) but in the large theological structure and system that sages framed.

That is why I insist that the hermeneutics defined the exegesis, the exegesis did not define the hermeneutics—as I have shown many times in my systematic analysis of the various Midrash compilations.[4] In most of the Midrash compilations of the Oral Torah, it is the simple fact that sages read from the whole to the parts, from the written part of the Torah outward to the oral part. That explains why nothing arbitrary or merely occasional, nothing ad hoc or episodic or notional characterized the sages' reading of Scripture, but a theology, formed whole in response to the whole. That explains why the sages did not think they imputed to Scripture meanings not actually there, and this account of their theology proves that they are right.

Sages read Scripture as a letter written that morning to them in particular about the world they encountered. That is because for them the past was forever integral to the present. So they looked into the written part of the Torah to construct the picture of reality that is explained by the world-view set forth in the oral part of the Torah. They found their questions in Scripture; they identified the answers to those questions in Scripture; and they then organized and interpreted the contemporary situation of holy Israel in light of those questions and answers. To that process the narrow focus of atomistic exegesis proves monumentally irrelevant, indeed, even incongruous. For the very category, proof text, reduces that elegant theology of the here and now to the trivialities of grammar or spelling or other nonsense details. It demeans sages' intellectual honesty, such as, on every page of the Talmud of Babylonia among many documents, is affirmed and attested by the very character of discourse. And it misses the fact that Scripture's corpus of facts, like nature's, was deemed to transcend the bounds of time. That explains why sages found in Scripture the main lines of structure and system that formed the architecture of their theology.

And it accounts for the fact that, in the heavenly academy to which corner of Eden imagination carried them, the great sages could amiably conduct arguments with God and with Moses. Not only so, but they engage in ongoing dialogue with the prophets and psalmists and the other saints of the Written Torah as well as with those of their masters and teachers in the oral tradition who reached Eden earlier (much as entire legions of participants in the Oral Torah in recent centuries aspire to spend an afternoon in Eden with Moses Maimonides). A common language joined them all, for in their entire engagement with the written part of the Torah, sages mastered every line, every word, every letter, sorting out matters of the day in response to what they learned in the written tradition.

That explains why we may justifiably say that on every page of the writings of the Oral Torah we encounter the sages' encompassing judgment of, response to, the heritage of ancient Israel's Scripture. There they met God, there they found God's plan for the world of perfect justice, the flawless, eternal world in stasis, and there in detail they learned what became of that teaching in ancient times and in their own day, everything seen in the same way. The sages' account of the Torah revealed by God to Moses at Sinai and handed on in tradition through the ages defines Judaism.

So if we ask, what if, in the timeless world of the Torah studied in the same heavenly academy, Moses and the prophets, sages, and scribes of Scripture were to take up the results of oral tradition produced by their heirs and successors in the oral part of the Torah? The answer is clear. They would have found themselves hearing familiar words, their own words, used by honest, faithful people, in familiar, wholly legitimate ways. When, for example, Moses heard in the tradition of the Oral Torah that a given law was a law revealed by God to Moses at Sinai, he may have kept his peace, though puzzled, or he may have remembered that, indeed, that is how it was, just so. In very concrete, explicit language the sages themselves laid their claim to possess the Torah of Moses. We recall how impressed Moses is by Aqiba, when he observed, from the rear of the study hall, how Aqiba was able to interpret on the basis of each point of the crowns heaps and heaps of laws. But he could not follow the debate and felt faint until he heard the later master declare, "It is a law given to Moses from Sinai," and then he regained his composure (Bavli tractate *Menahot* 3:7 II.5/29).

So it is entirely within the imaginative capacity of the Oral Torah to raise the question: what came before in relationship to what we have in hand? To state the matter more directly, are the rabbis of the Oral Torah right in maintaining that they have provided the originally oral part of the one whole Torah of Moses our rabbi? To answer that question in the affirmative, sages would have only to point to their theology in the setting of Scripture's as they grasped it. The theology of the Oral Torah tells a simple, sublime story.

1. God created a perfect, just world and in it made humans in God's image, equal to God in the power of will.
2. Humankind in its arrogance sinned and was expelled from the perfect world and given over to death. God gave humankind the Torah to purify its heart of sin.
3. Humans educated by the Torah in humility can repent, accepting God's will of their own free will. When they do, humans will be restored to Eden and eternal life.

In our terms, we should call it a story with a beginning, middle, and end. In sages' framework, we realize, the story embodies an enduring and timeless paradigm of humanity in the encounter with God: humankind's powerful will, God's powerful word, in conflict, and the resolution thereof.

But if I claim sages were right about the Written Torah, then what about the hermeneutics of others? If the sages claimed fully to spell out the message of the Written Torah, as they do explicitly in nearly every document and on nearly every page of the Oral Torah, so too did others. And those others, who, like the sages, added to the received Scripture other writings of a (to-them) authoritative character, set forth not only the story of the fall from grace that occupied sages but, in addition, different stories from those the sages told. They drew different consequences from the heritage of ancient Israel. Sages' critics will find their account not implausible but incomplete, a truncated reading of Scripture. They will wonder about leaving out nearly the entire apocalyptic tradition.[5] But, in the balance, sages' critics err. For no one can reasonably doubt that sages' reading of Scripture recovers, in proportion and accurate stress and balance, the main lines of Scripture's principal story, the one about creation, the fall of humanity and God's salvation of humankind through Israel and the Torah. In familiar, though somewhat gauche, language, "Judaism" really is what common opinion thinks it is, which is, "the religion of the Old Testament." If, as Brevard Childs states, "The evangelists read from the New [Testament] backward to the Old,"[6] we may say very simply, and, when I say, the sages were right, this is what I claim: *the sages read from the Written Torah forward to the oral one.*

So much for the *before* part of the Oral Torah. What about the *after* defined by synagogue piety? If the sages were right about the past, they assuredly commanded the future. In every synagogue in the world that addresses God in the words of the classical prayer book, the Siddur (and associated liturgies of synagogue and home), that privileges the Pentateuch and aspires to live by its law, the theology of the Oral Torah imparts shape and structure to holy Israel's address to God. We know that that is so, because sages' distinctive modes of thought and the connections that they made, the clusters of categories they formed and the connections they drew between one thing and another, would account for the character of Israel's liturgy. That is why I claim that, in the practiced piety of worship, not only is the Written Torah mediated through the oral, but the act and attitude of prayer are given theological substance in modes of thought particular to sages and in symbolic formulations distinctive to their account of God and the world. Accordingly, I am justified in claiming (in the language of history) that sages shaped the future of Judaism as much as they mediated its past.[7]

The order of prayer (*matbe'a shel tefillah*), with (1) recitation of the Shema ("Hear O Israel") with blessings fore and aft, (2) of the Eighteen Benedictions of the Prayer, and (3) the exit prayer, *Alenu* ("It is incumbent upon us . . .") rehearse in ways appropriate to the circumstance of prayer principal propositions about creation, revelation, and redemption, God, Torah, and Israel, that, in their theology the sages worked out. But that allegation is far too general to suffice. I identify as the definitive contribution of the Oral Torah very particular traits of mind on the one side, and formations of distinctive clusters of ideas on the other. These recapitulate the theology of the Oral Torah and impart to the liturgy the sages' indicative marker; intellectual traits of particular liturgies match modes of thought uniquely characteristic of the Oral Torah. Motifs or symbols or myths join together in conformity to the patterns established by the Oral

Torah but (by definition) not by the Written Torah. These two traits prominent in the liturgy of synagogue and home point toward the conclusion offered at the outset, that the Oral Torah exercised a particular and highly distinctive—and therefore the formative—influence upon the encounter between Israel and God that acts of faith and piety bring about.[8]

As to the dominance of modes of thought characteristic of sages in particular: in the liturgy, a timeless world of past, present, and future meet. That is how the sages recast history into paradigm. We recall how the sages re-framed Scripture's history into laws governing the social order, turning events from singular, sequential, onetime and unique happenings into exemplary patterns. These, we recall, encompass the past within the present and join future, present, and past onto a single plane of eternity. It is that mode of thought that brings about the formation of liturgies that have all the ages meet in one place, the great themes of existence coming together to reshape a very particular moment. It is that same mode of thought, moreover, that insists on the union of the public and the private, the communal and the individual, all things subject to the same principle, explained in the same way. Liturgies that form the intersection of events out of widely separated periods in the Scriptural narrative, the gathering of persons who in Scripture do not meet, realize sages' way of seeing Scripture.[9]

Two private liturgies exemplify the paradigmatic, as against the historical, formulation of matters. First, the particularly rabbinic mode of thought characterizes the prayer for the wedding of an Israelite man and woman, joining in one statement the motifs of creation, Adam, Eve, and Eden, the fall of Israel from the Land of Israel, and the hoped-for restoration of humankind to Eden and Israel to Jerusalem and the Land. The whole takes place out of time, in that "dream-time" characteristic of the theology of the Oral Torah. At a single moment the ages meet; discrete events intersect. Here we find fully exposed the matter of life in that timeless world of an ever-present past. So too, the private and the public meet as well when a new family begins. Individual lover and beloved celebrate the uniqueness, the privacy of their love. They turn out to stand for Adam and Eve and to represent the very public hope for the restoration of Israel to the perfection of Eden in the Land. That imposes upon their love a heavy burden for the young, infatuated couple.

Here is where the liturgy takes theological modes of thought and casts them into moments of realization and reprise. What is striking is how the theme of Eden and alienation, Land of Israel and exile, so typical of the theology of the Oral Torah, is reworked into a new pattern: from the loneliness and exile of the single life to the Eden and Jerusalem of the wedding canopy. So while the theme of exile and return is recapitulated, now it is reshaped by the message that the joy of the bride and groom—standing, after all, for Israel and God—is a foretaste of what is last, that final reprise of creation, now in eternal perfection. Adam at the end time, the Temple restored, Jerusalem rebuilt—that peculiar tableau certainly stands for sages' conception in particular. The personal and the public join, the individuals before us embody and reenact the entirety of Israel's holy life, past to future:

> Praised are You, O Lord our God, King of the universe,
>   Creator of the fruit of the vine.
> Praised are You, O Lord our God, King of the universe,
>   who created all things for Your glory.
> Praised are You, O Lord our God, King of the universe,
>   Creator of Adam.
> Praised are You, O Lord our God, King of the universe, who cre-
>   ated man and woman in his image, fashioning woman from
>   man as his mate, that together they might perpetuate life.
>   Praised are You, O Lord, Creator of man.
> May Zion rejoice as her children are restored to her in joy.
>   Praised are You, O Lord, who causes Zion to rejoice at her
>   children's return.
> Grant perfect joy to these loving companions, as You did to the
>   first man and woman in the Garden of Eden. Praised are You,
>   O Lord, who grants the joy of bride and groom.
> Praised are You, O Lord our God, King of the universe, who cre-
>   ated joy and gladness, bridge and groom, mirth, song, delight
>   and rejoicing, love and harmony, peace and companionship. O
>   Lord our God, may there ever be heard in the cities of Judah
>   and in the streets of Jerusalem voices of joy and gladness, voices
>   of bridge and groom, the jubilant voices of those joined in mar-
>   riage under the bridal canopy, the voices of young people feast-
>   ing and signing. Praised are You, O Lord, who causes the
>   groom to rejoice with his bride.[10]

The blessings speak of archetypal Israel, represented here and now by the bride and groom. They cover the great themes of the theology of the Oral Torah, excluding only one that does not fit. We find creation, Adam, man and woman in his image, after his likeness; then comes the restoration of Israel to Zion; then the joy of Zion in her children and the loving com-panions in one another; then the evocation of the joy of the restoration—past, present, future, all in the here and now. The sole critical component of the theology of the Oral Torah omitted here concerns justice on the one side; sin, repentance, and atonement on the other. That omission attests once more to sages' fine sense of what fits and what does not.

The theme of ancient paradise is introduced by the simple choice of the word "Adam," just as we should expect. The myth of humanity's creation is rehearsed: man and woman are in God's image, together complete and whole, creators of life, "like God." Woman was fashioned from man together with him to perpetuate life. But this Adam and this Eve—as we should expect in a rabbinic document!—also are Israel, children of Zion the mother, as expressed in the fifth blessing. Israel is in exile, Zion lies in ruins. It is at that appropriate point that the restorationist motif enters: "Grant perfect joy to the loving companions," for they are creators of a new line in humankind—the new Adam, the new Eve—and their home— May it be the garden of Eden. And if joy is there, then "praised are you for the joy of bride and groom."

The concluding blessing returns to the theme of Jerusalem. Given the focus of the system as a whole, that hardly presents a surprise. For the union of bridegroom and bride provides a foretaste of the new Eden that is coming. But that is only at the right moment, in the right setting, when Israel will have repented, atoned, and attained resurrection and therefore restoration to Eden/the world to come. How is all this invoked? The liturgy conveys these motifs when it calls up the tragic hour of Jerusalem's first destruction. When everyone had given up hope, supposing with the end of Jerusalem had come the end of time, exile, the anti-Eden, only Jeremiah counseled renewed hope. With the enemy at the gate, he sang of coming gladness:

> Thus says the Lord:
> In this place of which you say, "It is a waste, without man or
>   beast," in the cities of Judah and the streets of Jerusalem that
>   are desolate, without man or inhabitant or beast, there shall be
>   heard again the voice of mirth and the voice of gladness, the
>   voice of the bridegroom and the voice of the bride, the voice of
>   those who sing as they bring thank offerings to the house of the
>   Lord. . . . For I will restore the fortunes of the land as at first,
>   says the Lord.
>   Jeremiah 33:10–11 RSV

The intersection of characteristic motifs creates a timeless tableau. Just as here and now there stand before us Adam and Eve, so here and now in this wedding, the olden sorrow having been rehearsed, we listen to the voice of gladness that is coming. The joy of this new creation prefigures the joy of the Messiah's coming, inaugurating the resurrection and judgment and the final restoration. The joy then will echo the joy of bride and groom before us. So the small space covered by the marriage canopy is crowded indeed with persons and events. People who think historically and not paradigmatically can commemorate and celebrate. But they cannot embody, or even exemplify, eternity in the here and now, the presence and past and future all at once. In this context, only the sages of the Oral Torah have formed a mode of thought that is capable of imagining such a convocation of persons and concatenation of events.

The same mode of thought marks other liturgies that celebrate events of the life cycle. The entry of the male child into the covenant of Abraham through the rite of circumcision, yet another moment that is intensely personal (to the infant) and massively public (to all Israel), forms another moment of timeless eternity. Specifically, in the case of a boy child a minor surgical rite becomes the mark of the renewal of the agreement between God and Israel, the covenant carved into the flesh of the penis of every Jewish male—and nothing less. The beginning of a new life renews the rule that governs Israel's relationship to God. So the private joy is reworked through words of enchantment—once more, sanctification—and so transformed into renewal of the community of Israel and God. Those present find themselves in another time, another place. Specific moments out of the past are recapitulated, and specific personalities are called to attendance. In the present instant, eternity is invoked at the moment of cutting off the foreskin of the penis. Calling the rite, *berit milah*, the covenant of or effected through the rite of circumcision, invites Abraham to attend. *Berit milah* seals with the blood of the infant son the contract between Israel and God, generation by generation, son by son.

The words that are said evoke in the intimacy of the private life the being that all share together: Israel, its covenant with God, its origin in Abraham, Isaac, Jacob. In the rite God sees the family beyond time, joined by blood of not pedigree but circumcision, genealogy framed by fifty generations of loyalty to the covenant in blood and birth from the union of the womb of the Israelite woman with the circumcised penis of her Israelite husband: this is the holy fruit of the womb. There are four aspects in which the operation is turned into a rite. When the rite begins, the assembly and the *mohel* together recite the following:

> The Lord spoke to Moses saying, Phineas, son of Eleazar, son of
> Aaron, the priest, has turned my wrath from the Israelites by dis-

playing among them his passion for me, so that I did not wipe out the Israelite people in my passion. Say therefore [that] I grant him my covenant of peace.

Commenting on this passage, Lifsa Schachter states, "Phineas is identified with zealously opposing the . . . sins of sexual licentiousness and idolatry. He is best known for an event which occurred when the Israelites, whoring with Moabite women in the desert, were drawn to the worship of Baal-Peor. . . . Phineas leaped into the fray and through an act of double murder . . . quieted God's terrible wrath."[11]

Second, a chair is set called "the chair of Elijah," so that the rite takes place in the presence of a chair for Elijah, the prophet. The newborn son is set on that chair, and the congregation says, "This is the chair of Elijah, of blessed memory." Elijah had complained to God that Israel neglected the covenant (1 Kings 19:10–14). So he comes to bear witness that Israel observes the covenant of circumcision. Then, before the surgical operation, a blessing is said. Third, after the operation a blessing is said over a cup of wine. To understand the invocation of Elijah, for whom we set a chair, we first recall the pertinent biblical passage:

Behold, the word of the LORD came to him, and he said to him,
"What are you doing here, Elijah?"
He said, "I have been very jealous for the LORD, the God of hosts;
for the people of Israel have forsaken they covenant, thrown down
thy altars, and slain they prophets with the swords; and I, even I
only, am left; and they seek my life, to take it away."
And he said, "Go forth, and stand upon the mount before the
LORD." And behold, the LORD passed by, and a great and strong
wind rent the mountains, and broke in pieces the rocks before the
LORD, but the LORD was not in the wind; and after the wind an
earthquake, but the LORD was not in the earthquake.
And after the earthquake a fire, but the LORD was not in the fire; and
after the fire a still small voice.
And when Elijah heard it, he wrapped his face in his mantle and
went out and stood at the entrance of the cave. And behold, there
came a voice to him, and said, "What are you doing here, Elijah?"
He said, "I have been very jealous for the LORD, the God of hosts;
for the people of Israel have forsaken thy covenant, thrown down
thy altars, and slain thy rophets with the sword; and I, even I only,
am left; and they seek my life, to take it away."
1 Kings 19:9–14 RSV

This passage stands behind the story told in a medieval document, *Pirke deRabbi Eliezer*, that Elijah attends the rite of circumcision of every Jewish baby boy:[12]

> The Israelites were wont to circumcise until they were divided into two kingdoms. The kingdom of Ephraim cast off from themselves the covenant of circumcision. Elijah, may he be remembered for good, arose and was zealous with a mighty passion, and he adjured the heavens to send down neither dew nor rain upon the earth. Jezebel heard about it and sought to slay him.
>
> Elijah arose and prayed before the Holy One, blessed be he. The Holy One, blessed be he, said to him, "'Are you better than your fathers' (1 Kings 19:4)? Esau sought to slay Jacob, but he fled before him, as it is said, 'And Jacob fled into the field of Aram' (Hos. 12:12).
>
> "Pharaoh sought to slay Moses, who fled before him and he was saved, as it is said. Now when Pharaoh heard this thing, he sought to slay Moses. 'And Moses fled from the face of Pharaoh' (Ex. 2:15).
>
> "Saul sought to slay David, who fled before him and was saved, as it is said, 'If you save not your life tonight, tomorrow you will be killed' (1 Sam. 19:11)."
>
> Another text says, "And David fled and escaped" (1 Sam. 19:18). Learn that everyone who flees is said."
>
> Elijah, may he be remembered for good, arose and fled from the land of Israel, and he betook himself to Mount Horeb, as it is said, 'and he arose and ate and drank' (1 Kings 19:8).
>
> Then the Holy One, blessed be he, was revealed to him and said to him, "What you doing here, Elijah"?
>
> He answered him saying, "I have been very zealous."
>
> The Holy One, blessed be he, said to him, "You are always zealous. You were zealous in Shittim on account of the immorality. For it is said, 'Phineas, the son of Eleazar, the son of Aaron the priest, turned my wrath away from the children of Israel, in that he was zealous with my zeal among them' (Num. 25:11).
>
> "Here you are also zealous, By your life! They shall not observe the covenant of circumcision until you see it done with your own eyes."
>
> Hence the sages have instituted the custom that people should have a seat of honor for the messenger of the covenant, for Eli-

jah, may he be remembered for good, is called the messenger of the covenant, as it is said, 'And the messenger of the covenant, whom you delight in, behold he comes.'

(Mal. 3:1)

So too the "messenger of the covenant" (Mal. 1:23) is the prophet Elijah, and he is present whenever a Jewish son enters the *covenant* of Abraham, which is circumcision. God therefore ordered him to come to every circumcision so as to witness the loyalty of the Jews to the covenant. Elijah then serves as the guardian for the newborn, just as he raised the child of the widow from the dead (1 Kings 17:17–24). Along these same lines, on the Seder table of Passover, a cup of wine is poured for Elijah, and the door is opened for Elijah to join in the rite. Setting a seat for Elijah serves to invoke the presence of the guardian of the newborn and the zealous advocate of the rite of the circumcision of the covenant. Celebrating with the family of the newborn are not "all Israel" in general, but a very specific personage indeed. The gesture of setting the chair silent sets the stage for an event in the life of the family not of the child alone but of all Israel. The chair of Elijah, filled by the one who holds the child, sets the newborn baby into Elijah's lap. The enchantment extends through the furnishing of the room; what is not ordinarily present is introduced, and that makes all the difference.

We move, third, from gesture to formula, for there is a blessing said before the rite itself, that is, as the *mohel* takes the knife to cut the foreskin, these words are said:

> Praised are You . . . who sanctified us with Your commandments and commanded us to bring the son into the covenant of Abraham our father.

The explicit invocation of Abraham's covenant turns the concrete action in the here and now into a simile of the paradigm and archetype. The operation done, fourth, the wine is blessed, introducing yet a further occasion of enchantment:

> Praised are You, Lord our God, who sanctified the beloved from the womb and set a statute into his very flesh, and his parts sealed with the sign of the holy covenant. On this account, Living God, our portion and rock, save the beloved of our flesh from destruction, for the sake of his covenant placed in our flesh. Blessed are You . . . who makes the covenant.

The covenant is not a generality; it is specific, concrete, fleshly. It is more-over meant to accomplish a very specific goal—as all religion means to attain concrete purposes—and that is to secure a place for the child, a blessing for the child. By virtue of the rite, the child enters the covenant, meaning that he joins that unseen "Israel" that through blood enters an agreement with God. Then the blessing of the covenant is owing to the child, for covenants or contracts cut both ways.

After the father has recited the blessing, " . . . who has sanctified us by his commandments and has commanded us to induct him into the covenant of our father, Abraham," the community responds: "Just as he has entered the covenant, so may he be introduced to Torah, the *huppah* [marriage canopy] and good deeds." Schachter interprets those who are present as follows:

> In the presence of Elijah . . . Torah—as against idolatry; in the pres-ence of Phineas. . . . huppah, as against sexual licentiousness; in the presence of Abraham . . . to good deeds: "For I have singled him out that he may instruct his children and his posterity to keep the way of the Lord by doing what is just and right" (Gen. 18:18).[13]

In the transformation of the *now* of the birth of the son into the *then* of Abraham's covenant with God, people make a public event of a private joy. Many join the occasion: Elijah complaining to God, Abraham obediently circumcising his sons, Phineas calming God's wrath by an act of violence, and then making with God a covenant of peace.

So much for the way in which sages' mode of thought shapes the liturgy, imposing in concrete and personal form the pattern of an ever-present past upon the present and turning present-tense time into a paradigm of what will be. What of those distinctive clusters of themes that the theology of the Oral Torah calls together?[14] A glance at the *huppah*-liturgy defines what we should expect: Adam/Creation/Israel/Zion (land of Israel); or joy/Jerusalem; or image of God/image of humanity. Other such clusters will encompass Israel/Gentile, this age/world to come, Eden/world to come, and so on. But the Oral Torah yields a limited number of archetypal clusters, allowing for a nearly unlimited number of recombinations thereof. Within this theory of the character of the Oral Torah's theology, a certain few clusters should suffice to animate the liturgy. A determinate list ought to supply reference points, that is, encompass the liturgy within the boundaries of the Oral Torah in particular.

Let us begin with a simple test. If the Oral Torah imparts shape and structure to the liturgy, then whenever Israel the holy people forms the focus of prayer, the Gentiles must figure as well—and the same theory that defines the one has also to explain the other. To test that theory, we turn to the prayer, *Alenu,* recited at the conclusion of every act of public worship, three times daily, when the congregation, having embodied holy Israel, prays to depart. At the conclusion of worship, Israel thanks God for making Israel what it is: unlike the Gentiles, following a unique destiny. This prayer, celebrating Israel's difference as destiny but looking forward to the end of that difference, simply restates in terms of "you" the theology of Israel regarding the Gentiles that deems them to be idolaters—by definition, that defines Gentiles as those who reject the Torah of Sinai:

> Let us praise Him, Lord over all the world;
> Let us acclaim Him, Author of all creation.
> He made our lot unlike that of other peoples;
> He assigned to us a unique destiny.
> We bend the knee, worship, and acknowledge
> The King of kings, the Holy One, praised is He.
> He unrolled the heavens and established the earth;
> His throne of glory is in the heavens above;
> His majestic Presence is in the loftiest heights.
> He and no other is God and faithful King,
> Even as we are told in His Torah:
> Remember now and always, that the Lord is God;
> Remember, no other is Lord of heaven and earth.

So much for Israel, thanking God for making it what it is, God's assembly. Then predictably, Gentiles must follow. Here Israel prays for the end of idolatry, at which point the Gentiles will cease to be Gentile and become no other than Israel, living in God's kingdom. Integral to the same prayer is the next paragraph:

> We, therefore, hope in You, O Lord our God,
> That we shall soon see the triumph of Your might,
> That idolatry shall be removed from the earth,
> And false gods shall be utterly destroyed.
> Then will the world be a true kingdom of God,
> When all mankind will invoke Your name,
> And all the earth's wicked will return to You.
> Then all the inhabitants of the world will surely know
> That to You every knee must bend,
> Every tongue must pledge loyalty.

> Before You, O Lord, let them bow in worship,
> Let them give honor to Your glory.
> May they all accept the rule of Your kingdom.
> May You reign over them soon through all time.
> Sovereignty is Yours in glory, now and forever.
> So it is written in Your Torah:
> The Lord shall reign for ever and ever.[15]

The unique, the particular, the private become testimonies of divine sovereignty, pertinent to all people. When God's will be done, then all people will recognize that the unique destiny of Israel is intended for everyone. Israel by the theological definition will be no more, because everyone will be Israel. Here, then, the complementary antonym, Israel/Gentile, recapitulates the sages' theory of the Gentiles and idolatry within their theology of Israel and the Torah. And it is in so many words: "false gods . . . utterly destroyed . . . kingdom of God . . . all mankind invoke . . . ," and the like.

So much for a cluster that fits naturally its two opposed components. But in the main, the theology of the Oral Torah exhibits no sustained preference for antonymic or binary constructions. Rather, its intellectual ambition encompasses the power to combine many components into a single narrative statement. Creation, revelation, redemption form one such paramount cluster; land, liberation, covenant, Torah, another; Israel, Land of Israel, Jerusalem, restoration, a third; and so on. Above all, we must wonder, how do the several salvific symbols fit together in the larger mythic structure of creation, revelation, and redemption? In the Grace after Meals, recited whenever pious Jews eat bread, we see their interplay. To understand the setting, we must recall that in classical Judaism the table at which meals were eaten was regarded as the equivalent of the sacred altar in the Temple. Judaism taught that each Jew before eating had to attain the same state of ritual purity as the priest in the sacred act of making a sacrifice. So in the classic tradition the Grace after Meals is recited in a sacerdotal circumstance. That is why the entire theology of the Oral Torah comes to realization in this single, simple liturgy. I mark off its principal parts.

[1] Blessed art Thou, Lord our God, King of the Universe, who nourishes all the world by His goodness, in grace, in mercy, and in compassion: He gives bread to all flesh, for His mercy is everlasting. And because of His great goodness we have never lacked, and so may we never lack, sustenance—for the sake of His great Name. For He

nourishes and feeds everyone, is good to all, and provides food for each one of the creatures He created.

Blessed art Thou, O Lord, who feeds everyone.

[2] We thank Thee, Lord our God, for having given our fathers as a heritage a pleasant, a good and spacious land; for having taken us out of the land of Egypt, for having redeemed us from the house of bondage; for Thy covenant, which Thou hast set as a seal in our flesh, for Thy Torah which Thou has taught us, for Thy statutes which Thou hast made known to us, for the life of grace and mercy Thou hast graciously bestowed upon us, and for the nourishment with which Thou dost nourish us and feed us always, every day, in every season, and every hour.

For all these things, Lord our God, we thank and praise Thee; may Thy praises continually be in the mouth of every living thing, as it is written, And thou shalt eat and be satisfied, and bless the Lord thy God for the good land which He hath given thee.

Blessed art Thou, O Lord, for the land and its food.

[3] O Lord our God, have pity on Thy people Israel, on Thy city Jerusalem, on Zion the place of Thy glory, on the royal house of David Thy Messiah, and on the great and holy house which is called by Thy Name. Our God, our Father, feed us and speed us, nourish us and make us flourish, unstintingly, O Lord our God, speedily free us from all distress.

And let us not, O Lord our God, find ourselves in need of gifts from flesh and blood, or of a loan from anyone save from Thy full, generous, abundant, wide-open hand; so we may never be humiliated, or put to shame.

O rebuild Jerusalem, the holy city, speedily in our day. Blessed art Thou, Lord, who in mercy will rebuild Jerusalem. Amen.

[4] Blessed art Thou, Lord our God, King of the Universe, Thou God, who art our Father, our powerful king, our creator and redeemer, who made us, our holy one, the holy one of Jacob, our shepherd, shepherd of Israel, the good king, who visits His goodness upon all; for every single day He has brought good, He does bring good, He will bring good upon us; He has rewarded us, does regard, and will always reward us, with grace, mercy and compassion, amplitude, deliverance and prosperity, blessing and salvation, comfort, and a living, sustenance, pity and peace, and all good—let us not want any manner of good whatever.[16]

The context of grace is enjoyment of creation, the arena for creation is the land. The land lay at the end of redemption from Egyptian bondage.

Holding it, enjoying it is a sign that the covenant is intact and in force and that Israel is loyal to its part of the contract and God to his. The land, the Exodus, the covenant—these all depend on the Torah, statutes, and a life of grace and mercy, here embodied in and evoked by the nourishment of the meal. Thanksgiving wells up, and the paragraph ends with praises for the land and its food.

This cluster on its own does not demand identification with the Oral Torah. The restorationist dynamic is what (in the present context) reveals the hand of the sages. Here we have not merely a messianic prayer for the end of days, but a specific framing of the end in terms of the beginning, the restoration of Israel to the Land of Israel, that the liturgy bespeaks. The restorationist theme recurs throughout, redemption and hope for return, and then future prosperity in the land: "May God pity the people, the city, Zion, the royal house of the Messiah, the Holy Temple." The nourishment of this meal is but a foretaste of the nourishment of the messianic time, just as the joy of the wedding is a foretaste of the messianic rejoicing. Creation and re-creation, exile and return—these are the particular clusters that point to the substrate of the sages' theology.

Thus far, the first two clusters—dealing with Israel and the Gentiles, creation, revelation, redemption, and restoration—go over secondary matters. The primary claim of the Oral Torah concerns God's creation of a world order over chaos, and specifically, a world ordered by justice, a world ruled by God, and a world that would recover its original perfection. Here, in the third cluster of particular concern, we find the Judaic creed exactly as sages would have defined it. That is to say, the themes that converge here and the way in which they are articulated respond to the distinctive theological structure and system put forth by the sages. When I maintain that the Oral Torah imparted its imprint on all that came afterward, and that that is a matter not of historical influence based on political sponsorship but of inner logic, I point to formations such as the one before us here, the creed contained in the twice-daily recitation of the Shema.

Evening and morning, the pious Jew proclaims the unity and uniqueness of God. The proclamation is preceded and followed by blessings, two at the beginning, then the recitation of the Shema, then one at the end, in the sequence, creation, revelation, proclamation of God's unity and dominion, then redemption. The recital of the Shema is introduced by a celebration of God as Creator of the world. God daily creates an orderly world, a world ordered in goodness. That is what is important about creation. The Shema is recited morning and night, and the prayer varies for the occasion, though the message, the creation of world order, does not. In the morning, one says,

> Praised are You, O Lord our God, King of the universe.
> You fix the cycles of light and darkness;
> You ordain the order of all creation
> You cause light to shine over the earth;
> Your radiant mercy is upon its inhabitants.
> In Your goodness the work of creation
> Is continually renewed day by day. . . .
> O cause a new light to shine on Zion;
> May we all soon be worthy to behold its radiance.
> Praised are You, O Lord, Creator of the heavenly bodies.[17]

The blessing in the morning celebrates light, ending with the new light when creation is renewed. The corresponding prayer in the evening refers to the setting of the sun:

> Praised are You. . . .
> Your command brings on the dusk of evening.
> Your wisdom opens the gates of heaven to a new day.
> With understanding You order the cycles of time;
> Your will determines the succession of seasons;
> You order the stars in their heavenly courses.
> You create day, and You create night,
> Rolling away light before darkness. . . .
> Praised are You, O Lord, for the evening dusk.[18]

The natural order of the world in the liturgical setting elicits thanks and praise of God who created the world and who actively guides the daily events of nature. Whatever happens in nature gives testimony to the sovereignty of the Creator. And that testimony takes place in the most ordinary events: the orderly regularity of sunrise and sunset.

It is through the Torah that Israel knows God as not merely Creator, but purposeful Creator. There Israel encounters God as just, world order as a formulation of the benevolent, beneficent laws of life. Torah is the mark not merely of divine sovereignty and justice, but of divine grace and love, just as, in our account of complementarity, we saw mercy as the complement of justice. So goes the second blessing:

> Deep is Your love for us, O Lord our God;
> Bounteous is Your compassion and tenderness.

Now comes the pronouncement of the character of world order: reliable, guided by compassion, to be learned through God's self-manifestation in the Torah:

You taught our fathers the laws of life,
And they trusted in You, Father and king,
For their sake be gracious to us, and teach us,
That we may learn Your laws and trust in You.
Father, merciful Father, have compassion upon us:
Endow us with discernment and understanding.
Grant us the will to study Your Torah,
To heed its words and to teach its precepts. . . .
Enlighten our eyes in Your Torah,
Open our hearts to Your commandments. . . .
Unite our thoughts with singleness of purpose
To hold You in reverence and in love. . . .
You have drawn us close to You;
We praise You and thank You in truth.
With love do we thankfully proclaim Your unity.
And praise You who chose Your people Israel in love.[19]

God, the Creator, revealed his will for creation through the Torah, given to Israel his people. That Torah contains the "laws of life." In identifying the world order of justice as the foundation stone of sages' theology, I simply recapitulated the liturgical creed.

In the Shema, Torah—instruction through revelation—leads to the chief teaching of revelation, the premise of world order, the dominion of the one and only God. In proclaiming the following words, Israel accepts the rule of God the yoke of the dominion of heaven, and the yoke of the Torah and commandments:

Hear, O Israel, the Lord Our God, the Lord is One. This proclamation is followed by three Scriptural passages. The first is Deuteronomy 6:5–9: *You shall love the Lord your God with all your heart, and with all your soul, and with all your might.* And further, one must diligently teach one's children these words and talk of them everywhere and always, and place them on one's forehead, doorposts, and gates. The second Scripture is Deuteronomy 11:13–21, which emphasizes that if Jews keep the commandments, they will enjoy worldly blessings; but that if they do not, they will be punished and disappear from the good land God gives them. The third is Numbers 15:37–41, the commandment to wear fringes on the corners of one's garments.

Then comes the address to God, not as Creator or Revealer, but God as Redeemer. This prayer, predictably within the sages' framework, treats as comparable the redemption from Egypt and the redemption at the last, the one as the embodiment of the other:

> You are our King and our father's King,
> Our redeemer and our father's redeemer.
> You are our creator. . . .
> You have ever been our redeemer and deliverer
> There can be no God but You. . . .

Now we turn to the initial formation of the paradigm of redemption, the liberation from Egypt, through the passage through the sea:

> You, O Lord our God, rescued us from Egypt;
> You redeemed us from the house of bondage. . . .
> You split apart the waters of the Red Sea,
> The faithful you rescued, the wicked drowned. . . .
> Then Your beloved sang hymns of thanksgiving. . . .
> They acclaimed the King, God on high,
> Great and awesome source of all blessings,
> The ever-living God, exalted in his majesty.

As soon as redemption makes its appearance, the theme of arrogance and humility appears alongside, since, for sages, we need hardly remind ourselves, arrogance is the cause of sin and exile, and humility elicits God's favor and brings about restoration:

> He humbles the proud and raises the lowly;
> He helps the needy and answers His people's call. . . .
> Then Moses and all the children of Israel
> Sang with great joy this song to the Lord:
> Who is like You O Lord among the mighty?
> Who is like You, so glorious in holiness?
> So wondrous your deeds, so worthy of praise!
> The redeemed sang a new song to You;
> They sang in chorus at the sore of the sea,
> Acclaiming Your sovereignty with thanksgiving:
> The Lord shall reign for ever and ever.
> Rock of Israel, arise to Israel's defense!
> Fulfill Your promise to deliver Judah and Israel.
> Our redeemer is the Holy One of Israel,
> The Lord of hosts is His name.
> Praised are You, O Lord, redeemer of Israel.[20]

That God not only creates but also redeems is embodied in the redemption from Egyptian bondage. The congregation repeats the exultant song of Moses and the people at the Red Sea as participants in the salvation of old and of time to come. The stories of creation, the Exodus from Egypt, and the revelation of Torah at Sinai are repeated, not merely to re-count what once happened but rather to re-create out of the reworked materials of everyday life the "true being"—life as it was, always is, and will be forever.

The final and most important liturgical exercise in reworking sages' theology brings us to the main principle of world order, God's just rule over creation. No more eloquent and powerful statement of that principle occurs than in the liturgy of the New Year, *Rosh Hashanah*, and the Day of Atonement, Yom Kippur, which together mark the Days of Awe, of solemn penitence, at the start of the autumn festival season. These occasions work out in concrete terms how the world order of justice extends to the here and now of patterned, orderly, everyday life. For on the first of these occasions, the New Year, each person is inscribed for life or death in the heavenly books for the coming year, and on the Day of Atonement the books are sealed. The synagogues on that day are filled with penitents. The New Year is called the birthday of the world: "This day the world was born." It is likewise a day of remembrance on which the deeds of all creatures are reviewed. On it God asserts God's sovereignty, as in the New Year Prayer:

> Our God and God of our Fathers, rule over the whole world in Your honor . . . and appear in Your glorious might to all those who dwell in the civilization of Your world, so that everything made will know that You made it, and every creature discern that You have created him, so that all in whose nostrils is breath may say, "The Lord, the God of Israel is king, and His kingdom extends over all."[21]

The themes of the liturgy are divine sovereignty, divine memory, and divine disclosure. These correspond to creation, revelation, and redemption. Sovereignty is established by creation of the world. Judgment depends on law: "From the beginning You made this, Your purpose known. . . ." And therefore, since people have been told what God requires of them, they are judged:

> On this day sentence is passed upon countries, which to the sword and which to peace, which to famine and which to plenty, and each creature is judged today for life or death. Who is not judged on this day? For the remembrance of every creature comes before You, each man's deeds and destiny, words and way. . . .

The theme of revelation is further combined with redemption; the ram's horn, or *shofar*, which is sounded in the synagogue during daily worship for a month before the *Rosh Hashanah* festival, serves to unite the two:

> You did reveal yourself in a cloud of glory. . . . Out of heaven you made them [Israel] hear Your voice. . . . Amid thunder and lightning You revealed yourself to them, and while the shofar sounded You shined forth upon them. . . . Our God and God of our fathers, sound the great Shofar for our freedom. Lift up the ensign to gather our exiles. . . . Lead us happily to Zion Your city, Jerusalem the place of Your sanctuary.

The complex themes of the New Year, the most "theological" of Jewish holy occasions, thus recapitulate a familiar cluster of themes.

The most personal, solemn, and moving of the Days of Awe is the Day of Atonement, Yom Kippur, the Sabbath of Sabbaths. It is marked by fasting and continuous prayer. On it, Israel makes confession:

> Our God and God of our fathers, may our prayer come
> before You. Do not hide yourself from our supplication,
> for we are not so arrogant or stiff-necked as to say
> before You. . . . We are righteous and have not sinned.
> But we have sinned.
> We are guilt laden, we have been faithless, we have
> robbed. . . .
> We have committed iniquity, caused unrighteousness, have
> been presumptuous. We have counseled evil, scoffed,
> revolted, blasphemed. . . .[22]

The Hebrew confession is built on an alphabetical acrostic following the letters of the Hebrew alphabet, as if by making certain every letter is represented, God, who knows human secrets, will combine them into appropriate words. The very alphabet bears witness against us before God. Then:

> What shall we say before You who dwell on high? What shall we tell You who live in heaven? Do You not know all things, both the hidden and the revealed? You know the secrets of eternity, the most hidden mysteries of life. You search the innermost recesses, testing men's feelings and heart. Nothing is concealed from You or hidden from Your eyes. May it therefore be Your will to forgive us our sins, to pardon us for our iniquities, to grant remission for our transgressions.[23]

A further list of sins follows, built on alphabetical lines. Prayers to be spoken by the congregation are all in the plural: "For the sin which we have sinned against You with the utterance of the lips. . . . For the sin which we have sinned before You openly and secretly. . . ." The community takes upon itself responsibility for what is done in it. All Israel is part of one community, one body, and all are responsible for the acts of each. The sins confessed are mostly against society, against one's fellow human beings, few pertain to ritual laws. At the end comes a final word:

> O my God, before I was formed, I was nothing. Not that I have been formed, it is as though I had not been formed, for I am dust in my life, more so after death. Behold I am before You like a vessel filled with shame and confusion. May it be Your will. . . . that I may no more sin, and forgive the sins I have already committed in Your abundant compassion.[24]

Israelites, within all Israel, see themselves before the just and merciful God: possessing no merits, yet hopeful of God's love and compassion. Where, then, shall we look for an address to God that is not framed within the theology of the Oral Torah?

Now readers ought rightly to object, but is this corpus of liturgy not a mere reprise of Scripture? Why invoke the oral part of the Torah to make sense of the synagogue worship, when that liturgy simply reworks the main lines of thought of the written part of the Torah, indeed constantly recites verses of Scripture within the act of worship? And I hasten to concede, as would the sages in whose behalf I have claimed so much, readers do not err. A liturgy that recapitulates the themes of creation, revelation, and redemption, that speaks of exile from and return to the Land in a plan of restoration, that celebrates God's sovereignty and invokes God's justice in judgment, surely reworks the themes of Scripture. And one that constantly makes reference to the Torah as the emblem of God's love and to Israel as the people of the Torah, that perpetually invokes the correspondence of world order in the heavens with peace on earth (as in the Qaddish prayer)—such a liturgy surely rests squarely on the Written Torah, which from its opening lines says no less.

A single, seamless statement, the Siddur and Mahzor, the Oral Torah, and the Written Torah, severally and jointly say the same few things. That is why the worship of the synagogue, in the Siddur and the Mahzor, with its enchanted and timeless world of ever-present eternity, is beyond all comprehending except within the framework of the oral part of the Torah. But so too, sages will have insisted, the oral part of the Torah for its part restates precisely the message, in exact balance and proportion, of the written part. It too makes sense only within the framework of the written part of the Torah. So, in sequence, the sages read from the Written Torah to the oral one. And, reflecting on that reading, the theologians of the liturgy composed prayer to re-frame in the second-person "you" of prayer personally addressed to the person of God precisely the result of that same reading: what the Torah teaches about God that Israel may bring in prayer to God.

So that is why, as I claimed at the outset, when we define the theology of the Oral Torah, we state Judaism pure and simple, no more, no less. And once we state Judaism, we realize, we cannot at any point engage with Christianity or Islam. Each in its way parts company from the Torah of Sinai. And that suffices. That is why Judaisms and Christianities do not meet and cannot meet: because they cannot afford a common prayer and do not share a common revelation.

Here in Judaism alone we encounter the one, the only, the unique God, who speaks to Israel in the Torah, creates a world ordered by justice, and sustains and restores that world order, every day, making peace, as the Qaddish says, both in heaven and on earth. That is what revealing the justice of God in the world order requires: God's rule in the chaos of the here and now. So in the words of the Qaddish, invoking heaven and earth at once:

> Magnified and sanctified be the great Name in the world that he cre-
> ated as he willed, and may his dominion come in your life and in your
> days and in the life of the whole house of Israel, speedily and soon . . .
> May he who makes things whole on high make things whole for us . . .

Chapter 11

Jesus, a Galilean Rabbi

Bruce Chilton

U ntil recently, Jewish Galilee has been as mysterious as Jesus himself has been. Known from the pages of Josephus as a proud region, resistant to the occupying force of Roman rule and its customs, envied for the fertility of its land and the quality of its produce, Galilee nonetheless had no voice of its own. Even Josephus speaks as a Judean, a southerner, and as the general who had tried and failed to subdue this proud people. No written source, no body of rabbinic literature, no scroll discovered in the midst of archaeological work, has been attributed to a Galilean of the first century. An oral culture, as resistant to change as it was to the Romans who occupied it, Jewish Galilee condemned itself to silence from the point of view of history by its loyalty to the spoken word.

In 1997 a book appeared, supported by a grant from the Tisch Family Foundation, which conveys the extraordinary range of excavations that have been conducted in Galilee.[1] That new evidence both underscores the isolation of rural Galilee from Hellenistic culture and attests the cultural integrity of Galilean Judaism. Some of the most interesting evidence comes from what might have been thought to suggest that Galilee was well integrated within the Roman Empire: hordes of coins. After all, that must at first sight suggest commercial contact. But these hordes of coins, in find after find, turned out to be local stashes of *various kinds of coins*, whether in circulation among Romans or from defunct regimes.[2]

Galilean peasants engaged in financial transactions so sporadically, they had no regular method of storing coins (and much less of banking them). Further, these tiny villages persistently attest a great concern for purity, the definition of who exactly belongs to Israel and of how contact with those outside Israel should be regulated. Stone vessels for carrying water for purificatory washing are typically found. They are characteristic of Jewish villages, and quite unlike vessels for cooking or the large cisterns used to store water for drinking. They are more persistent in Galilee than

154

the *miqveh*, the stepped bathing pool, or the synagogue, but all of them have been found, and they lead to one conclusion. Jewish Galilee had established institutions and practices that put it outside any supposed assimilation within Graeco-Roman culture.

These are not isolated finds. In village after village, artifacts testify to institutions that attest the distinctiveness of Galilee. The example of the water jars is revealing:

> A unique item in the material culture of the Early Roman Jewish world was a class of soft, white stone vessels which appear in no less than sixty-five sites all over ancient Palestine. At least fourteen of these sites are in Upper and Lower Galilee (Gush Halav, Nabratein, Meiron, Kefar Hananiah, Capernaum, Yodfat, Jotapata, Ibelin, Kefar Kenna, Sepphoris, Reina, Nazareth, Bethlehem of Galilee, Migdal Ha-Emeq, and Tiberias). . . .These vessels were evidently designed to meet the requirements of laws of purity. They seem to be distinctively Jewish, as they only superficially resemble the marble vessels well known in the Roman world.[3]

Evidence of this kind cannot be pinned down to a single artifact, such as the ossuary of Caiaphas,[4] and that makes it difficult to assess. Where the ossuary of Caiaphas simply had to be put into its historical context in order to be appreciated, the many new artifacts of Galilee need to be arranged into a cultural context that is still under construction.

All these finds have shattered the myth of a purely or mostly Hellenistic Jesus.[5] Until a synagogue was found in Galilean Gamla, it was routinely claimed that synagogues were only a post-Christian institution.[6]

Before *miqvaoth* were discovered in several towns, bathing was often dismissed as purely the elitist practice of Pharisees in Judea. Indeed, it was often said that Jesus spoke Greek rather than Aramaic, but the discovery of the Dead Sea Scrolls shows that Aramaic was used during the first century and earlier, and the discovery of other scrolls near Qumran establishes that the usage of Aramaic persisted there until the second century C.E.

The archaeological Galilee is a Jewish Galilee, as far as Jesus and his movement are concerned; philo-Roman urban enclaves such as Sepphoris are notable for their absence from Jesus' itinerary in the Gospels.[7] Judaism has long been thought to be what is taught in the Mishnah and the Talmud. But those documents are much later than the New Testament. So the attempts by scholars of the previous generation to characterize Jesus in terms of Mishnah and Talmud run into a simple chronological problem. Sadly, it is all too easy for partisans of the

Hellenistic Jesus to dismiss Mishnah and Talmud as being too late to be relevant, and to ignore the Jewish identity of Jesus altogether. But the Dead Sea Scrolls, already mentioned, have rendered that gambit untenable. In the case of the Scrolls, anyone can see that the group that produced those documents focused on maintaining the correct purity and the accurate teaching which would assure that members of the community were included when God acted to vindicate his people. The archaeological and textual scholarship of the past decade has revolutionized how we should think about Galilee and about Judaism, and that means the once fashionable (and in some circles, still fashionable) picture of Jesus as an Athenian in Jewish dress must change.

The Scrolls opened a window on the extraordinary pluralism of early Judaism. Judaism in the time of Jesus was not fixated as it later was on the issue of how to keep the Torah, central though the Torah and the Scriptures always were. That was the program of a later day, the time of the Mishnah during the second century, to some extent part of an effort to compensate for the destruction of the Temple by the Romans by fire in 70 C.E., and then by demolition (stone by stone) in 135 C.E. The Judaism of the rabbis, with its emphasis on promulgating and interpreting the Torah as the center and boundary of any true definition of Israel, was constructed on the ashes of the Temple. Before then, various forms of Judaism vied with one another, and in their competition they shared a single kind of hope: the hope that God would personally and actively intervene on behalf of his people. That was just the hope that Jesus articulated when he announced, in the Galilean dialect of Judaism, the kingdom of God. His dialect of Judaism was one among many, and they were to varying degrees Hellenistic (as well as Egyptian and Ethiopian and Latin and Libyan and Persian, among other cultural influences). Judaism was an international religion during the first century, and it is impossible to reduce it to a single cultural form.

The evaluation of Judaism has long perplexed Christianity. Galilee has been a particular stumbling block. Because little was known of it, researchers once claimed it was essentially non-Jewish. In 1940, a scholar named Walter Grundmann insisted that Galilee had no real Judaic identity and that Jesus was not in any real sense Jewish.[8]

He was awarded by preferment during the Third Reich, and continued to have his work published (and respectfully reviewed) after World War II. Increasingly, however, the New Testament has been understood in a totally different light. For years, scholarship stagnated in a sterile debate between those who took the Bible as literally true history and those who regarded the Bible as the fiction of the few authors who wrote it. But we have learned that the Gospels emerged in an oral environment, such as when rabbis taught their students just what the best perspectives were. The collection of Jesus' sayings, although subject to a great deal of interpretation, began with Jesus himself. As a rabbi, he taught his own people what his views were.

Anti-Semitism has been the stock in trade for many superficial forms of Christianity, which have attempted to denigrate Judaism rather than stand up to the hard test of explaining the distinctive genius of Christianity. But Christianity is about that genius: his name is Jesus, and he cannot be comprehended outside the environment of his own Judaism. He was Jewish not only in the circumstances of his life, but in his dedication to that identity. Confronted with the increasing certainty that he was to die for his beliefs, Jesus taught his followers a carefully crafted teaching (a *kabbalah*) of suffering. *Kabbalah* refers particularly to a discipline of the vision of God which can be passed on from one person to another, and Jesus' characteristic *kabbalah* made human hardship into a crucible for experiencing the divine.

Of course, scholarly discussion about archaeology, about the nature of early Judaism, and about the emergence of the New Testament is far from over. But the fact that debate continues does not mean that no progress has been made. We now know that Jewish Galilee was not just an outpost of Hellenistic culture: it was rather a deeply proud and resistant representative of an alternative culture, whose emblem was "the kingdom of God." We now know that, in its proud individuality, the diverse Judaism of Galilee was not just the same as the Essenes' of Qumran or the Pharisees' in Jerusalem, but that it was in active debate with them. And we know, at the end of the day, that this Galilean Judaism gave birth, through Jesus, to Christianity. For that reason, we need to begin with Galilee. Galilee was the beginning, not just in the happenstance of Jesus' life, but at the center of his religious identity. Once we have understood his upbringing within the context of Galilee, we can then place him within the great unfolding of his unique religious vision. By properly valuing the Jewishness of Jesus, we will see him in his all his distinctiveness, and at the same time come to appreciate the fundamental commonality of Judaism and Christianity.

Jesus' religious environment is also better understood today than previously because textual work has been pursued on an intensive basis. The Aramaic translations of the Bible, called the Targums, illuminate the Jewish interpretation of Scripture as never before, because they are free renderings, *paraphrases* which reveal how the Scripture was understood, not just what it said. The project of publishing the Targums in English (the first time they were rendered as a whole into any language other than Aramaic) was started in 1987, and is about to be completed. Indeed, after my work on Jesus' preaching of the kingdom, Targumic study took up most of my professional time for a number of years.[9]

The discovery and translation of texts have played their part recently in the study of Christianity, as well as in the study of Judaism. At the same time one young man discovered the caves of Qumran, another found a cave full of Coptic documents near Nag Hammadi in Egypt. These sources from the fourth century C.E. include works such as the *Gospel according to Thomas*, a work first written during the second century that includes some sayings of Jesus which many regard as authentic,[10] a few of which are not contained in the canonical Gospels. In addition to providing us with interesting new material, these documents have taught us even more important things. It was once the case that scholars were left to choose between two extremes in a sterile debate: one side treated the Gospels as literal history, and the other insisted they were fictions. But to readers now familiar with ancient history and ancient novels, as well as with Jewish and early Christian literature, it becomes apparent that the Gospels are neither simple chronicles nor simple inventions. Rather, they deliberately represent interpretations of Jesus for their respective communities.

We are presented in our principal sources (the Gospels of the New Testament and, with caution, *Thomas*) with ways of seeing Jesus within the communities for which each Gospel was intended. Identifying the view of Jesus each one takes, we can infer how Jesus must have acted to have produced that view of him, together with the distinct views of him the other sources take. We are dealing, not only with four or five documents— Matthew, Mark, Luke, John, and *Thomas*—but with the groups of followers of Jesus that produces materials for those documents. Figures such as Barnabas (the companion of Paul), James (the brother of Jesus), Paul, Peter, as well as the circle of the twelve apostles, all had their parts in producing the texts as we can read them today. So the issue of how Jesus stands in relation to the Gospels cannot be resolved by imagining Jesus on the one hand and four or five authors composing documents on the other. Between Jesus and the texts there were groups of teachers, each of which generated its own view of Jesus. We need to address the generative question, how the texts emerged, by attending to how Jesus must have acted in order to have produced the complex documents before us. The unfolding of the sources themselves is a fascinating question, but our concern here is only with the initial stage: what we must infer of Jesus within his Jewish environment to explain how the texts emerged in their variety and in their agreement?

But we need one more dimension to understand Jesus, the Judaism of his time, and the Christianity that emerged from his activity (albeit only after his death). That dimension is the proper perspective of biography: how Jesus developed and changed, what the pivots of transition were in his unlikely journey from a Galilean boy accused of irregular birth to a respected rabbi who challenged the operation of the Temple in Jerusalem, directly confronting both the high priest of the time and the representative of Rome's power in the process. How was that possible, and why should the shameful result of that confrontation, Jesus' crucifixion, have resulted in the conviction that God had raised him from the dead?

Biography concerns transition. The focus cannot be just what is usually called "the life and personality of Jesus." Typically, studies of Jesus deal only with the public side of his activity in the year or two prior to his death. The result is that Jesus becomes like a two-dimensional icon: there is the height of his teaching and the breadth of his influence, but no depth of character. Now that we know more about Judaism and about Galilee, we no longer have to accept that situation. Rather, we can enter into Jesus' life, and join his experience, given the sources we have access to, so that we can understand how he emerged as the figure he did, how he developed and changed over time, and how his activity set in motion the generation of those sources.

The Gospels are without question the best sources for understanding Jesus, although what they have to say needs to be evaluated carefully. Between Jesus' death in 32 C.E. and the date of the first of the written Gospels (Mark, c. 71 C.E.) there lies a full generation of Christian teaching activity, designed to make, initiate, and keep converts within the new faith. Each of the Gospels was written in and for a predominantly non-Jewish community in a Hellenistic city: Mark in Rome, Matthew in Damascus (c. 80 C.E.), Luke in Antioch (c. 90 C.E.), and John in Ephesus (c. 100 C.E.).[11] The first three Gospels follow so closely the same basic order of preaching that they are called the Synoptic Gospels: they can be laid out side by side so that they can be compared (in a layout called a "Synopsis"). Their preaching is largely based on the oral preaching of Peter, supplemented by a collection of Jesus' teaching called "Q" (an abbreviation of the German term *Quelle*, "source," the closest thing there is to a mishnah of Rabbi Jesus) and by traditions stemming from followers such as James, Jesus' brother, and Barnabas, a prominent Hellenistic Jew.

The purpose of the Synoptics is to prepare people for baptism in Jesus' name, after a careful training. Christians in the environment of Roman persecution in which they lived needed to be wary of the damage which informers and loose-lipped groupies could inflict: mastery of the materials in the Synoptic Gospels became a requirement of baptism, which assured that only serious converts joined the movement. Once they were in, they looked for more advanced, mystical teaching, which is exactly what the Gospel according to John provides, as well as *the Gospel according to Thomas* (from about fifty years later).

Because the Gospels present either baptismal teaching (in the case of the Synoptics) or mystical teaching (in the case of John and *Thomas*), it should be obvious that they cannot be taken as objective history and as nothing else. A critical understanding of Jesus is possible only if one allows for the aims that produced the Gospels. In addition, we need to distinguish the urban, Hellenistic setting of the Gospels from the rural, Galilean environment of Jesus. In adjusting both for the aims and the cultural drift of the Gospels, the writings of Josephus are useful. Still, Josephus was no objective observer but a Jewish general who became one of the most famous turncoats ever. He is so concerned with his own reputation and his own, laundered version of Judaism, his claims need to be evaluated with extreme care. Bias is also evident in the famous Dead Sea Scrolls. The Scrolls were produced by a group called the Essenes which was so sectarian, they believed that everyone who did not agree with them (including the majority of the Jewish people) would be killed in the final, holy war when the angels would come to their aid. So although the Scrolls are immensely informative when they reflect common elements of Judaism (such as their conception of God's kingdom and their usage of Aramaic), no serious scholar would try to make them into the index of Judaism or Christianity in the first century. Finally, rabbinic literature is also helpful in assessing Jesus, but it, too, must be used with care. The earliest document of rabbinic literature, the Mishnah, was not produced until 200 C.E., well after Christianity and Judaism had gone their separate ways, and after a prolonged period of tension, sometimes violence, between the two. The Mishnah and later rabbinic literature frames a new definition of Judaism, for the epoch after the Temple had been destroyed by the Romans (in 70 C.E.) and after Christianity was one of Judaism's competitors. So no one could really expect that the Mishnah or the Talmud, a later commentary on the Mishnah, would *directly* reflect Judaism in the first century.

The fundamental character of Christianity is revealed only in its relationship to Judaism, whether one's viewpoint is that of faith or no faith.

In my work as a priest, I have become skeptical of the claim that belief and unbelief are diametrically opposed. Rather, inquiry seems to me to be characteristic of people who are engaged by the entire issue of God. Whether they will adhere to a given creed or not during the course of their lives will vary with a large number of circumstances. They might call that creed after the name of a religion, or refer to it as a denial of religion. (Atheism is a theological position and usually denies particular views of God.) Whether from an atheistic position or its opposite (a theistic position), the biography of Jesus lies at the heart of religion as we know it. As we uncover that biography, we will encounter not only vivid new images of Jesus which emerge from artifacts and texts critically considered, but also the emotional ferment, the hopes and fears and longings, which fed Rabbi Jesus and made him the most influential visionary the world has ever known.[12]

Conclusion

Craig A. Evans

The dialogue between Peter Zaas and William Craig has probably generated more discussion and debate than either imagined. In their limited allotments of time, they touched on a few issues. These issues and others have been explored by several scholars, both Jewish and Christian, who were invited to comment on the dialogue. To be sure, the responses overlap here and there, but for the most part they move into distinctive but related areas. The upshot is a discussion that touches on many of the issues that divide and draw together Jews and Christians.

This brief conclusion offers a few comments on the response essays, summarizing and in a few cases qualifying various statements made within them. No matter what position readers of this book may take—whether supporting a Christian assessment of Jesus or supporting a Jewish assessment of Jesus—readers will find much to ponder and digest. At the very least, they will discover that the questions that lie behind the central question of this book, "Who was Jesus?," are complicated and not easily answered. But knowing the questions and becoming better acquainted with the complexities facilitate understanding and encourage ongoing dialogue.

Donald Hagner writes the first essay in response to the dialogue between Peter Zaas and William Craig. At the outset he qualifies the claim made by Zaas that there is no Jewish position on Jesus. Hagner rightly counters that there really is widespread agreement among Jews as to who Jesus *was not*. Christians believe that Jesus was and is God's Son, Israel's Messiah, and the Savior of the world. Jews (unless they are Christians or "Messianists") do not believe this. Jesus may have been a prophet or a teacher, perhaps even a messianic claimant who hoped to reform or liberate Israel, but he was not the Messiah for whom some of the Jewish faithful still await. Thus, the unofficial Jewish position on Jesus is essentially the opposite of the Christian position.

In the balance of his essay, Hagner addresses himself to three areas that he thinks are very important in this dialogue. These topics are important for discussion not only with Jews but with anyone interested in what Christians believe about Jesus.

First, Hagner challenges the negative findings of the Jesus Seminar, with respect to the Gospels as historical sources. He rightly questions the conclusion that only 18 percent of the sayings in the Gospels are authentic. Curiously, many Jewish scholars are not nearly so skeptical. In this regard, conservative Christian scholars share more common ground with Jewish scholars than they do with the highly skeptical scholars from non-conservative Christian circles. There is some irony in this, to be sure.

Second, Hagner speaks to the question of the aims of Jesus. The portrait of Jesus as teacher or healer, which some Jewish scholars and writers will accept, is inadequate; Jesus was not simply a reformer of Judaism. Hagner is correct here, and Craig would agree wholeheartedly. The problem here is that such banal portraits square neither with the sources themselves (primarily the Gospels, though also some parts of other New Testament writings) nor with the beliefs and actions of the first Christians. Postmortem appearances of a beloved teacher or healer would in themselves not lead to ideas of resurrection, eschatology, and messianic identity, much less to notions of divine sonship. These ideas must have been rooted in Jesus' teaching and actions, and the impressions he made on those around him.

Hagner agrees with Zaas that Jesus was thoroughly Jewish, and he agrees with Craig that Jesus assumed and exhibited great authority. We see this authority in Jesus' invitation to come to him (instead of coming to the Torah), in taking his yoke (not the yoke of Torah) on him, or in the idea that to acknowledge Jesus will result in his acknowledging that one to God. Hagner rightly states that "the teaching of Jesus is ultimately inseparable from his personal claims" and that Jesus is not "one messiah among many," as Zaas puts it. We have examples of various would-be messiahs in the approximate time of Jesus. Their respective ministries, the impact they had on their contemporaries, and the results of their efforts stand in stark contrast to the character of Jesus' ministry and the impact he had on those around him.

This leads to Hagner's third point, the birth of the church. He supports Craig's contention that the resurrection is ultimately what makes Jesus stand out and what certainly explains the origin of the church. Alternative explanations (such as theories about going to the wrong tomb, hallucinations, the theft of Jesus' body) are inadequate and implausible. What took place was resurrection, not revivification, and this resurrection fulfilled Israel's scriptures and hopes. It is accordingly very relevant for Jews, not only for Christians.

Consequently, when Zaas argues that there is nothing at stake for the Jewish people, so far as beliefs about Jesus are concerned, he is wrong. The implications of Jesus—his teaching, his person, his resurrection—are as relevant for the Jewish people as they are for all other peoples. To say that who Jesus was doesn't matter begs the question; it assumes that Jesus was in fact no one of importance. But the evidence of history and experience suggests otherwise.

The essay by Craig Evans attempts to clarify the conceptual and methodological disagreements, be they conscious or unconscious, between the positions of Zaas and Craig. The burden of Evans's essay is to underscore the importance of situating Jesus fully into his Jewish context. He argues that Jesus accepted all of the major tenets of the Jewish faith: the unity and sovereignty of God, the value and sanctity of the Temple of Jerusalem, the authority of the Jewish Scriptures, the election of the people of Israel, and the hope of Israel's redemption. Jesus observed many of the practices of Jewish piety of his day, such as giving alms, prayer, and fasting. Evans qualifies Craig's assertion that Jesus set his own authority over against that of Torah. Rather, Jesus accepted the authority of Torah but set his own interpretation of it over against scribal interpretation and authority. Indeed, Jesus' hermeneutic seems to have been essentially that of the prophets of the Old Testament.

Jesus functioned as a prophet, anointed by the Spirit of God. He proclaimed God's reign (or "kingdom") and—in a less explicit manner— claimed to be God's Son. For Jesus it was Daniel's vision of the mysterious personage, the one "like a son of man," who from God received kingdom and authority, that seemed to underlie his self-understanding. Possessed of this authority, Jesus proclaimed the reign of God and the demise of Satan's sphere of authority, but he also proclaimed judgment upon the Temple establishment. It was these claims and actions that led to the inevitable collision with the authorities, both Jewish and Roman. Jesus died not because of his views of Torah, or because of quarrels with the Pharisees, but because he threatened the Temple establishment and justified his criticisms by an appeal to his divine sonship. Not only were his views understandably offensive to Jewish authorities, they were also seditious in the eyes of the Roman governor and so warranted capital punishment.

Evans concludes his essay in agreement with Craig, claiming that it was indeed the resurrection that brought the church into existence. Jesus was resurrected, and it was the church's duty to proclaim his message and his person until he should return. It was for this basic reason that the Gospels were eventually composed. Although selective in their coverage and obviously written from the perspective of faith, they are essentially reliable and historical.

Scot McKnight focuses his comments on how Jesus fit into first-century Judaism in all its diversity. The understandings of Judaism seen in Qumran's Teacher of Righteousness or in Philo of Alexandria amply demonstrate this diversity in the time of Jesus. Yet, there is an important unifying core centered on the observance of the Sabbath, circumcision, food laws, and avoidance—even suppression—of prohibited images. Christianity's problem, says McKnight, is that it is not "Jesus" enough; that is, it is not sufficiently anchored in his teaching and because of that has drifted far from its Jewish heritage.

McKnight emphasizes the meaning of Jesus' baptism and death, but he also treats several other elements as well (such as Jesus' prophetic actions, his use of the name of God, his ethics, emphasizing righteousness, love, and peace). McKnight considers the meaning of John's baptizing ministry, his call to Israel to repent and purify itself as preparation for God's visitation. Jesus' ministry is thus founded squarely on Jewish restorative hopes, which in various ways and by various people were championed in late antiquity. McKnight offers much insight with respect to Jesus' death. Jesus was executed not for challenging any of the tenets of Judaism, though he did disagree with some religious teachers over various matters of interpretation and halakhah, but because Jewish and Roman authorities saw in him a serious threat to peace and stability. McKnight believes that Jesus acted as he did knowing full well the danger that would result. Jesus threw himself into the danger and suffering of the last days, offered himself as a sacrifice for Israel, in the firm belief that God would vindicate him. McKnight finds that these actions and the thinking that underlies them are fully intelligible in the context of the Jewish Palestine of Jesus' day. Jesus was a Jew within that Judaism that was faithful to God's covenant with Israel.

Carsten Claussen explores the factors that led to Christianity's separation from Judaism. He begins his discussion with the meaning of Jesus' proclamation of the kingdom of God, which he believes stands within Jewish apocalypticism. Claussen then discusses Jesus and the Spirit and how important the shared experience of the Spirit was for the early Christian community. Claussen moves on to the names and terminology given to Jesus' followers. Christians were called a "sect" (or *hairesis*), a word

Josephus uses to describe Pharisees, Sadducees, Essenes, and Zealots, Nazarenes, *Christianoi* (or Christians), just as Herod's partisans were called *Hērōdianoi* (or Herodians). Christians were given these names to distinguish them from other groups of *Ioudaioi* (or "Judeans," i.e., Jews).

Claussen also considers Jesus, Paul, and the law. Like Jesus, Paul's theology is eschatological, and its point of departure is Judaism, particularly as seen in the synagogue. As did Hagner, Claussen questions Zaas's claim that there is no normative Judaism in the first century. Claussen considers Jimmy Dunn's "fourfold foundation on which all these more diverse forms of Judaism built, a common heritage which they all interpreted in their own ways." These four elements are monotheism, election, Torah, and Land focused in Temple. Although Christianity is rooted in important ways to these elements, it stretched them significantly, making separation inevitable. The divinity of Jesus was especially controversial. Claussen concludes that Jewish-Christian separation has its roots in Jesus' proclamation of the kingdom and accelerated in the exaltation of Jesus and the abandonment, even denigration of aspects of the Jewish heritage.

Herbert Basser provocatively suggests that a wide gulf exists between the Jewish Jesus and the non-Jewish Gospels that tell his story. Indeed, the Gospels are not simply non-Jewish in perspective; they are downright anti-Semitic. Basser asserts that a "central goal of the Gospel writers was to instill contempt, an odium, against Judaism: Jews were children of hell, their leaders a brood of vipers."

Does Basser's understanding reflect the perspective of the evangelists themselves, or does it reflect what tragically so many Christian theologians and apologists did with the Gospels in later generations? Jewish people are called a "brood of vipers" in Matthew and Luke. In Matthew 3:7 the harsh epithet is directed against the religious leaders ("Pharisees and Sadducees," the contextualization to which Basser refers), while in Luke 3:7 the epithet is directed against the people in general ("the multitudes"). But are these words of John the Baptizer reflective of early Christianity's contempt for the Jewish people and/or its leadership, or do they derive from John himself, a Jewish charismatic committed to the reform and restoration of Israel? Most critical scholars think the latter. John's words in later contexts may have been used by Gentile Christians against the Jewish people (much as the equally harsh words of the prophets could be hijacked and used against the Jewish people), but in their original setting there was nothing anti-Semitic about them.

Indeed, New Testament polemic pales in comparison to the harsh polemic we find in the Hebrew Bible and in Jewish writings from the approximate time of the New Testament. We see this especially in the Dead Sea Scrolls and in some of the other intertestamental writings. The prophet Isaiah rails against his own people: "Ah, sinful nation, a people laden with iniquity, offspring of evildoers, sons who deal corruptly" (Isa. 1:4 RSV). Jerusalem, he says, "has become a harlot" (Isa. 1:21 RSV). Later in this book we hear of "offspring of the adulterer and the harlot" (Isa. 57:3 RSV). Jeremiah and Hosea describe Israel as a harlot (Jer. 3:6; Hos. 1:2 RSV). In many places in the Hebrew Bible, Israel is described as stubborn, rebellious, stiff-necked (Deut. 29:1–3 [Eng. 29:2–4]; Jer. 7:25–26; 11:7–8; 2 Chron. 36:11–16). None of this is anti-Semitic, of course; it is in-house prophetic criticism, in which the prophet and biblical writer calls Israel to repentance. John the Baptizer and Jesus of Nazareth did the same. But these angry prophetic denunciations in the hands of outsiders take on a completely different dynamic, and this is precisely where Christians must take heed.

Further, Basser rejects too facilely Craig's inferential arguments to explain the resurrection in favor of skepticism about the historicity of the Gospels and any sound information about Jesus they may provide.[1]

Jacob Neusner surprises his readers with an opening statement even bolder than what we find in Basser's essay: "Judaisms and Christianities never meet anywhere. That is because at no point do Judaism, defined by the Torah, and Christianity, defined by the Bible, intersect." This statement is followed by a series of categorical denials. One's first impression is that Neusner is talking about Christianity and Judaism far removed from the first century; but no, he declares that they were "incompatible from the beginning."

Neusner's stimulating and controversial essay touches on many issues, especially those that concern Judaism itself, its diversity, as well as its coherent system as worked out in what we call rabbinic Judaism. He offers his essay more as a challenge to Zaas than as a challenge to Craig. Neusner's essay is instructive throughout and in many places will command assent. But I will offer one challenge of a hermeneutical nature.

The specific point that in my judgment especially requires qualification is the claim near the beginning of the essay: "Much that Jesus taught, and still more that his disciples taught, does not meet that criterion [i.e., the criterion of the Torah] but violates the teaching of Moses our rabbi." In a carefully qualified sense this may well be true (and much of Neusner's essay offers such qualification). But let's take another look, a look that takes into account some of the "Judaisms" current in the time when "Christianities" began to emerge.

Those who made up the community of the new covenant at Qumran believed that their story was rooted in Torah and was faithful to the letter of the law. It was they, not the "seekers after smooth things" (*dereshei halaqoth*), by which we probably should understand the Pharisees, the "seekers after legal decisions" (*dereshei halakoth*), who obeyed Moses truly and uprightly. It was they, not their opponents, who understood Torah, both written and oral, from beginning to end, as it should be understood. Their hermeneutic was eschatological, prophetic, and centered on the restoration of the cultus. But this group came to an end in the first major war with Rome, and so its hermeneutic did not become foundational for the Judaism that survived. Their legacy remained locked in time, one could almost say hermetically sealed, until its accidental uncovering in the discovery of the Dead Sea caves.

Samaritans believed (and still believe) that they are the true descendants of the tribes of Israel. They have their Torah, which is more than 90 percent the same as the Masoretic Text, and await the *Taheb* (the "restorer"), a prophet "like Moses," who will return and make things right. Of all forms of Judaism in this period, they alone adhered strictly to Torah as sacred Scripture: Torah and Torah alone, no Prophets and Writings.[2]

Philo of Alexandria offered a hermeneutic by which Torah could be understood as philosophy, a philosophy more intelligible to his Hellenistic contemporaries. Philo doubtless believed that his interpretation of Torah was true to Moses, for surely all that was true and good in Greek philosophy is in fact taught by the great lawgiver. But Philo's system did not take hold in Judaism, although, ironically, aspects of it did in some of the Christian fathers (notably in Origen).

Early Christians also believed that the story of Jesus not only was rooted in the Torah but was a fulfillment of it. The Lukan evangelist's Septuagintalizing style seems to suggest that the Gospel story should be viewed as a continuation of the story of Israel, from the first "son of God" (Adam) to the second "son of God" (Jesus). But there is an important Mosaic overlay as well, for Jesus is explicitly identified as the "prophet like Moses" (Deut. 18:15–18; cf. Acts 3:22–23; 7:37), who when tempted responds with the words of Torah (Deut. 8:3; 6:16, 6:13 in Matt. 4:4–10; Luke 4:4–12). The Matthean evangelist declares at the outset of his work that Jesus is "the son of David, the son of Abraham" (Matt. 1:1). By this, the evangelist implies that Jesus has fulfilled the covenant expectations associated with David (in that he is Israel's royal Messiah) and Abraham (in that in him all the nations will be blessed). However, the Matthean evangelist does not neglect to work out a Mosaic typology in which the infant Jesus is nearly slain by a fearful despot, flees to and from Egypt, and hands down his interpretation of Torah on a mount (Matt. 5–7) and utters his teaching in five major blocks of material (Matt. 5–7, 10, 13, 18, 24–25).

The charge that what Jesus taught "violates the teaching of Moses" is true only in the sense of the qualification Neusner supplies: "Moses our rabbi." Yes, that is true; Jesus and his apostolic successors do violate the teaching of Moses, but only after Moses has been presented as the great rabbi who taught the Oral Torah, as the sages taught it. But Jesus and his successors believed that they, as surely as did the covenanters of Qumran, interpreted Moses correctly. They believed that the great lawgiver foretold the coming of the prophet like himself, even the word that would come down from heaven (Deut. 30:11–14). Early Christians believed that Jesus fulfilled these expectations. What Neusner appears to overlook is how a very early high Christology emerged among Jewish Christians (e.g., the Aramaic prayer to Jesus, *Marana tha*, or Jesus' being identified as the "one Lord" by the Jew Paul) while they held tenaciously to monotheism—and this is simply *uncontested* in early Christian communities. Yahweh in the prophets is depicted as a God of "new things"; while the New Testament introduces *novelty* to be sure, it is founded on the requisite *continuity*.[3]

Neither Judaism nor Christianity today obeys the Torah as practiced prior to 70. No one can. No one slaughters animals and offers them on the Temple altar; the Temple is no more. Spiritual and metaphorical equivalents have been found. Here Christianity and Judaism parallel one another, as also Qumran did, when the community separated itself from the Temple establishment. Without a Temple, deeds of righteousness and prayers are offered up as sacrifices and incense. In the words of Paul, Christians are "living sacrifices" (Rom. 12:1). A whole host of other pieces of Mosaic legislation simply cannot be observed today. This is where hermeneutics comes in. The meaning, relevance, and applications of Torah can be extracted by means of allegory (so Philo), midrash (so the sages and rabbis), pesher (so Qumran), and prophetic typology (so Christianity). Each hermeneutical system attempts to lay claim and appropriate the riches of the Torah. Moses becomes "our rabbi" for each Judaism and Christianity (excepting Marcionism, which Christianity quite properly repudiated).

The sages have indeed developed a coherent system that explains and makes sense of Torah. The logical outcome is rabbinic Judaism, centered on Torah, written and oral. "The sages' account of the Torah revealed by God to Moses at Sinai and handed on in tradition through the ages," says

Neusner, "defines Judaism." Well said. Later Neusner says that the "sages' reading of Scripture recovers . . . the main lines of Scripture's principal story, the one about creation, the fall of humanity and God's salvation of humankind through Israel and the Torah." Quite so. But I wonder, does not Christianity do the same thing? Christianity is centered on Jesus' account of the Torah revealed by God to Moses and the Prophets, also inspired by God. Apart from Torah, the story of Jesus is meaningless (for Jesus and for his followers).

In the end, I wonder if it is really necessary to conclude, as has Neusner, that "Judaisms and Christianities do not meet and cannot meet: because they cannot afford a common prayer and do not share a common revelation." It seems to me that both hold in common God's revelation at Sinai, extended and developed by the rabbis into a given worldview and system, and extended and developed by Jesus and his followers into a somewhat different, yet overlapping worldview and system. Both share the vision of the Prophets, who envision restoration and renewal. Both share the Prayer—the Qaddish and the Lord's Prayer—whereby petition is made for God's sanctity and coming kingdom. Christianities and Judaisms are not identical, and they do differ significantly at many points, but they do overlap in important ways, and in that overlap, it seems to me, they *do* and *can* meet.

Bruce Chilton highlights an important feature in Jewish-Christian dialogue: the Jewishness of Jesus. Chilton rightly and emphatically situates Jesus in Galilee and correctly describes his activities and occupational self-understanding as a rabbi. The Jewishness of Jesus and especially his rabbinic orientation underscore the common roots of Judaism and Christianity. Chilton also emphasizes, in contrast to some of the scholarship that has emanated from the North American Jesus Seminar, the Jewishness of Galilee itself, as so firmly documented in recent years through archaeology. We find Jesus interested in purity, frequenting synagogues, employing Aramaic, which is the language of Galilee, the synagogue, and the paraphrased and interpreted Bible of his day.

Chilton concludes by making the important statement that the "fundamental character of Christianity is revealed only in its relationship to Judaism, whether one's viewpoint is that of faith or no faith." He is quite correct. It is here that Jewish-Christian dialogue may begin and may continue. As Christians come to recognize the systemic Jewish identity and character of Jesus, they will come to a deeper and richer understanding of their faith. Recognition of the Jewishness of Jesus will also enable Jews to appreciate, even reclaim, Rabbi Jesus and evaluate his contribution to the complex matrix of Judaisms in the first century, before the vicissitudes of war and history began driving apart communities of faith.

The Zaas-Craig dialogue and the essays that have responded to it, and to one another as well, have laid bare the essential issues with which Jews and Christians must grapple if understanding is to grow. Common to all of the essays is the recognition that Judaism itself must be understood if there is to be any meaningful dialogue. If Christians wish to disagree with aspects of Judaism, they need to know accurately and fairly what Judaism is all about. The same is true with regard to Jews: if they are to disagree with Christian beliefs, they need to know accurately and fairly what Christianity is all about.

Notes

Preface

1. As found in *b. Sanh.* 43a and *b. Sanh.* 107b.
2. The year 135 marks the end of the Bar Kokhba war.
3. James D. G. Dunn, ed., *Jews and Christians: The Parting of the Ways: A.D. 70 to 135* (Grand Rapids: Wm. B. Eerdmans, 1999), 368.
4. Some contributors to this volume (obviously) believe that the threads of Judaism and Christianity *should* be pulled apart and kept separate.

Introduction

1. Zaas notes this in a discussion (published at Siena College) with Kevin Tortorelli, OFM: "A Dialogue: Can the New Testament Be a Text for Jewish-Christian Understanding?" *Voices* (Fall 1983), 36.
2. Peter Zaas, "Protology and Eschatology in the Jewish-Christian Dialogue" in *Torah and Revelation*, Daniel Cohn-Sherbok, ed. (Lewiston, N.Y.: Edwin Mellen, 1992), 135f.
3. Not that all these scholars believe Jesus rose from the dead—only that they accept these three facts of history.

Chapter 1. Who Was Jesus? A Jewish Response

1. I am very grateful to the Siena College students who invited me to be part of this dialogue, especially to Kati Tucker.
2. Rabbi Schneersohn has since died, although his death has not stilled the yearnings of those who still consider him the Messiah.

Chapter 2. Who Was Jesus? A Christian Perspective

1. James D. G. Dunn, *Jesus and the Spirit* (London: SCM Press, 1975), 86.
2. Wolfhart Pannenberg, "Jesu Geschichte und unsere Geschichte," in *Glaube und Wirklichkeit* (München: Chr. Kaiser, 1975), 92–94.
3. Joachim Jeremias, *Die Abendmahlsworte Jesu* [Eng. trans.: *The Eucharistic Words of Jesus*], 4th ed. (Göttingen: Vandenhoeck & Ruprecht, 1967), 95–98.
4. Norman Perrin, *The Resurrection According to Matthew, Mark, and Luke* (Philadelphia: Fortress, 1977), 80.
5. A. N. Sherwin-White, *Roman Society and Roman Law in the New Testament* (Oxford: Clarendon, 1963), 188–91.
6. Rudolf Pesch, *Das Markusevangelium*, 2 vols., HTKNT 2 (Freiburg: Herder, 1976–77), 2.519–20.

7. *y. Sot.* 19a; *b. Qidd.* 82b.

8. Jacob Kremer, *Die Osterevangelien—Geschichten um Geschichte* (Stuttgart: Katholisches Bibelwerk, 1977), 49–50.

9. D. H. van Daalen, *The Real Resurrection* (London: Collins, 1972), 41.

10. R. H. Fuller, *The Formation of the Resurrection Narratives* (London: SPCK, 1972), 2.

11. Joachim Jeremias, "Die älteste Schicht der Osterüberlieferung," in *Resurrexit*, ed. Edouard Dhanis (Rome: Libreria Editrice Vaticana, 1974), 194.

12. C. F. D. Moule and Don Cupitt, "The Resurrection: A Disagreement," *Theology* 75 (1972), 507–19.

13. C. F. D. Moule, *The Phenomenon of the New Testament*, SBT 2/1 (London: SCM, 1967), 3, 13.

14. Wolfhart Pannenberg, *Jesus: God and Man*, trans. L. L. Wilkins and D. A. Priebe (London: SCM, 1968), 67.

Chapter 3. Interactive Discussion

1. Ahad ha'Am, "Judaism and the Gospels," in *Nationalism and the Jewish Ethic*, ed. H. Kohn (New York: Schocken Books, 1962), 298.

2. Jacob Neusner, *A Rabbi Talks with Jesus* (New York: Doubleday, 1993).

3. Robert J. Hutchinson, "What the Rabbi Taught Me about Jesus," *Christianity Today* (September 13, 1993), 28.

4. Since the discussion in 1993, this ruling has been changed by the Israeli judicial system.

Chapter 4. Questions and Answers

1. Horst Georg Pöhlmann, *Abriss der Dogmatik*, 3d rev. ed. (Düsseldorf: Patmos Verlag, 1966), 230.

2. Ibid.

Chapter 6. The Jesus of History and the Christ of Faith: Toward Jewish-Christian Dialogue

1. I am alluding here to P. Lapide's provocative book, *Auferstehung: Ein jüdisches Glaubenserlebnis* (Stuttgart: Calwer, 1977); ET: *The Resurrection of Jesus: A Jewish Perspective* (Minneapolis: Augsburg, 1983). What is placed in quotation marks represents my summary of one aspect of Lapide's book. These are not Lapide's actual words.

2. As quoted in *Time* (7 May 1979), 91.

3. For discussion of the issues and positions involved in this debate, see C. F. Evans, *Resurrection and the New Testament* (SBT 2; London: SCM Press, 1970); S. T. Davis, D. Kendall, and G. O'Collins (eds.), *The Resurrection* (Oxford: Oxford University Press, 1997); S. E. Porter, M. A. Hayes, and D. Tombs (eds.), *Resurrection* (JSNTSup 186; RILP 5; Sheffield: Sheffield Academic Press, 1999).

4. For discussion of this dimension of the debate, see P. Perkins, *Resurrection: New Testament Witness and Contemporary Reflection* (Garden City, N.Y.: Doubleday & Co., 1984); idem, "The Resurrection of Jesus of Nazareth," in B. D. Chilton and C. A. Evans (eds.), *Studying the Historical Jesus: Evaluations of the State of Current Research* (NTTS 19; Leiden: Brill, 1994) 423–42.

5. N. T. Wright, *Who Was Jesus?* (London: SPCK, 1992; Grand Rapids: Wm. B. Eerdmans, 1993). Wright criticizes B. Thiering, *Jesus and the Riddle of the Dead Sea Scrolls: Unlocking the Secrets of His Life Story* (San Francisco: HarperCollins, 1992); A. N. Wilson, *Jesus*

(London: Sinclair-Stevenson, 1992); and J. Spong, *Born of a Woman* (San Francisco: HarperCollins, 1992).

6. E. P. Sanders, *Jesus and Judaism* (London: SCM; Philadelphia: Fortress, 1985). For an earlier and broader criticism of Christian misinterpretation of first-century Judaism, see Sanders, *Paul and Palestinian Judaism* (London: SCM; Philadelphia: Fortress, 1977). For several studies that attempt to discover how Jews and Christians "defined" themselves, see E. P. Sanders et al. (eds.), *Jewish and Christian Self-Definition* (3 vols., Philadelphia: Fortress, 1980–82).

7. As capably demonstrated in B. D. Chilton, *A Galilean Rabbi and His Bible: Jesus' Use of the Interpreted Scripture of His Time* (GNS 8; Wilmington, Del., Glazier, 1984).

8. Another famous example is Isaiah's deliberate allusion to the Davidic Covenant (2 Sam. 7:12–16): "If you do not believe, you will not be established" (Isa. 7:9). Both words, "believe" and "establish," derive from the verb *aman* (from which we get the word "amen"—let it be established or made sure), which is the word found in 2 Sam. 7:16: "And your house and your kingdom *shall be made sure* forever before me." With prophetic boldness Isaiah has declared that the promise made to David is not unconditional (as one might interpret 2 Samuel 7), but is conditioned on faith and obedience.

9. As seen, for example, in one of the Dead Sea Scrolls (cf. 11QMelchizedek).

10. There are many other examples where Jesus challenged the conventional wisdom of his day, a wisdom based in large part on traditional understanding of Scripture.

11. G. Vermes, *Jesus the Jew: A Historian's Reading of the Gospels* (London: Collins; Philadelphia: Fortress, 1973); idem, *Jesus and the World of Judaism* (London: SCM, 1983; Philadelphia: Fortress, 1984); idem, *The Religion of Jesus the Jew* (London: SCM; Minneapolis: Fortress, 1993). Honi the Circle Drawer, mentioned in the Mishnah (*m. Ta'anit* 3:8) and in Josephus (*Ant.* 14.22), was remembered to have called down rain from heaven by refusing to leave the circle which he drew on the ground. God answered his prayer and sent rain. Hanina ben Dosa is remembered for many mighty deeds, including stopping and starting rain, healing, surviving the bite of a poisonous reptile, and banishing demons (*m. Ber.* 5:5; *m. Sota* 9:15; *b. Ber.* 33a–34b; *b. Pesah.* 112b).

12. Sanders, *Jesus and Judaism*, 239–40. Theudas promised to lead Israelites across the Jordan, in the fashion of Joshua of old, apparently as a prelude to a new conquest of the holy land (Josephus, *Ant.* 20.97–98). The Egyptian Jew promised his following, who gathered around him atop the Mount of Olives, overlooking the Temple Mount, that at his command the walls of Jerusalem would collapse (Josephus, *Ant.* 20.169–170). Again, it seems that we have another example of a Joshua-like figure who, as the successor to Moses (cf. Deut. 18:15–18), would usher in a new golden age. Both Theudas and the Egyptian Jew are mentioned in the book of Acts (5:36; 21:38).

13. B. D. Chilton, *The Temple of Jesus: His Sacrificial Program within a Cultural History of Sacrifice* (University Park: Penn State Press, 1992). Chilton cites and discusses the tradition about the teaching of Hillel, who insisted that the supplicant take possession of the sacrificial animal before having it offered up at the Temple. For two works by Jewish scholars who see important parallels between Jesus' teachings and those of the rabbis, see A. Finkel, *The Pharisees and the Teacher of Nazareth* (AGSU 4; Leiden: Brill, 1964), and P. Sigal, *The Halakah of Jesus of Nazareth according to the Gospel of Matthew* (Lanham, Md.: University Press of America, 1986).

14. C. A. Evans, *Jesus and His Contemporaries: Comparative Studies* (AGJU 25; Leiden: Brill, 1995), 437–56. See also A. E. Harvey, *Jesus and the Constraints of History* (London:

Duckworth, 1982), 120–53. I think Isaiah 35:5–6, 61:1–2, and possibly 52:7 were very informing passages for Jesus. Jesus' message was very much in step with the ideals of Israel's classic prophets. In this connection I completely agree with Zaas's description of Jesus' ministry: "Jesus stood against the sin of religiosity, the notion that what God desires is religiousness rather than justice, the notion that the person whose religiousness is a mask for their viciousness is the worst sinner. This idea, born among the Hebrew prophets but expressed with Jesus' characteristic simplicity and vigor in the Gospels, links this teacher with what is best in Jewish ethical thinking."

15. For a technical presentation of aspects of comparison, see my *Jesus and His Contemporaries*. For a popular presentation, see J. H. Charlesworth, *Jesus within Judaism* (ABRL; New York: Doubleday, 1988).

16. The Hebrew word "rabbi," which literally means "my great one," is often found in the Gospels in its Greek form "teacher."

17. On this, see H. Lapin, "Rabbi," *ABD* 5.600–602.

18. Indeed, this could explain the appearance of Matthew 23:6–8 RSV ("they love . . . being called rabbi by men. But you are not to be called rabbi") in a Gospel that is sharply critical of the Pharisees, the principal Jewish teachers who after 70 opposed early Christianity.

19. Bultmann and others thought that Jesus did not understand *himself* as the "son of man," but that this figure would come from heaven coincident with the arrival of the kingdom of God. This point remains hotly debated today.

20. See J. J. Collins, "The Works of the Messiah," *DSD* 1 (1994), 98–112.

21. It is not at all apparent that the resurrection in itself would have led Jesus' disciples to confess Jesus as "Messiah," if he had never claimed or accepted such an identification during his ministry. Would the followers of Rabbi Aqiba have proclaimed their beloved teacher Messiah, had he been resurrected following his martyrdom (ca. 135 AD)? I doubt it.

22. In later Christian tradition the idea of Jesus sharing God's throne is expressed explicitly, as seen in Revelation 3:21 (RSV): "He who conquers, I will grant him to sit with me on my throne, as I myself conquered and sat down with my Father on his throne."

23. Whether or not it was blasphemous in the technical sense of the discussion of capital blasphemy in the Mishnah tractate *Sanhedrin* 6–7 is an open question. Here the divine name has to be pronounced, and in a vain or obscene context. Even if Jesus had uttered the divine name ("You will see the son of man seated at the right hand of Yahweh"), it is not clear that that in itself would have constituted blasphemy according to *Sanhedrin* 6–7. But in the first century the word "blasphemy" was used in a more informal sense and could apply much more broadly than what is allowed in the Mishnah. On this topic, see D. L. Bock, *Blasphemy and Exaltation in Judaism and the Final Examination of Jesus: A Philological-Historical Study of the Key Jewish Themes Impacting Mark 14:61–64* (WUNT 2.106; Tübingen: Mohr [Siebeck], 1998; repr. Grand Rapids: Baker, 2000).

24. For an English translation of some of his work, see C. H. Talbert (ed.), *Reimarus: Fragments* (Philadelphia: Fortress, 1970).

25. A. Schweitzer, *The Quest of the Historical Jesus: A Critical Study of Its Progress from Reimarus to Wrede* (London: Black, 1910 [German orig., 1906]).

26. For the classic statement of the new quest, see J. M. Robinson, *A New Quest of the Historical Jesus* (SBT 25; London: SCM, 1959). For a brief but helpful summary of the major contributors to the third quest, see Wright, *Who Was Jesus?*, 12–18. For a more technical assessment of the third quest and its relationship to the former quests, see C. A. Evans, "Life-of-Jesus Research and the Eclipse of Mythology," *TS* 54 (1993), 3–36; idem, *Jesus and His Contemporaries*, 1–49.

27. See R. T. France, "Jesus the Baptist?" in J. B. Green and M. Turner (eds.), *Jesus of Nazareth: Lord and Christ. Essays on the Historical Jesus and New Testament Christology* (Carlisle: Paternoster; Grand Rapids: Wm. B. Eerdmans, 1994), 94–111. On the probability that Jesus continued important aspects of John's call for repentance, see B. D. Chilton, "Jesus and the Repentance of E. P. Sanders," *TynBul* 39 (188), 1–18.

28. See C. A. Evans, "Jesus' Ethic of Humility," *TrinJ* 13 (1992), 127–38.

29. Most scholars accept the *titulus* as authentic. They reason, and I think cogently, that had Christians invented the *titulus*, the wording would have been different. Christians did not regard Jesus as the "king of the Jews." They regarded him as the Lord of the Church, as the Savior of the World, as the Son of God, and as the Messiah.

30. Here I disagree with W. L. Lane, *The Gospel of Mark* (NIC; Grand Rapids: Wm. B. Eerdmans, 1974), 536. That a messianic claim was not in itself blasphemous, see J. Marcus, "Mark 14:61: 'Are You the Messiah-Son-of-God?'" *NovT* 31 (1989), 125–41. I have to disagree to some extent with Bill Craig's comments about the role blasphemy may have played in Jesus' death. I think Pannenberg's statement, which Craig quotes and with which he is in agreement, exaggerates the blasphemy charge. Jesus may have been accused of blasphemy, but the primary accusation, and the one in which Pilate took interest, was his messianic claim. Here I agree with Peter Zaas. But I do not agree that the blasphemy charge was a Markan invention. If Jesus claimed that he would sit upon the divine throne, next to God, Caiaphas's shout of blasphemy is not unexpected. Where I think Zaas goes wrong is in his assumption that the question should be settled by an appeal to the rules found in the Mishnah. We should not assume that the rules spelled out in this early third-century source were observed, or even known, in the early part of the first century. Some of them may have been, but corroboration is required, not assumption. Zaas is correct to object to statements to the effect that "the Jews rejected Jesus." This smacks of later anti-Jewish polemics. It is more accurate to say that part of the Jewish leadership, for understandable reasons, rejected Jesus.

   I might also add, in response to Question 2 during the discussion time, that the assertion that "the Romans didn't want to crucify Jesus" is problematic. Even if we take the Gospels' accounts at face value (and many Gospel critics at this point do not), Pilate's hesitation may have been due to a variety of factors. Normally the governor did not hesitate to use brutal force to eliminate various prophets and deliverers (see Josephus). In the case of Jesus, Pilate's hesitation may have been due to a desire to avoid stirring up the crowds, with which Jerusalem was swollen during the Passover season. Once he had determined that Jesus was not in fact heading up an armed following bent on violent overthrow, he may have wondered why execution was necessary. Why not beat and release him, or beat and throw him in prison? Naturally, the Gospels, written and circulated in the Roman Empire, would have had every reason to emphasize Pilate's hesitation. Christians were not eager to have Jesus portrayed as an enemy of the state. In my judgment, the truth lies somewhere in the middle. Pilate may very well have been reluctant to execute a popular charismatic figure, especially when he learned that he posed no military threat. The Gospels then exaggerate Pilate's hesitance, leaving the reader with the impression that it was a battle between the wills of the governor (whose judgment was proper) on one side and the ruling priests (whose judgment was improper) on the other.

31. Three such individuals are mentioned in Acts (5:36–37; 21:38), all three of which, along with a host of other would-be liberators, are discussed, usually with contempt, by Josephus.

32. The word is *lestai*, which the King James Version translates "thieves" (Mark 15:27). A

more literal translation is "robbers." But Josephus's use of the word suggests that it probably is better to translate it "insurrectionists" or "rebels."

33. I have found Bill Craig's publications on the resurrection of Jesus to be solid and well considered; I recommend them highly.

34. For recent discussion of the "criteria of authenticity," see J. P. Meier, *A Marginal Jew: Rethinking the Historical Jesus* (vol. 1; New York: Doubleday, 1991), 167–95; Evans, *Jesus and His Contemporaries*, 13–26.

35. See R. W. Funk and R. W. Hoover (ed.), *The Five Gospels: The Search for the Authentic Words of Jesus* (New York: Macmillan, 1993); R. W. Funk (ed.), *The Acts of Jesus: What Did Jesus Really Do? The Search for the Authentic Deeds of Jesus* (San Francisco: HarperCollins, 1998).

36. See my essay, "Luke and the Rewritten Bible: Aspects of Lukan Hagiography," in J. H. Charlesworth and C. A. Evans (eds.), *The Pseudepigrapha and Early Biblical Interpretation* (JSPSup 14; SSEJC 2; Sheffield: JSOT Press, 1993), 170–201.

37. See T. Elgvin (ed.), *Israel and Yeshua* (Jerusalem: Caspari Center, 1993); K. Kjaer-Hansen and B. F. Skjøtt, *Facts & Myths about the Messianic Congregations in Israel* (Jerusalem: United Christian Council, 1999).

Chapter 7. Jesus' New Vision within Judaism

1. Judaism at one time was sketched by Christian scholarship as Pharisaic Judaism, and that sketch was drawn from the rabbinic sources, especially the Mishnah and Babylonian Talmud. Scholarship today has chased this conceptualization into the deep thicket and, instead, has grown comfortable with diversity, even Judaisms. See, e.g., M. S. Jaffee, *Early Judaism* (Englewood Cliffs, N.J.: Prentice-Hall, 1997), for a recent sketch of how Judaism is now being understood. See also S. J. D. Cohen, *The Beginnings of Jewishness: Boundaries, Varieties, Uncertainties* (Berkeley, Calif.: University of California Press, 1999); "Judaism at the Time of Jesus," in *Jews and Christians Speak of Jesus* (ed. A. E. Zannoni; Minneapolis: Fortress, 1994), 3–12, who balances the issues of diversity and identity.

2. On this conceptualization of the data, see M. O. Wise, *The First Messiah: Investigating the Savior before Jesus* (San Francisco: HarperSanFrancisco, 1999).

3. E. P. Sanders, *Paul and Palestinian Judaism: A Comparison of Patterns of Religion* (Philadelphia: Fortress, 1977); *Judaism: Practice and Belief. 63 BCE–66 CE* (Philadelphia: Trinity Press International, 1992), 241–78.

4. See S. J. D. Cohen, "Judaism," 3–12; P. Fredriksen, *Jesus of Nazareth, King of the Jews* (New York: Alfred A. Knopf, 1999), 61–65.

5. See J. D. G. Dunn, *The Partings of the Ways: Between Christianity and Judaism and their Significance for the Character of Christianity* (Philadelphia: Trinity Press International, 1991). I have taken one cross section through this history in "A Parting within the Way: Jesus and James on Israel and Purity," in *James the Just and Christian Origins* (eds. B. Chilton, C. A. Evans; SupplNovTest XCVIII; Leiden: E. J. Brill, 1999), 83–129.

6. A definitive essay here is G. B. Caird, *Jesus and the Jewish Nation* (London: Athlone, 1965).

7. See here T. Wright, *The Original Jesus* (Grand Rapids: Wm. B. Eerdmans, 1996), 44–55.

8. See A. Geiger, *Judaism and Its History* (trans. C. Newburgh; New York: Bloch, 1911 [=1864]). Pinchas Lapide, *The Resurrection of Jesus: A Jewish Perspective* (trans. W. C. Linss; Minneapolis: Augsburg, 1983).

9. One of the most compelling features of N. T. Wright's portrait of Jesus is that his Jesus is anchored in a credible Jewish context (read: story). See *The New Testament and the People of God* (Minneapolis: Fortress, 1992), 145–338.

10. See, e.g., L. T. Johnson, "The New Testament's Anti-Jewish Slander and the Conventions of Ancient Polemic," *JBL* 108 (1989), 419–41; C. A. Evans and D. A. Hagner, eds., *Anti-Semitism and Early Christianity: Issues of Polemic and Faith* (Minneapolis: Fortress, 1993). Herb Basser's essay unfortunately fails to engage Christian—and Jewish—scholarship of this sort.

11. See my *A New Vision for Israel: The Teachings of Jesus in National Context* (Grand Rapids: Wm. B. Eerdmans, 1999).

12. I do not hereby imply that "restoration movements" is a code term for the "hasidic movements," a theory that has recently fallen out of favor in light of newer research into the Maccabean period.

13. On this, see J. H. Charlesworth, ed., *The Messiah: Developments in Earliest Judaism and Christianity* (Minneapolis: Fortress, 1992); J. J. Collins, *The Scepter and the Star: The Messiahs of the Dead Sea Scrolls and Other Ancient Literature* (ABRL; New York: Doubleday, 1995); D. Cohn-Sherbok, *The Jewish Messiah* (Edinburgh: T & T Clark, 1997); J. Neusner, W. S. Green, E. Frerichs, eds., *Judaisms and Their Messiahs at the Turn of the Christian Era* (Cambridge, Mass.: Cambridge University Press, 1987).

14. See S. McKnight, "John the Baptist," *New Dictionary of Biblical Theology* (Leicester: Inter-Varsity Press, 2000) 602–4; idem, *A Light among the Gentiles: Jewish Missionary Activity in the Second Temple Period* (Minneapolis: Fortress, 1991), 82–85.

15. On this see R. L. Webb, *John the Baptizer and Prophet: A Socio-Historical Study* (JSNTSup 62; Sheffield: JSOT, 1991), 219–348.

16. An entire tractate of the Mishnah is devoted to these pools and how purifications were to take place (*Miqvaoth*).

17. An excellent survey of the evidence and its meaning is E. P. Sanders, *Jewish Law from Jesus to the Mishnah: Five Studies* (Philadelphia: Trinity Press International, 1990), 214–27; see also J. J. Rouseau and R. Arav, *Jesus and His World: An Archaeological and Cultural Dictionary* (Minneapolis: Fortress, 1995), 236–40.

18. See B. Chilton, *Jesus' Baptism and Jesus' Healing: His Personal Practice of Spirituality* (Harrisburg: Trinity Press International, 1998), 1–29.

19. See esp. J. Klawans, *Impurity and Sin in Ancient Judaism* (Ph.D. disseration; Columbia University, 1997; UMI #9728236), 47–58. I differ with Klawans on John's rite as purificatory for two reasons: (1) I do not think Josephus's distinction between a ritual and moral purification is anything but apologetics, and (2) I cannot see how a watery act to remove sins can be anything but some kind of purification, even if it is moral. But see his discussion at pp. 288–98. C. Brown gives other arguments against a purification orientation; see his "What Was John the Baptist Doing?," *BBR* 7 (1997), 37–50, here pp. 41–42. See also J. E. Taylor, *The Immerser: John the Baptist within Second Temple Judaism* (Grand Rapids: Wm. B. Eerdmans, 1997), 49–100.

20. See C. H. Kraeling, *John the Baptist* (New York: Scribner's, 1951); Webb, *John the Baptizer*, 203–5.

21. See 4QMMT; also cf. C. A. Evans, "Jesus' Action in the Temple and Evidence of Corruption in the First-Century Temple," in *SBL Seminar Papers 1989* (ed. D. J. Lull; Atlanta: Scholars, 1989), 522–36.

22. See Brown, "What Was John the Baptist Doing?," upon whom I am dependent here.

23. On this, cf. S. McKnight, "Jesus and Prophetic Actions," *BBR* 10 (2000), 197–232. In this article, I detail a complete listing of the prophetic actions of Moses, the prophets, and the popular leadership prophets and compare them to Jesus' similar prophetic actions.

24. Apart from my study in the previous footnote, see especially W. D. Stacey, *Prophetic*

Drama in the Old Testament (London: Epworth, 1990); K. G. Friebel, *Jeremiah's and Ezekiel's Sign-Acts: Rhetorical Nonverbal Communication* (JSOTSup 283; Sheffield: Sheffield Academic Press, 1999); M. D. Hooker, *The Signs of a Prophet: The Prophetic Actions of Jesus* (Harrisburg: Trinity Press International, 1997).

25. See S. McKnight, *A New Vision for Israel*, 15–69.

26. I mention a sampling: D. Ben-Amos and J. R. Mintz, trans., *In Praise of the Baal Shem Tov [=Shivhei ha-Besht]: The Earliest Collection of Legends about the Founder of Hasidism* (Northvale, N.J.: Jason Aronson, 1993); A. Green, *Tormented Master: The Life and Spiritual Quest of Rabbi Nahman of Bratslav* (Woodstock, Vt.: Jewish Lights, 1992); I. G. Marcus, *Rituals of Childhood: Jewish Acculturation in Medieval Europe* (New Haven, Conn.: Yale University Press, 1996); E. Kaplan and S. H. Dresner, *Abraham Joshua Heschel: Prophetic Witness* (New Haven, Conn.: Yale University Press, 1998); E. Wiesel, *All Rivers Run to the Sea: Memoirs* (New York: Alfred A. Knopf, 1995); and G. G. Schmidt, *Martin Buber's Formative Years: From German Culture to Jewish Renewal, 1897–1909* (Tuscaloosa, Ala.: University of Alabama Press, 1995).

27. *Die Geschichte des Christus* (Stuttgart: Calwer, 1977 [=1923]), 140. Author's translation.

28. See McKnight, *A New Vision for Israel*, 197–237.

29. See McKnight, *A New Vision for Israel*, 200–206; idem, "Justice, Righteousness," in J. B. Green, S. McKnight, and I. H. Marshall, eds., *Dictionary of Jesus and the Gospels* (Downers Grove, Ill.: InterVarsity, 1992) 411–16; B. Przybylski, *Righteousness in Matthew and His World of Thought* (SNTSMS 41; Cambridge, Mass.: Cambridge University Press, 1980).

30. The best definition I know of today, especially as a result of the advances in Pauline studies in light of the advances in study of Judaism, is J. D. G. Dunn, *The Theology of Paul the Apostle* (Grand Rapids: Wm. B. Eerdmans, 1998) 334–89.

31. *What Is Christianity?* (trans. T. B. Saunders; New York: Harper, 1957 [=1901]).

32. See L. H. Schiffman, "The Jewishness of Jesus: Commandments Concerning Interpersonal Relations," in *Jews and Christians Speak of Jesus* (ed. A. E. Zannoni; Minneapolis: Fortress, 1994), 37–53.

33. See E. P. Sanders, "Jesus and the First Table of the Jewish Law," in *Jews and Christians Speak of Jesus*, 55–73; here pp. 55–59.

34. See P. S. Alexander, "Jesus and the Golden Rule," in *Hillel and Jesus: Comparative Studies of Two Major Religious Leaders* (ed. J. H. Charlesworth and L. L. Johns; Minneapolis: Fortress, 1997), 363–88.

35. On this, see esp. M. Borg, *Conflict, Holiness and Politics in the Teachings of Jesus* (forew. N. T. Wright; rev. ed.; Harrisburg: Trinity Press International, 1998), 139–46.

36. See D. A. Hagner, *Matthew 1–13* (WBC 33A; Dallas: Word, 1993), 381–84, 391–95.

37. See E. P. Sanders, *Jesus and Judaism* (Philadelphia: Fortress, 1985), 294–318.

38. On this, cf. M. Hengel, *Crucifixion* (trans. J. Bowden; Philadelphia: Fortress, 1977).

39. On this, cf. D. C. Allison, Jr., *The End of the Ages Has Come: An Early Interpretation of the Passion and Resurrection of Jesus* (Philadelphia: Fortress, 1985), 5–25, 115–41. I am dependent here on this research by Allison.

40. See here G. B. Caird, *New Testament Theology* (ed. L. D. Hurst; New York: Oxford, 1994), 369–84.

41. See the very helpful volume of W. H. Bellinger and W. R. Farmer, eds., *Jesus and the Suffering Servant: Isaiah 53 and Christian Origins* (Harrisburg: Trinity Press International, 1998), especially the essays of Otto Betz, Morna Hooker, and N. T. Wright.

42. See here N. T. Wright, *Jesus and the Victory of God*, 540–611.

43. Jacob Neusner and Bruce Chilton, *Jewish-Christian Debates: God, Kingdom, Messiah* (Minneapolis: Fortress, 1998) 86; see also Wright, *Jesus and the Victory of God*, 554–63.
44. On the broader, sociological issue, cf. J. H. Elliott, "Temple versus Household in Luke-Acts: A Contrast in Social Institutions," in *The Social World of Luke-Acts: Models for Interpretation* (ed. J. H. Neyrey; Peabody, Mass.: Hendrickson, 1991), 211–40.
45. See S. Heschel, *Abraham Geiger and the Jewish Jesus* (Chicago Studies in the History of Judaism; Chicago: University of Chicago Press, 1998); R. P. Ericksen, *Theologians under Hitler: Gerhard Kittel, Paul Althaus and Emanuel Hirsch* (New Haven, Conn.: Yale University Press, 1985).
46. See Dunn, *Partings*.
47. See Neusner and Chilton, *Jewish-Christian Debates*, 215–16.
48. Dunn, *Partings*, 258.

Chapter 8. Early Christianity and the Synagogue: A Parting of the Ways

1. I am grateful to Prof. A. J. M. Wedderburn and Dr. Paul Copan for their helpful critical comments and for kindly correcting my English.
2. All quotations from the Bible follow the New International Version (NIV).
3. Cf. C. A. Evans, *Jesus and His Contemporaries: Comparative Studies* (AGJU 25; Leiden/New York/Köln: E. J. Brill, 1995), 307: "Jesus apparently understood his power as an exorcist as evidence of the presence and power of the kingdom."
4. Cf. William Lane Craig, *Reasonable Faith: Christian Truth and Apologetics* (Wheaton, Ill.: Crossway Books, 1994), 249: "Thus, most NT critics acknowledge that the historical Jesus acted and spoke with a self-consciousness of divine authority and that furthermore, he saw in his own person the coming of the long-awaited kingdom of God and invited people into its fellowship."
5. Cf. M. Hengel and A. M. Schwemer, *Königsherrschaft Gottes und himmlischer Kult* (WUNT 55; Tübingen: Mohr Siebeck, 1991), 3.
6. J. D. G. Dunn, *The Partings of the Ways between Christianity and Judaism and Their Significance for the Character of Christianity* (London: SCM/Philadelphia: Trinity Press International, 1991) 279; cf. idem, *Jesus and the Spirit* (London: SCM Press, 1975), 183.
7. Dunn, *Partings*, 279.
8. But see C. J. Hemer, *The Book of Acts in the Setting of Hellenistic History* (WUNT 49), ed. C. H. Gempf (Tübingen: Mohr, 1989); M. Hengel, *Acts and the History of Earliest Christianity* (London: SCM, 1979).
9. J. Neusner et al. (ed.), *Judaisms and Their Messiahs at the Turn of the Christian Era* (Cambridge, Mass.: Cambridge University, 1987); A. F. Segal, *The Other Judaisms of Late Antiquity* (BJS 127; Atlanta: Scholars, 1987).
10. The earliest use of *christianos* as a Christian self-designation is by Ignatius (*Eph.* 11:2; *Rom.* 3:2; *Magn.* 10:3; *Pol.* 7:3) in the early second century.
11. Mark 3:6; 12:13 = Matt. 22:16; cf. Josephus, *Ant.* 14.450.
12. For a more extensive discussion regarding the origin and use of the name 'Christians' in Antioch and elsewhere, see M. Hengel/A. M. Schwemer, *Paul between Damascus and Antioch: The Unknown Years* (London: SCM, 1997), 225–30.
13. P. Stuhlmacher, *Biblische Theologie des Neuen Testaments. Band 1: Grundlegung. Von Jesus zu Paulus* (Göttingen: Vandenhoeck & Ruprecht, 1992), 236.
14. Rom. 14:17; 1 Cor. 4:20; 6:9–10; 15:50; Gal. 5:21; cf. 1 Thess. 2:12; 2 Thess. 1:5.
15. E. Käsemann, *Paulinische Perspektiven* (Tübingen: Mohr, 1969), 145.

16. Cf. A. J. M. Wedderburn, "Paul and Jesus: The Problem of Continuity," in: idem (ed.), *Paul and Jesus. Collected Essays* (JSNT.S 37; Sheffield: Sheffield Academic, 1989), 99–115.
17. 2 Sam. 8:15=1 Chron. 18:14; 1 Kings 10:9=2 Chron. 9:8; Ps. 72:1–3; Prov. 16:12; 25:5; Qoh. 5:8–9; Isa. 9:7; 32:1ff; Jer. 22:2–3, 15; 33:15; Ezek. 45:9, etc.
18. Wedderburn, "Paul," 108. See Ps. 9:7–8; 96:13; 97:2; 98:9; 99:4, etc.
19. Dunn, *Partings*, 18.
20. These are the headings in Dunn, *Partings*, 19–36.
21. Although monotheism and covenant people (as part of the election) are not "eradicated" but redefined.
22. J. D. G. Dunn, "Works of the Law and the Curse of the Law (Galatians 3.10–14)," *NTS* 31 (1985), 523–42, here: 524–27; cf. M. Limbeck, *Die Ordnung des Heils. Untersuchungen zum Gesetzesverständnis des Frühjudentums* (Düsseldorf: Patmos, 1971), 34; J. Neusner, *Judaism: The Evidence of the Mishnah* (BJS 129; Atlanta: Scholars Press, 2nd ed., 1988) 72–75; W. A. Meeks, *The First Urban Christians* (New Haven, Conn./London: Yale University Press, 1983), 97.
23. "Sabbath": Josephus, *Ant.* 14.214–216, 227, 235, 257f., 260f.; "food": Josephus, *Ant.* 14.226, 245, 261.
24. Cf. M. Hengel, "'Sit at My Right Hand!' The Enthronement of Christ at the Right Hand of God and Psalm 110:1," in idem, *Studies in Early Christology* (Edinburgh: T & T Clark, 1995), 119–225.
25. For a still up-to-date overview, see P. W. van der Horst, "The Birkat ha-minim in Recent Research," *ExpTim* 105 (1994), 363–68.
26. Cf. C. K. Barrett, *The Gospel According to St. John: An Introduction with Commentary and Notes on the Greek Text* (Philadelphia: Westminster Press, 2nd. ed, 1978), 361–62.
27. W. Horbury, "The Benediction of the *Minim* and Early Jewish-Christian Controversy," *JTS* 33 (1982), 19–61, here 59; for a more cautious treatment, see J. Maier, *Jüdische Auseinandersetzung mit dem Christentum in der Antike* (EdF 177; Darmstadt: Wissenschaftliche Buchgesellschaft, 1982), 136–41.
28. Ignatius, *Magn.* 10:1, 3; *Rom.* 3:3; *Phld.* 6:1.
29. M. Hengel, "Das früheste Christentum als eine jüdische messianische und universalistische Bewegung," *Theologische Beiträge* 28 (1997), 197–210, here 202.
30. Origen, *in Lev. hom.* 5.8 (GCS 6, 349. 4ff.); *in Exod. hom.* 12.46 (PG 12, 285).
31. Origen, *in Gen. hom.* 10.5 (GCS 6, 100. 4ff.); *in Lev. hom.* 10.1–2 (GCS 29, 442, 10ff.–445).
32. Chrysostom, *Homilies against the Jews* 1.5 (PG 48, 851); 1.8 (PG 48, 855); 4.7 (PG 48, 881); 5.12 (PG 48, 904); 6.6 (PG 48, 913); 6.7 (PG 48, 914f.); 8.8 (PG 48, 940).
33. Chrysostom, *Homilies against the Jews* 1.3 (PG 48, 847f.).
34. Chrysostom, *Homilies against the Jews* 1.1 (PG 48, 844).
35. Chrysostom, *Homilies against the Jews* 1.3 (PG 48, 847): "*Multi, scio, reverentur Judaeos, eorumque ritus hodiernos censent esse honestos.*"

Chapter 9. The Gospels Would Have Been Greek to Jesus

1. Craig claims all rabbis objected to women studying the Torah. He is ignorant of another view in *m. Sota* 3:4: Ben Azzai says: "A man is obligated to teach his daughter Torah." This opinion accords with early literary accounts in Susanna (who learned from her parents) and in Tobit (who learned from his grandmother). See the *Apocrypha: An American Translation* (trans. E. J. Goodspeed; New York: Modern Library, 1959), 349, 109. Later Palestinian sources also note such study by women. See *t. Ber.* 2.12; *m. Ber.* 4:3 (many texts), *y. Ketubot* 5.2, *t. Kelim* (A) 4.9, (B) 1.3.

2. For one example see *m. Yebamot* 15:4, which lists the few women in a particular case who might have reason to hide the truth. All other women may testify.

3. See *m. Sanh.* 10:1.

4. See *b. Megilla* 3a.

5. See Deut. 13:2–15.

6. James Parkes, *The Conflict of the Church and the Synagogue: A Study in the Origins of Antisemitism* (London: Soncino, 1934), and Jacob Katz, *From Prejudice to Destruction: Antisemitism, 1700–1933* (Cambrdige, Mass.: Harvard University Press, 1980).

7. See further H. W. Basser, "The Acts of Jesus," *Frank Talmage Memorial Volume Part I* (Haifa: Haifa University Press, 1993), 274–82.

8. See *b. Shab.* 128b and *t. Shab.* 15.1.

9. Permission to override scribal Sabbath law where an object is of great value to its owner.

10. See *b. Shab.* 154b.

11. See *b. Shab.* 153a.

12. And likewise allows untying such knots. See also *b. Bezah* 31b.

13. See *b. Shab.* 112a–b and 113a.

14. See *b. Shab.* 53a, 153b, *t. Shab.* 14.8–9; 18.4.

15. Aside from New Testament sources.

16. CD 11:13.

17. *t. Shab.* 14.3.

18. See *b. Shab.* 128b.

19. See *b. Babba Metzia* 32b.

20. Concerning an animal under stress, Exodus 23:5 states, "You must [surely] help."

21. In Matthew, Jesus will always criticize Pharisees for lack of compassion; in mentioning sacrifice, Matthew adds that the Pharisees neglect compassion, but that is not central to the argument here at all. It is an aside.

22. S. Zeitlin (*Rise and Fall of the Judean State: A Political, Social, and Religious History of the Second Commonwealth* [3 vols., Philadelphia: Jewish Publication Society of America, 1962–78] 2.324) is of a wholly other opinion. He thinks this "plucking" conflict represents a real Jesus dispute. Jesus flagrantly broke biblical law and justified himself in ways foreign to Pharisaic teachings. He appeared to be an arrogant renegade to the Pharisees. See D. M. Cohn-Sherbok, "An Analysis of Jesus' Arguments concerning the Plucking of Grain on the Sabbath," *JSNT* 2 (1979), 31–41; repr. in C. A. Evans and S. E. Porter (eds.), *The Historical Jesus: A Sheffield Reader* (BibSem 33; Sheffield: Sheffield Academic Press, 1995) 131–39. Cohn-Sherbok thinks the incident is historical but that Jesus' justification for plucking grain reveals faulty understanding of rabbinic law and midrash.

23. See *b. Shab.* 128a. In Mark we must assume that the text reads "plucking" and "rubbing" of the kernels to show the kernels were hard and taken from the field in an ad hoc way. See *t. Shab.* 14.12, which permits *kotem* and *molel*, plucking and rubbing. The idea here is more the idea of plucking out the kernel from the ear and then rubbing it, which might be the idea in Luke (rather than uprooting the whole ear of grain, as might be suggested in the other versions).

24. Compare *t. Shab.* 9.14–16.

25. According to an ancient tradition in *b. Menahot* 96a and *Yalkut Shimoni* on 1 Samuel 130, David was stricken by a disease brought about by starvation and ate the Shew Bread because he would likely die if he did not eat huge amounts and there was no other food available in huge amounts. The tradition learns from the story of David the general principle that only the possible saving of life can override the Sabbath. It is not claimed in the

Gospels that the disciples were on the verge of death—but "tsad heter" is correctly implied: there are cases (when in dire need) of eating that override the biblical law stipulating non-priests may not eat the Shew Bread. "Tsad heter" is a technical phrase that means there is one case in the category of forbidden rules when certain rules are relaxed (viz., to save a life), so (the inference of the Gospels is that in the application of scribal legislation to guard the Sabbath, the scribes certainly provided certain times when the rules may be relaxed (viz., under conditions of watchfulness). Matthew adds the case of the Temple because that model was directly connected to the Sabbath, whereas the more original story of David's consumption of Shew Bread requires the intervention of abstract generalizations for its Sabbath connection.

26. See *b. Beza* 11b and *b. Shab.* 20a.

27. The Gospels are useful here in providing the scribal thinking behind *eyn shvut bamikdash* and *kohanim zrizim hem*, which are principles applied by later authorities to early laws. The Gospel evidence shows the aptness of these applications.

28. It is unlikely that the idea of permitting laxity in that place was the invention of the Talmud's editors. The whole idea of such laxity runs counter to the thrust of talmudic civilization and proves embarrassing in its permissive attitudes. The very next line in the Talmud criticizes the elders in the upper chamber for remaining silent in the face of one taking liberties with scribal laws. Rabbi Moses Feinstein, in his *Dibrot Moshe* commentary to *b. Shab.* 29b, cannot accept the words as given in the Talmud without his positing very unlikely circumstances to account for the permissive attitude. Hence, it is unlikely the point that this chamber was exempted, on this occasion, from a rabbinic Sabbath law, has been added by an editor. It is the type of thing a censor would remove, not add. Rather, it likely reflects ancient scribal notions concerning relaxing non-biblical legislation. It seems obvious that the scribes, open to the accusation that they were hypocrites by enacting rules and then exempting themselves, would have abolished this questionable practice. But the vestiges of such exemptions (in places of vigilant authority) are preserved in the talmudic version of the Tosephta and the Gospels.

29. This passage is similar to *t. Shab.* 2, which, however, lacks mention of the vigilance of the court. The Tosepta may be an edited version since the old idea that rabbinic rulings might in some cases be suspended is nowhere else to be found. The language of the Palestinian teaching in the Talmud is also suspect as it utilizes Babylonian Aramaic. The reading in the commentary of Rabbi Hananel is superior, and it is likely that there was some such teaching in early times that fell out of the Tosephta. Similarly we find cases where certain rabbinic laws are suspended for priests (because they are diligent) and among the groups at Passover sacrificial meals (where people are watchful). We note certain rabbinic laws may be suspended in these cases but never biblical laws.

30. H. W. Basser, *Pseudo Rabad: Commentary to Sifre Deuteronomy* (Atlanta: Scholars Press, 1994).

Chapter 10. At What Points Do Judaisms and Christianities Meet?

1. But it is the fact that sages discuss liturgy, whether the Shema, or the Prayer, or other rules of synagogue worship and conduct. But only a few liturgical compositions are attributed in the Oral Torah to the authorship of sages, and these always take their place around the fringes of the worship service, never at the center. So while the Siddur and Mahzor in their principal parts speak with sages' approval, we require evidence that, in addition, they speak in behalf of sages in particular. Only with the evidence of that very particular kind can I claim that the Oral Torah takes up that mediating position that I impute to it.

2. *The Theology of the Oral Torah: Revealing the Justice of God* (Kingston and Montreal: McGill-Queens University Press, 1998; second edition, 2000).

3. If I were engaged in constructive systematic theology, not just the historical kind, I should further claim that the sages' system is the only possible system that the Hebrew Scriptures sustain. Whether or not other theologies built on the Hebrew Scriptures may be deemed congruent with those Scriptures is not at issue here, only the claim that the sages' is. But I think a powerful case can be made in behalf of the congruity with Scripture, in proportion, balance, and also detail, of the sages' retelling of the Scriptural tale. Even here, in a mere description of the theological system of the Oral Torah, it should be said that how sages diverge from Scripture in their basic theological structure and system I simply cannot discern. In my view, transcending the promiscuous use of proof texts is the evidence on the surface of matters. At no point can I find important differences between the sages' and Scripture's respective theological systems and structures. In that sense, I argue that sages are right about the Written Torah (Christianity's Old Testament) and everyone else is wrong. That is because the sages read outward and forward from Scripture, and the other, competing heirs of Scripture read backward to Scripture. So, in that simple sense, sages say what Scripture means, and no one else does.

4. To give a single example, I point to *Judaism and Scripture: The Evidence of Leviticus Rabbah* (Chicago: University of Chicago Press, 1986), I have dealt systematically with the atomistic reading of the Midrash compilations in *The Documentary Foundation of Rabbinic Culture. Mopping Up after Debates with Gerald L. Bruns, S. J. D. Cohen, Arnold Maria Goldberg, Susan Handelman, Christine Hayes, James Kugel, Peter Schaefer, Eliezer Segal, E. P. Sanders, and Lawrence H. Schiffman* (Atlanta: Scholars Press for South Florida Studies in the History of Judaism, 1995).

5. That is with two exceptions, for, so far as that tradition can be naturalized into the framework established by sages' structure and system, sages do so, as in the case of Daniel. Second, they take over as fact and accept apocalyptic expectations, as with the war of Gog and Magog.

6. *Biblical Theology of the Old and New Testaments*, 720.

7. But whether or not the same sages who formed the Oral Torah bear principal responsibility, also, for the character of synagogue liturgy as we know it has no bearing on my argument. Many take for granted that they do. When I claim that the theology of the Oral Torah is realized in the liturgy of the synagogue, that is not a historical-temporal but a theological judgment. Why do I think it also is a historical fact? Certainly, the sages in the Oral Torah evinced the ambition to define the liturgy. Their *halakhah* extends to the order of common worship, defining its principal parts. The *aggadah* contains compositions of prayers in the name of various sages, and some of these are incorporated in the liturgy—the Siddur and Mahzor, the prayer books for every day, Sabbath, and festivals on the one side, and for the Days of Awe on the other. But whether or not the sages of the Oral Torah bear responsibility for the liturgy as it is first attested in detail is another question, and one that has no bearing on my claim in behalf of the sages' theology and its impact. That claim forms an intellectual judgment about the power of ideas, not a historical one about the politics of public worship and who was in control thereof. The detailed wording of both the Siddur and the Mahzor is first attested centuries after the close of the Talmud of Babylonia, but the fixed order of prayer, as we know that order of prayer in the earliest written Siddurim, conforms to the law of the Talmud. Some prayers in both documents are assigned in the Talmud to named sages; others are merely alluded to, without a clear claim of sages' authorship in particular. But my point of insistence, that

the liturgy responds to sages' theology, is to be evaluated in its own framework, which is phenomenological, not historical.

8. It seems to me self-evident that, when it comes to generative modes of thought and distinctive clusters of motifs, we do well to limit our inquiry into formative influences to the dual Torah.

9. A fair test of this allegation of the particularity of sages' reading will address the liturgies found in the library at Qumran and compare those of the synagogue with the prayers that the group represented by that library offered. Other such tests are readily to be imagined.

10. *A Rabbi's Manual*, ed. Jules Harlow (New York: The Rabbinical Assembly, 1965), 45. The "seven blessings" said at a wedding are printed in traditional Jewish prayer books. All of the translations of liturgies set forth here derive from Rabbi Harlow's superlative translations.

11. Lifsa Schachter, "Reflections on the Brit Mila Ceremony," *Conservative Judaism* 38 (1986), 38–41.

12. *Pirke deRabbi Eliezer*, trans. by Gerald Friedlander (London, 1916), 212–14.

13. *op. cit.*, p. 41.

14. In *The Theological Grammar of the Oral Torah* (Binghamton: SUNY Press, 1997), II. *Syntax: Connections and Constructions*, I have catalogued 150 of them.

15. *Weekday Prayerbook*, ed. by the Rabbinical Assembly of America Prayerbook Committee, Rabbi Jules Harlow, Secretary (New York: Rabbinical Assembly, 1962), 97–98.

16. Judah Goldin, trans., *The Grace after Meals* (New York: The Jewish Theological Seminary of America, 1955), 9, 15ff.

17. *Weekday Prayerbook*, ed. by the Rabbinical Assembly of American Prayerbook Committee, Rabbi Jules Harlow, Secretary (New York: Rabbinical Assembly, 1962), 42.

18. Ibid., p.141.

19. Ibid., pp. 45–56.

20. Ibid., pp. 50ff.

21. Traditional prayer; author's translation from the Hebrew.

22. Jules Harlow, trans., *Mahzor* (New York, rep. 1995: Rabbinical Assembly).

23. ibid.

24. ibid.

Chapter 11. Jesus, a Galilean Rabbi

1. See Douglas R. Edwards and C. Thomas McCollough (eds), *Archaeology and the Galilee. Texts and Contexts in the Graeco-Roman and Byzantine Periods*, South Florida Studies in the History of Judaism 143 (Atlanta: Scholars, 1997).

2. See Richard A. Horsley, *Archaeology, History, and Society in Galilee. The Social Context of Jesus and the Rabbis* (Valley Forge, Pa.: Trinity Press International, 1996), 67–70.

3. James F. Strange, "First Century Galilee from Archaeology and from the Texts," *Archaeology and the Galilee: Texts and Contexts in the Graeco-Roman and Byzantine Periods*, ed. Douglas R. Edwards and C. Thomas McCollough (Atlanta: Scholars Press, 1997), 39–48, 54.

4. In a major archeological discovery in 1990, a bulldozer took the top off a cave half a mile south of Mount Zion, uncovering a mausoleum. An adult, even a short adult, could not have stood erect in the cave, but a pit had been dug near its entrance to allow mourners to stand while tending to their dead and praying. Corpses were laid out on a shelf, and after the flesh had decomposed, the bones were gathered and stored. Bone storage for

the anonymous poor was in a pit dug in the cave's floor, while the bones of wealthier, prominent people were kept in small limestone ossuaries, which were placed in the shafts that ran outward from the central cave like spokes.

One such ossuary had the name "Caiaphas" carved roughly into its side and back, once in Aramaic and once in Hebrew (never in Greek!). A coin discovered in the cave is dated 42/43 C.E. (during the reign of Herod Agrippa I). If the ossuary were for Caiaphas the high priest, he would have been about sixty when he died (c. 46): and, inside the ossuary marked with Caiaphas's name, the bones of a man aged around sixty years old were indeed found, along with the bones of an adult female, two infants, a small child, and a young adult. Death apparently came to them all from natural causes. The ossuary's elegant carving distinguishes it from most ossuaries of that place and period. It is carved with a pattern of five floral designs, for the most part in spirals, arranged around a central, spiraling flower. The palm design that surrounds the circles on Caiaphas's ossuary picks up a motif in the Temple's decoration. Placed in the tunnel to the south of the cave, his ossuary was in fact oriented to face that Temple. His status, and his connection to the Temple, the preeminent sacred place in Judaism, is attested by this find, and the ossuary is an eloquent witness of Judaism in the first century: a vibrant religion, centered on the Temple and passionately devoted to the worship of God through sacrifice in that holy place. Although Israeli archaeologists have identified the name on this ossuary with that of Joseph called Caiaphas of the New Testament Gospels and Josephus, other scholars have raised questions; see W. Horbury, "The 'Caiaphas' Ossuaries and Joseph Caiaphas," *PEQ* 126 (1994), 32–48; E. Puech, "A-t-on redécouvert le tombeau du grand-prêtre Caïphe?" *Le monde de la Bible* 80 (1993), 42–47; idem, *La croyance des Esséniens en la vie future*, vol. 1 (EBib 21; Paris: Gabalda, 1993), 193–95. The inscription raises doubt whether the inscribed name should be pronounced "Caiaphas" (or Cayapha); it may well be "Qopha" or "Qepha."

5. As is very forcefully shown, for example, by Richard A. Horsley in *Archaeology, History, and Society in Galilee.*

6. For what archaeology has now taught us about synagogues and *miqvaoth*, see Dan Urman and Paul V. M. Flesher, *Ancient Synagogues. Historical Analysis and Archaeological Discovery*, Studia Post-Biblica (Leiden: Brill, 1995). A synagogue dating from first-century B.C. Jericho has also been recently announced.

7. In any case, more recent archaeological reports indicate that prior to 70, Sepphoris also may have been primarily a Jewish city.

8. *Jesus der Galiläer und das Judentum*, Veröffentlichungen des Instituts zur Erforschung des jüdischen Einflusses auf das deutsche kirchliche Leben (Leipzig: Weigand, 1940).

9. See *The Glory of Israel. The Theology and Provenience of the Isaiah Targum*, Journal for the Study of the Old Testament, Supplement 23 (Sheffield: JSOT, 1982); *The Isaiah Targum. Introduction, Translation, Apparatus, and Notes*, The Aramaic Bible 11 (Wilmington, Del.: Michael Glazier; Edinburgh: T. & T. Clark, 1987).

10. This issue is debated, with many scholars concluding that *Thomas* contains nothing outside the New Testament Gospels that is authentic. Although the present writer believes *Thomas* probably does contain primitive, authentic material, he does recognize the need for careful, critical study of it.

11. And some will date the Gospels a few years earlier or later.

12. This is the narrative perspective that I have developed in *Rabbi Jesus. An Intimate Biography* (New York: Doubleday, 2000).

Conclusion

1. In addition to Craig's *Assessing the New Testament Evidence for the Resurrection of Jesus*, Studies in the Bible and Early Christianity (Lewiston, N.Y.: Edwin Mellen, 1989), see Craig's responses to similar criticisms in Paul Copan, ed., *Will the Real Jesus Please Stand Up?* (Grand Rapids: Baker, 1998), 156–79; Paul Copan and Ronald K. Tacelli, ed., *Jesus' Resurrection: Fact or Figment?* (Downers Grove, Ill.: InterVarsity Press, 2000), 160–204.

2. To be sure, the Samaritans do have other writings that are regarded as authoritative. But only the Torah (or "Samaritan Pentateuch"), which like the Masoretic Text is preserved in Hebrew, is Scripture.

3. For an example of how this novelty and continuity are played out, see Richard Bauckham, *God Crucified: Monotheism and Christology in the New Testament* (Grand Rapids: Wm. B. Eerdmans, 1998).

Index of Ancient Writings

Bible

Author Index

197

Subject Index

79, 83, 85–86, 90–91, 93, 96,
106, 136, 142, 144, 149, 154, 163,
165–69, 171

Jacob, 125, 138, 140
James, 21, 105, 158–59
Jeremiah, 45, 82, 127, 136, 168
Jericho, 79, 187
Jerusalem, vii, 61, 69, 79–80, 85, 91,
94, 101, 123, 135–36, 142, 144,
157, 165, 168, 177
Jesus, 1–11, 15–19, 21–28, 29–42,
passim
ethics of, 89–93, 94
Jesus Seminar, 48, 71, 164, 171
Jesus, son of Ananias, 69
Jewish Christians.
See Ebionites
Jewish prophet from, 62
Egypt
Jews, 1–11, 15–21, 24–27, 30–35,
passim
Joash, 82
John the Baptist, 45, 64, 67, 78–81, 84,
94, 99, 167–68
John, Gospel of, 17, 30, 41, 48, 63,
106–7, 111, 124, 159, 160
Jordan River, 80–82
Josephus, 74, 79, 154, 160, 177–79
Joshua, 80–81, 83–84, 175
Joshua ben Levi, 116
Jotapata, 155
Judaism, 1–11, 15–20, 30–35,
passim
Judea, 80
Julius Caesar, 102

Kabbalah, 157
Kemp, Jack, 20
Kefar Hananiah, 155
Kerygma, 17
Khirbet Qumran, 73
kingdom of God, Heaven, 4, 17, 41,
50, 52, 62–65, 67, 70–71, 76–78, 85,
88, 91, 93, 97–99, 103, 106, 160, 165–66,
171, 181

Kofer ba-ikar, 114, 157–58, 160
Kyrios, 46, 106

Lamb of God, 36
land, 8, 81, 89, 96, 104, 115, 130, 135,
144, 167
Law, Torah, 4, 6, 9–10, 32–33, 42,
48–49, 50, 61–62, 68, 74, 87–88,
95, 98, 101, 103–5, 109, 118–21,
125–26, 128–35, 142–43, 146–48,
152–53, 156, 164–65, 167–71,
185–86, 188
Lazarus, 39
legend, 23, 112–13
Lehotsi et hadavar melibam, 114
Lord's (Last) Supper, 53, 94
Lord's Prayer, 84, 171
love, 88–90
Luke, 118, 159, 169
Luther, 75, 114

Maccabean Period, 104, 122
Machaerus, 81
Magog, 185
Mahzor, 126, 152, 184–85
Maimonides, Moses, 121, 132
manna, 83
marana tha, 106, 170
Marcionism, 170
Mark, Gospel of, 30, 37, 40–41, 86,
159
Mathe'a shel tefillah, 134
Matthew, Gospel of, 50, 86, 113, 117,
120, 159, 169, 183
Meiron, 155
Meshumad, 122
Messiah, Messianism, 1–2, 4–11, 34–35,
passim
Middle Ages, 112
Midrash, 123, 131, 170
Migdal, 155
Minim, 107
See Birkat Haminim
Miqveh, Miqvaoth, 79, 155, 179
Mishnah, 10, 66, 155, 160, 175–79
monotheism, 74, 104